D0188937

The Moral
Construction
of Poverty

The Moral Construction of Poverty

Welfare Reform in America

Joel F. Handler
Yeheskel Hasenfeld

SAGE Publications
International Educational and Professional Publisher
Newbury Park   London   New Delhi

Copyright © 1991 by Sage Publications, Inc.

All rights reserved. No part of this book may be reproduced or utilized in any form or by any means, electronic or mechanical, including photocopying, recording, or by any information storage and retrieval system, without permission in writing from the publisher.

For information address:

SAGE Publications, Inc.
2455 Teller Road
Newbury Park, California 91320

SAGE Publications Ltd.
6 Bonhill Street
London EC2A 4PU
United Kingdom

SAGE Publications India Pvt. Ltd.
M-32 Market
Greater Kailish I
New Delhi 110 048 India

Printed in the United States of America

Library of Congress Cataloging-in-Publication Data

Handler, Joel F.
  The moral construction of poverty : welfare reform in America / Joel F. Handler, Yeheskel Hasenfeld.
      p.   cm.
  Includes bibliographical references.
  ISBN 0-8039-4197-8.   —   ISBN 0-8039-4198-6 (pbk.)
  1. Public welfare—United States—Moral and ethical aspects.
  2. Poor—Government policy—United States.   I. Hasenfeld, Yeheskel.
  II. Title.
  HV95.H259   1991
  361.6'8'0973—dc20   91-6939
                                                                          CIP

95 96 97 98 99 10 9 8 7 6 5 4 3

Sage Production Editor: Judith L. Hunter

Contents

Acknowledgments

This book represents a true collaborative effort. We have not hesitated to openly and candidly challenge each other's ideas as we struggled jointly to develop a coherent understanding of the history of welfare reform in the United States. In this process we have forged an everlasting friendship for which we are most grateful. Throughout this project we have benefited from the insight and comments of many colleagues at UCLA, Wisconsin, and Michigan. We are especially thankful for the help we received from Tom Brock, Sheldon Danziger, William Forbath, Mark Greenberg, Leonard Schneiderman, and Lucie White. Finally, we want to dedicate our book to our respective wives, Betsy and Helen, and to our children, Stephen, Joanne, Kate, Adam, Ann, and Frances Handler, and Rena and Rachel Hasenfeld.

Introduction

What accounts for the convoluted history of America's response to poverty, particularly of single mothers and their children? Throughout U.S. history, single women and their children have been overwhelmingly represented among the poor, and, despite a long history of social welfare reform, they are still disproportionately poor. Although we have had considerable success in reducing poverty among the elderly, this has not been the case with single mothers and their children. To be sure, not all poor single mothers and their children fare badly. If the mother has survived a husband who qualified under the social security system, then the family receives a relatively generous pension. However, if the family needs public aid because the mother has been divorced or separated, or if the mother was never married, the family receives Aid to Families with Dependent Children (AFDC), popularly known as "welfare"—a program mired in controversy and moral ambiguity. The social security widow and her children are treated with respect and dignity. The AFDC mother is, more often than not, viewed with suspicion and contempt.

There is a profound paradox about welfare.[1] Although the public expenditure on welfare represents a small fraction of all social welfare expenditures under public programs, it has had the dubious distinction of being almost continuously on the national domestic agenda since the late 1950s.[2] Indeed, few other social policies attract so much public attention, and are subject to such heated attacks from all sides of the political spectrum. It is a policy that has marginal legitimacy and is steeped in negative images and controversy. Why is it that welfare policy is so charged with moral and political controversy, and how can we best understand the forces that shape it? We discuss below some of the theories that have been advanced to explain welfare policy, the limitations of these theories, and our own theoretical approach. Current theories can be classified as follows: (a) social need theories, which view welfare policy as a response to poverty arising from changing demographic and economic conditions; (b) subjugation theories, which see the roots of welfare policy in class, gender, and race subjugation; (c) political interest theories, which explain welfare policy as a function of political negotiations and bargaining among contending interest groups; and (d) moralistic theories, which perceive welfare policy as a reflection of moral choices, and attribute its presumed failure to moral laxity.

SOCIAL NEED THEORIES

Industrialization, migration, urbanization, and demographic trends such as the changing structure of the family and the aging of the population are factors frequently cited as conditions that precipitate poverty among certain groups of people. It is implicitly assumed that welfare policy is generally a rational response to the objective conditions of poverty, once the conditions of poverty are scientifically documented, researched, and understood. For example, Durman (1973) has argued that the expansion of the welfare rolls in the 1960s was a function of the expanded pool of single-parent families and the resulting liberalization of welfare policy. Danziger, Haveman, and Plotnick (1986) show how the welfare policies of the Great Society were a response to the persistence of poverty—especially among the elderly, female-headed households, and nonwhites—which was further aggravated by slow economic growth. In analyzing the effects of such policies, these authors conclude that, indeed, welfare policies significantly reduced poverty in the period between 1964 and 1983, but with some negative effects on the supply of labor, and lack of success in increasing earning and self-sufficiency among the able-bodied poor. Garfinkel and McLanahan (1986) offer a thorough analysis of the economic plight of female-headed families, which they attribute to shifts in the relative earning opportunities of men and women. Their findings point to welfare reform based on strengthening the enforcement of child-support obligations and establishing work-relief and guaranteed jobs programs.

Thus from a social needs perspective welfare reform is seen as an incremental process in response to changing demographic and economic conditions. Ellwood (1988) epitomizes this approach in his cogent analysis of poverty among American families and in his proposed welfare reforms. Because poverty among two-parent families is mostly due to low wages or unemployment, he advocates, in addition to universal medical protection, wage subsidies through the earned income tax credit, liberalized unemployment insurance, and a small jobs program. Poverty among single-parent families is partly due to insufficient income from work or from the inability to work. For such families, he proposes a welfare policy that strengthens and guarantees child-support payments and provides transitional assistance to jobs through welfare-work programs. Finally, he points to the problems of ghetto poverty, which are due to extreme deprivation, concentration, and isolation of the poor from other segments of society. For them he suggests the addition of extensive investments in education and training, the creation of jobs, and the imposition of an obligation to work.

The difficulty with a social needs perspective lies in its underlying assumptions. It is indeed questionable whether poverty policy is a response to scientifically determined objective conditions. The social construction of "problems" or "needs" is a matter of ideology and political interests (Edelman, 1988). Social science findings about poverty can be interpreted from many different ideological perspectives, and it is precisely the role of ideologies in shaping welfare policy that the social needs perspective ignores. Only in the broadest sense does social policy respond to social needs. Ideology and politics determine the specifics of the response to particular needs and the choices among different alternatives.

SUBJUGATION THEORIES

What is common to all subjugation theories—whether based on class, gender, or race—is that they view welfare policy as an instrument of domination and social control by elites. Taking a neo-Marxian approach, Piven and Cloward (1971) argue that in a capitalist economy the function of welfare policies is

(to regulate labor, and they do so in two general ways. First, when mass unemployment leads to the outbreak of turmoil, relief programs are ordinarily initiated or expanded to absorb and control enough of the unemployed to restore order; then, as turbulence subsides, the relief system contracts, expelling those who are needed to populate the labor market. (p. 3)

They go on to explain much of the history of welfare policy from this perspective, and propose that the rapid expansion of welfare in the 1960s was an attempt to control urban disorders.

Isaac and Kelly (1981) found, as Piven and Cloward had predicted, that racial insurgency was consistently important in influencing public assistance expenditures in the postwar years. At a more abstract level, Quadagno (1988) argues that "the social organization of production determines the nature and form of relief programs. If poor laws are a product of feudalistic agrarian societies requiring an immobilized labor force, then national welfare systems emerge from the conflicts generated by the commodification of labor under industrial capitalism and the need for a mobile labor force" (pp. 6–7). However, she adds an important political dimension, namely, the accessibility of social classes to power to shape the social agenda.

The general notion that welfare policy serves to maintain social control and industrial discipline has been used by several historians. Boyer (1978), for example, argues that much of the system of philanthropy during the Jacksonian era was initiated as an effort at social control in the face of increasing fears about industrialization, class division, immigration, and family disruptions. Katz (1986), while acknowledging that welfare policy attempts to alleviate misery, nonetheless suggests that the preservation of social order and discipline and the regulation of the labor market have been the prime movers of welfare reform.

Undoubtedly, there is historical validity to the social control and labor regulation propositions. Nonetheless, the neo-Marxian analysis is flawed in several ways. The general assumption of a unified capitalist class with a common set of interests that conspires to set welfare policy is not tenable in light of the historical evidence. As we shall show, much of the history points to fragmented and disjointed policies that are often contradictory. The neo-Marxians tend to dismiss the role of ideologies as mere reflection of capitalist class interests. To the contrary, ideologies and cultural symbols are much more complex systems of belief that transcend class interests, and are powerful in their own right in influencing welfare policy. In this connection, neo-Marxians dismiss the importance of the norm of charity, deeply ingrained in the Judeo-Christian ethos, as a mere reflection of the struggle of the lower classes for equality. The neo-Marxians also fail to recognize that welfare policy in itself has "feedback effects" on subsequent formations of interest groups and the political processes affecting welfare reform (Weir, Orloff, & Skocpol, 1988). Moreover, the welfare bureaucracy itself becomes an important actor whose interests must be considered in order to understand the evolution of welfare policy. In addition, welfare policy reflects the political economy of the community in which it is implemented. Irrespective of the presumed class struggle, rich states have more generous and liberal welfare policies than do poor states. Finally, as we shall point out, welfare policy is not a very effective mechanism of social control; in fact, it tends to fail quite often in regulating the poor.

Taking exception to the narrow class analysis, feminists argue that "gender, more than race or class, structures every aspect of human nature and social life" (Abramovitz, 1988, p. 23), including, of course, welfare policy. Fraser (1989) argues that there is a gender subtext to the U.S. welfare system. Despite the fact that the overwhelming majority of U.S. families no longer conform to the normative ideal of the two-parent household with the husband as the primary breadwinner, the various combinations of social welfare programs are structured on this sexual division of labor. One set of welfare programs is related primarily to the labor market (e.g., social security, unemployment compensation) and the other to family or household (AFDC, food stamps, Medicaid). The latter—the "feminine" programs—are based on the family, but a defective family (i.e., without a male breadwinner), with the adult member making her claim on the basis of her status as an unpaid domestic homemaker, not as a paid worker in the labor market. This is in contrast to the "masculine" programs, which are based on participation in the paid labor force. The system is not only separate, in terms of gender, but also unequal. The masculine programs are national, generous, and, generally, nonintrusive; the beneficiaries are "rights-bearing" citizens. In contrast, the feminine programs are inadequate, intrusive, and humiliating; the clients are effectively denied the attributes of social citizenship. The AFDC program, by failing to provide child care, job training, and a decent income, constructs these women exclusively as homemakers, but instead of honoring them, the program stigmatizes and humiliates them. AFDC, both ideologically and structurally, institutionalizes the feminization of poverty; the structure of the program is "system-conforming," which actually "reinforce[s] rather than challenge[s] basic structural inequalities" (Fraser, 1989, p. 145). In short, the U.S. welfare system perpetuates fundamental gender relations; taken as a whole, the system has created "public patriarchy" from "private patriarchy" (p. 145).

In an analogous way, it is argued that welfare policy also functions to regulate patterns of racial domination. As Orfield (1988) puts it, "In a society with intense racial consciousness and a rigid color line, all kinds of resources and opportunities are distributed in ways that benefit the dominant group" (pp. 314–315). Prior to the civil rights movement, the role of welfare policy in maintaining the economic and political subjugation of African-Americans in the South was quite apparent. Yet, less apparent is the use of welfare policy to blame the urban ghetto ethnic minorities for their poverty predicament. African-American feminists, including welfare recipients active in the National Welfare Rights Organization, view welfare policy as strategy to denigrate African-American women, to blame them for their marital status and dire poverty, and to force them into menial labor (Jones, 1985). In his study *The Negro Family: The Case for National Action*, published in 1965, Moynihan argues that African-American male unemployment gave rise to female-headed families in the black community, and created a female culture that undermined the male role. This vicious cycle resulted in a "tightening tangle of pathology," condemning the women to a life on welfare. Serving as a blueprint for welfare reform, Moynihan's argument is viewed by African-American feminists as a condemnation of African-American women, especially the poor, and as an intellectual rationale for their continued racial oppression (Jones, 1985, p. 315).

It is undeniable that welfare policy is inextricably intertwined with gender and race. Indeed, as we argue throughout this book, because welfare policy is part of the larger ideological and normative order, it necessarily reflects and reinforces fundamental gender and race beliefs. AFDC, as Fraser says, is family policy; as such, it validates dominant intrafamily and family-work relations. And because minority men and women are disproportionately poor, welfare policy is also racial policy; in race, as in gender, welfare reflects and reinforces moral and social markers.

However, gender and race are necessary, but not sufficient, explanatory elements in an attempt to understand the evolution of welfare policy. As we shall show, it is the overriding need to distinguish between the able-bodied and the disabled poor, between the "undeserving" and the "deserving" poor, be they men or women of any racial or ethnic origin, that is the driving force behind welfare policy. It is the able-bodied poor, whatever their ascriptive status, that present the moral dilemma to the modern capitalist state, because they challenge the legitimacy of its economic and civic order. Indeed, historically, poor able-bodied men, particularly from racial and ethnic minorities, have been viewed as extraordinary threats to the economic and social order, thus becoming the target of highly repressive welfare policies. Even today, programs for able-bodied men are miserly, harsh, and mean-spirited. To be sure, race and gender are intertwined with the social construction of deservingness. For most of our welfare history, African-Americans were simply excluded altogether; many are still excluded today. Single poor women and their children were also excluded during most of the history of AFDC. They carried their gender- and race-based moral condemnation with them in their massive entry into the AFDC program during the last three decades.

Thus, to understand welfare policy, it is important to understand the full range of ideological constructs. Where the state draws the line is a function of the confluence of many factors—normative, political, economic, and organizational.

POLITICAL INTEREST THEORIES

Welfare policy has also been viewed as an outcome of political processes. One approach emphasizes the role of electoral politics, namely, the existence of democratic political institutions; the relations among local, state, and federal electoral institutions; the roles of political parties and other interest groups; and political competition (e.g., Schneider, 1982; Sharkansky & Hofferbert, 1969). Much of Moynihan's (1973) analysis of the failure of the Nixon administration's welfare reform initiative uses this perspective (see also Leman, 1980). A related approach is to emphasize the role of the state itself and its bureaucracy in influencing welfare policy (Skocpol, 1986). The fiscal strength of the state and its bureaucratic capacity are seen as particularly important variables. Amenta and Carruthers (1988) found that the adoption of social policies such as old-age pensions and unemployment compensation by the various states is, in part, a function of the administrative powers of the state (e.g., the existence of appropriate state bureaucracies and effective tax mechanisms).

Moreover, the welfare bureaucracy itself becomes a powerful interest group aiming to preserve and enhance itself. Through its administrative discretion it can shape the implementation of welfare policy (Lipsky, 1980), and through its close linkages with key legislative bodies, it uses the information and expertise it controls to shape welfare policy (e.g., Cates, 1983).

We concur with the emphasis of the political interest theories on the interplay among interest groups, electoral politics, and state bureaucracy in understanding welfare policy. However, these theories omit an important and powerful force in policy-making, namely, the role of symbols, images, and myths that provide legitimacy to interests to be considered seriously in the electoral political process. Put differently, unless political interests can garner broad legitimacy through attachment to dominant cultural symbols, they are unlikely to enter the public agenda. This is especially true for welfare policy because inherently it is a policy about morality, and thus the success of welfare reform hinges, in no small measure, on the attainment of political consensus, however temporary, concerning its underlying moral stance. The "moralization" of political interests occurs through the construction of social problems. As Edelman (1988) puts it:

Problems come into discourse and therefore into existence as reinforcement of ideologies not simply because they are there or because
they are important for wellbeing. They signify who are virtuous and
useful and who are dangerous or inadequate, which action will be
rewarded and which penalized. They constitute people as subjects
with particular kinds of aspirations, self concepts, and fears, and they
create beliefs about the relative importance of events and objects.
They are critical in determining who exercises authority and who ac-
cepts it. They construct areas of immunity from concern because those
areas are not seen as problems. Like leaders and enemies, they define
the contours of the social world. (pp. 12–13)

By tracing the history of welfare policy, we show the importance
of symbols in defining and redefining the different moral categories
of the poor and in framing the responses to them. Symbols, for
example, were an important factor in thwarting attempts to enact
social insurance legislation that was truly redistributive, providing
a minimal guaranteed income. Despite pressures from powerful political interest groups, both liberal and conservative, advocating income support based on a "flat system" (i.e., guaranteed minimal
income), the framers and administrators of the Social Security Act
successfully invoked the private insurance metaphor to delegitimate such proposals (Cates, 1983). They constructed the problem of
income support as an individual responsibility to contribute to a
pension system based on one's earnings. In so doing, they framed
public assistance as the enemy and ascribed to it a morally inferior
status.

MORALISTIC THEORIES

The normative underpinnings of welfare policy have always provoked debates about its ethical justification and, more important,
about its moral consequences on both the poor and society at large.
There has been, of course, a long tradition of moralistic thinking
about poverty and welfare, much of it emanating from early Judeo-
Christian theologies. Contemporary approaches are anchored in the
moral philosophies of Adam Smith, Bentham, and Malthus, among
others (see Himmelfarb, 1984).

Justifying or debunking welfare policy on moral grounds while
using social science research and theory to buttress the moral argu-

ment is the key attribute of moralistic theories. This approach is exemplified in several recent studies of welfare policy. Murray (1984), in his book *Losing Ground*, argues that the Great Society programs of the 1960s were responsible for the increase in unemployment, the decline in educational attainment, the rise in crime, and the increase in rates of illegitimacy and female-headed households among African-Americans. He attributes these results to ideological changes in the 1960s that linked poverty to faults in the social system rather than in the individual. Accordingly, this led to an income transfer policy that rewarded the "undeserving" poor at the expense of the "deserving" poor. Although much of the validity of Murray's findings has been convincingly refuted (e.g., Danziger & Gottschalk, 1985), it is important to understand how a moralistic argument would lead to such a conclusion. It is based on an implicit assumption that many people are poor because they choose a way of life that makes them poor. Therefore, a social policy that attempts only to induce them out of poverty actually rewards their undesirable behavior, and indeed may attract others who might not otherwise have chosen to engage in such behavior. Hence, unless the undeserving poor are coerced to participate in social programs aimed at changing their behavior, these policies are likely to cause more harm than good.

In a somewhat similar vein, Mead (1986) argues that welfare policies of the 1960s failed to reduce dependency because they were based on entitlement without reciprocal obligations. Again, the moral culprit is social policies that treat problems among the poor, such as nonwork or family breakup, as if they were outside forces acting on the poor, and thus shift the responsibility from the individual to the government. As a result, welfare policies result in the erosion of the work ethic. According to Mead, welfare reforms fail because they remain ambivalent regarding the work requirement; thus the solution to the "welfare mess" must include a firm imposition of authority requiring able-bodied welfare recipients to work for their relief.

The moralists are correct in pointing out the moral imperative of welfare policy, and how moral choices play a key role in shaping the policy itself. There is no doubt that the welfare reforms of the 1960s and beyond echoed significant moral and ideological shifts as expressed in the civil rights movement, the women's rights movement, the extension of citizenship rights to previously disfranchised social groups, and the conservative reaction. Yet, the analysis of welfare policy is colored by the morally prescribed lenses through which the moralists view the world, and in viewing the world as they do, they commit two fundamental errors. First, they tend to attribute to welfare policy a moral coherence and consistency that seldom exists. As we shall point out, welfare policy is fraught with moral ambiguities and contradictions. Second, they tend to assume a one-to-one correspondence between the moral aspects of the policy and its actual operation. As we shall show, there are major disjunctures between the two. In this sense, the moralists fail to see the symbols and myths of the policy for what they are, namely, affirmation of cultural beliefs that are only loosely connected to the policy implementation itself.

OVERVIEW OF THIS BOOK

The approach we take in this book centers on two major arguments. The first is that social welfare policy cannot be fully understood without recognizing that it is fundamentally a set of symbols that try to differentiate between the deserving and undeserving poor in order to uphold such dominant values as the work ethic and family, gender, race, and ethnic relations. In this sense welfare policy is targeted not only at the poor, but equally at the nonpoor, through the symbols it conveys about what behaviors are deemed virtuous or deviant. These symbols, nonetheless, are quite ambiguous, reflecting contending moral systems. Hence welfare policy itself is fraught with contradictions, making the design and administration of programs problematic. One consequence is that the administration of welfare policy is loosely related to the symbols of the policy. Because much greater emphasis is placed on the symbolic than on the substantive consequences of welfare policy, its implementation tends to focus on structural features designed to affirm the distinctions between deserving and undeserving poor, and to certify eligibility for welfare benefits. We term these features *myths* and *ceremonies* because their main function is to confirm the dominant cultural norms about the poor (Meyer & Rowan, 1977). This is not to ignore the fact that the policy does commit public resources to relieve some of the misery the poor experience. Rather, we suggest that such a commitment is limited mostly to giving sufficient credence to the symbols in the eyes of their beholders. Rarely are these resources adequate to alleviate the economic misery of poor single women and their children, let alone to meet their expectations and hopes. The gaping discrepancy between the symbols and the committed resources is camouflaged by the myths and ceremonies.

The myths and ceremonies, nonetheless, have profound consequences for the lives of welfare recipients. They determine how much relief recipients will get, and under what conditions; they curtail citizenship rights and are morally degrading; and they subject recipients to frequent administrative regulations. At the same time, they send a message to the poor who are not on welfare, by signifying the types of ceremonies they are likely to be subjected to if they do apply for welfare.

Within these broad and ambiguous constraints, the substance of welfare policy is greatly influenced by economic and political forces occurring in the very communities in which the poor live. These forces include class, gender, and ethnicity; actual or imagined manifestations of social unrest; the fiscal strength of the community and the structure of its labor market; the interests of the political groups that control local electoral institutions; the degree of political competition and protest; and the bureaucratization of relief. These forces are often in conflict with one another, creating internal contradictions in the administration of welfare at the local level. The poor themselves also resist, mostly passively but occasionally violently, because they have to survive. As these forces shape the administration of welfare, they contribute further to the decoupling of the policy from its administration.

Moreover, because welfare policy is an expression of a moral system, it defines who are the "deviants." Hence our second major argument is that federalism is used to control the "deviants" and to manage the conflicts that such control generates. Throughout welfare history, conflicts over the undeserving poor have been delegated to local units of government. Contemporary work programs provide a major example. Under the Reagan administration, the states were given additional discretion to experiment with work programs. A careful analysis of the Family Support Act of 1988 shows that this delegation has been codified and strengthened. Federal requirements are few, and often have loopholes. Thus a major form of social control still remains at the local level.

Periodically, the disjunctures between the symbols and the administration of welfare policy become sufficiently ominous as to threaten the validity of the symbols themselves, thus creating an impetus for welfare reform. This may occur when there are significant shifts in the cultural norms themselves, such as the role of women in the labor force, or when social controls break down, as in the case of the rapid rise in the welfare rolls in the 1960s.

We are, of course, not devoid of an ideological stance regarding welfare policy, and we state our views explicitly. We are in favor of job training, educational, and work programs, with expanded health and child care and child support. But, as distinguished from both conservatives and liberals, we object to coercive requirements on the grounds that they are unnecessary, unfair, unworkable, and serve the purpose of segregating and stigmatizing the welfare recipient. Nonpoor mothers work, but they have a choice; poor mothers should have the same option.

In Chapter 1, we present in greater detail our theoretical orientation. Chapters 2 and 3 may be considered prologue. They trace the history of how our major themes—industrial discipline, family policy and child protection, and race and ethnicity—formed the ideology and structure of the American social welfare state. The English heritage, particularly the poorhouse experiment, was very influential in the United States. That experience provides an exceptionally clear illustration of the major elements of our theoretical perspective: the construction of social problems, the definition of the poor as enemy, the requirements of liberal capitalism, and the crucial role of lower-level administration. We then describe the pre-New Deal period and the rise of the categorical programs—AFDC, aid to the blind, and old-age assistance—as well as workers' compensation. This period formed the basic ideologies and jurisdictional allocations of the modern social welfare state, which were then refined, but basically confirmed, by the Social Security Act of 1935. That act sharply distinguished between the deserving and the undeserving poor by creating contributory social insurance for those who had satisfied their moral obligation to work from the others—the dependents. Of particular importance during this period were the New Deal work-relief programs and the ambivalent unemployment insurance program. That entire generative period confirmed the central importance of industrial discipline in American social welfare.

Chapters 4, 5, and 6 tell the contemporary story—the vast changes in the demographic and legal characteristics of AFDC, and the consequent rise of work requirements. Chapter 5 discusses the tension among four strategies designed to cope with the "welfare crisis" through six administrations, from Eisenhower through Carter—social services, incentives, regulatory work requirements, and the negative income tax—and the emergence of the regulatory work test as the dominant policy choice. Chapter 6 is concerned with the 1981 Omnibus Budget Reconciliation Act of the Reagan administration, the work demonstration projects, and the two most important state programs, Employment and Training (ET) Choices in Massachusetts and Greater Avenues for Independence (GAIN) in California, the latter considered one of the important models for the Family Support Act of 1988. We compare GAIN with experiences in some of the other important state programs. In Chapter 6, we discuss the current welfare reform consensus and the Family Support Act, and present our views concerning the likely unfolding of the present reform effort.

NOTES

1. Throughout this book, we will use the terms *AFDC* and *welfare* interchangeably.

2. In 1987, expenditures for public assistance (which includes AFDC, Medicaid, and general assistance), were approximately 9% of all social welfare expenditures (*Social Security Bulletin, Annual Statistical Supplement*, 1989, Table 3.A3).

1

What Is Welfare Policy?

Who the poor are and what to do about their poverty form the basis of welfare policy. For most of human history, such questions were never asked; the poor were considered part of the natural order. Why, then, do the poor emerge as a social problem? Why do particular categories of the poor become social problems? These are moral questions. The construction of the nature, causes, and remedies for poverty reflect fundamental values as to how society should be organized, how people should act, how to assign blame, and when to relieve misery.

Responses to poverty are designed to perform a number of social purposes. We tend to focus on the practical, social control, regulatory interests of the state—maintain labor discipline, relieve misery, or, when necessary, quell disorder. But welfare programs perform other functions as well. They define values and confirm status; they are expressive and symbolic. Poverty is a social problem. Conditions become social problems, enter political language, not because they suddenly materialize or change in character; usually they have always been present. Rather, conditions become social problems for ideological purposes. Social problems are constructed. They serve the interests of those who define them. The distinction between the "deserving" poor and the "undeserving" poor is a moral issue; it affirms the values of the dominant society by stigmatizing the outcasts. The meaning ascribed to events is thus reciprocal; observers construct themselves by constructing others.[1] The definition of problems creates authority and status; it allocates resources and rewards. Explanations rationalize particular actions and justify authority in people who claim competence in dealing with particular causes; explanations will endure if they comport with dominant ideologies (Edelman, 1988). We construct problems and symbols to further our interests; interests, in turn, may be both symbolic and tangible.

Welfare policy is part of the larger normative order of society—in our society, the capitalist market economy. The normative order justifies itself by providing for the well-being of its citizens in exchange for work. The state offers protection, comfort, and material rewards for those who participate in the productive system. For those who cannot participate, because of conditions beyond their control, the state provides relief. This is the moral contract of citizenship: rewards for those who are productive, care for those who are unable to work. The persistence of poor people inevitably calls into question the economic order; after all, how can the state command allegiance if so many of its citizens are not being provided for? The relief of those who cannot work legitimates the state.

Thus the heart of welfare policy centers on the question of who is excused from work—who can claim material support that is not the product of his or her own effort. In short, when is the failure to support oneself and one's family justified? Ultimately, this is a moral question. Although simply stated, this question is deeply mired in contradiction and ambiguity. It involves deciding the nature and extent of the work ethic; the causes and extent of disability; the impact, both real and perceived, of incentives and disincentives on human behavior; and the consequences of failure to abide by conventional norms on the individual, the family, and the community. Much of the moral ambiguity present in granting relief to the poor centers on the relationship between welfare and work. Historically, welfare was always viewed as having the potential to erode motivation to work. A persistent feature of welfare policy has been to set the poor to work as a condition for receiving welfare. Needless to say, the moral determination of deservingness is contested at least passively if not overtly by the poor themselves.

When specific categories of the poor are considered—such as the single mother and her children—the moral questions become even more complex. Issues of gender, family, and child rearing are part of the larger normative order of work, welfare, and social control. In the particular context of the United States, race and ethnicity are inextricably connected. The single mother and her children are not only poor, they are also disproportionately members of a minority or ethnic group. Gender, class, race, and ethnicity evoke powerful meanings in American society; they feed into and make more complicated the moral construction of poverty and welfare policy.

Welfare policy, then, to a large extent, may be understood as the institutionalized production of *symbols* whose primary purpose is to affirm the dominant social values of work, family and gender roles, and social status. At the same time, welfare policy does real things—it selects and rejects applicants, spends public money, and regulates behavior. Thus welfare policy is also a system of *regulation*; as such, it reflects the structural demands of federalism, the political economy, and bureaucracy. Both systems—the production of symbols and regulation—are ambiguous and contradictory internally and as they interact with each other over the construction and implementation of welfare policy.

In this chapter, we discuss the major features of both the symbolic and the regulatory systems; this will provide the analytic framework for the historical development of welfare policy (Chapters 2 and 3), the analysis of 25 years of work programs (Chapters 4 and 5), and the contemporary consensus on welfare reform (Chapter 6).

THE INSTITUTIONALIZED PRODUCTION OF SYMBOLS

What are the interests served by welfare policy? Why does society care about poverty?

The Work Ethic

The "problem of poverty" has been, and is today, defined primarily in terms of the moral values of work. The most consistent, animating part of welfare policy is to reinforce the work ethic. This is the principle of "less eligible": The conditions of relief have to be made less desirable than the conditions of the lowest-paid work (Katz, 1986, p. 33). The idea is to make sure that those who can work will not choose welfare. Those who fail to support themselves or their families through work are morally deviant. Stigmatizing those who fail to conform affirms the moral worth of those who do.

The failure to support oneself and one's family through paid labor is constructed in terms of three basic principles. First, productive work is an *individual* responsibility. With rare exceptions (for example, during the Great Depression), blame for the failure to find an adequate job is placed on the individual. Second, this failure is considered to be a *moral* one. Those who fail to work, without a socially approved excuse, at a socially approved job are condemned. They are defined as deviant. The chronically unemployed, able-bodied malingerers, paupers, bums, tramps, and those who work in socially disapproved jobs are considered threats to the ideology of labor discipline—hard work, thrift, and reward through individual effort. Third, *moral degradation* of the poor is used as a negative symbol to reinforce the work ethic.

The very categorization of the poor reflects these moral attitudes. The poorhouses created many offenses against the poor—the separation of families, forced labor, terrible living conditions—but one of the most salient offenses was the deprivation of liberty; this was the ultimate denial of citizenship, the ultimate stigma, and a great rallying cry for the poorhouse foes (Himmelfarb, 1984). One of the most common regulatory techniques that is still used today is forced menial labor for relief recipients—pauper labor—justified on deterrence grounds.

Conversely, when work is not at issue, the symbols of welfare are deliberately designed to avoid the relief stigma. The most common symbol is the absence of a means test, or the presence of a simplified, nonintrusive one. In the nineteenth century, when states such as Wisconsin created institutions for the blind and the deaf, means tests were rejected on the grounds that they were "certificates of pauperism" (State Board of Control, 1939, p. 77). Pensions for Civil War veterans were administered by separate agencies to distinguish these worthy beneficiaries from paupers. A major controversy over New Deal work programs centered on the means test. The reformers wanted to avoid the stigma of relief; capitalists insisted that the test be used. Humiliation is a conscious creation of relief policy. As an alternative to the means test, support is granted on some form of social contract theory. Thus the proponents of an expanded old-age assistance program for the needy aged in the 1930s tried to abolish the means test, or scale it back, and establish a flat-grant system, called a "pension." The paradigm program, of course, is the social security program of Old-Age and Survivors Insurance (OASI). Despite the fact that its insurance features are attenuated and the program has strong redistributive effects, it has always been sold on the basis of "insurance" and "contributions." A deliberate attempt has been made to distinguish social security beneficiaries from the dependent poor. There is no means test for social security.

Throughout the long history of welfare policy, it has proved to be difficult to administer relief that would relieve misery but not undermine the moral value of work (Himmelfarb, 1984; Katz, 1986). Because the failure to earn one's living was considered an individual moral failure, and because this failure would lead to other, even more serious forms of deviant behavior, welfare policy had to be extremely careful not to encourage dependency. Relief would be given *only* to those who would not thereby be encouraged to become permanently dependent. Those in the *category* of the potentially eligible, those presumptively in the labor market, the able-bodied, were not to be given relief for the asking. The category was presumptively "undeserving" or "unworthy" of public aid. This is not to say that all persons within the class were to be denied—the relief of misery, as we shall see, was also a goal—but welfare administrators had to pick and choose carefully as to who would be helped, how much, and under what conditions. This decision involved not only a determination of the *reasons* for poverty, but also a prediction as to the likely effects of relieving poverty. The nineteenth-century campaigns to abolish outdoor relief (relief given outside of institutions) in favor of the poorhouse were justified on the grounds that the difficulty in deciding between the deserving and undeserving applicant at the local level was contributing to the spread of pauperism. The poorhouse was a simplified means test; because conditions were so awful, the act of relief itself became the test of necessity.

The example of the poorhouse illustrates the third part of the ideological construction of the work ethic, the moral degradation of the poor. Despite the fact that throughout most of welfare history, only the truly desperate received help—the aged, the seriously disabled, widows, and small children—the conditions of their relief were deliberately miserable to deter the able-bodied from seeking relief. The poorhouse, the stone pile, and the wood yard were pauper labor, as distinguished from market labor, to stigmatize the former. The moral degradation of the truly desperate served as symbolic support for the liberal capitalist order.

Moral degradation is, of course, concrete in the lives of the truly desperate—they suffered the poorhouse and menial labor, and they suffer the harshness of programs today. In other words, symbols are made creditable by specific acts—whether by sometimes relieving misery or by onerous conditions. This is what we mean by welfare as a system of myth and ceremony. The myths are the ideological constructions of the problem of poverty and the solutions. The ceremonies—the concrete acts—serve two functions: They lend credence to the beholders of the dominant order that something is being done, and at the same time they serve as examples to deter the poor from seeking welfare rather than work.

The structures of specific welfare programs are part of the system of myth and ceremony. The different structures reflect moral attitudes toward the category of poor to be served. We ask, Why is this particular person (category) poor and what, if anything, should be done about that poverty? If the category is considered deviant, then the program will be one of social control; it will seek to modify what society considers to be inappropriate behavior. On the other hand, if the person (category) is considered to be faultless, then misery will be relieved. In welfare policy jargon, the latter is *deserving* and the former *undeserving*. While these terms encompass many characteristics, as we shall see, the core concept is whether or not the category is *morally excused from work*. If the category is not morally excused from work, then the relief of misery cannot conflict with the moral value of work; members of the category will be either excluded or, if admitted, subject to work requirements.

Programs for the deserving poor are *inclusive*; they reach out and try to bring in members of the category. Social control programs are *exclusive*; they try to enforce social control either by the conditions of relief or by denying entry altogether. In analyzing particular welfare programs, it is important to look at the *category* of potential clientele and to determine who is excluded as well as who is included. General relief is exclusive: It is considered the major line of defense, the principal enforcer of labor discipline, when confronted by its category of potential applicants—historically, the able-bodied poor; today, the stereotype is the African-American, urban male. Unemployment insurance is also selective. Benefits are quite limited as to both amount and duration, and the majority of the unemployed, for a variety of reasons, are excluded. Unemployment insurance, in the United States, is more in the nature of temporary relief at subsistence levels. Throughout most of its history, Aid to Families with Dependent Children was also very exclusive, primarily serving white widows. Since the 1960s, as a result of the civil rights movement, welfare rights campaigns, and the development of legal rights, AFDC has largely lost the power to exclude; but this does not mean that AFDC has become a deserving poor program. As we shall argue, the program is adopting more social control characteristics to regulate its new, deviant clients. In contrast to these three programs are the social security programs OASI and Supplemental Security Income (SSI). The clients of these programs are morally excused from work; these programs are inclusive.[2]

Who is excluded from particular programs, and why, tells us a great deal about social attitudes toward various categories of the poor. Failure to focus on the category (both the excluded as well as the included) has led to a major misinterpretation of what our social attitudes toward the female-headed household in poverty have been and are today. For example, contrary to interpretation (Garfinkel & McLanahan, 1986; Katz, 1986), the early aid to dependent children (ADC) programs—called "mothers' pensions"—did not represent a major change in policy toward the poor single mother, because, in fact, the vast majority of poor single mothers were excluded. As discussed in the next chapter, the mothers' pension program was myth and ceremony. The myth was that now worthy single mothers would be excused from the paid labor force and their homes would not be broken. This salved the consciences of the program's proponents. The ceremony consisted of granting small amounts of relief to a select group of white widows. White widows were defined in terms of the Other—the *excluded* single mothers; the latter were still part of the paid labor force. The myths and ceremonies of the mothers' pension movement thus spoke to *both* the nonpoor and the poor. The values of patriarchy and the "proper" female role were rewarded; and the nonconforming poor, those who were morally degraded to begin with (people of color, never marrieds, and those who were divorced, separated, or deserted) need not apply.

Family and Gender Roles

As the early mothers' pension programs illustrated, the position of women in the paid labor force and the implications of that position for the ideologies of family policy and child rearing are central to the analysis of welfare policy. Three major themes interact. There is, first, the overarching policy of labor discipline. Second, there is the role of women—singles, wives, and mothers—in the industrial order in light of the domestic code. And, third, there is the theme of child rearing. Labor discipline forced poor mothers to work by restricting relief. Patriarchy and the domestic code condemned them for working. Child protection declared them socially deviant and threatened to take away their children.

The family is pivotal in regulating sexual relations and procreation, in socializing children to adult roles, and in defining adult gender roles especially in relation to the labor market. Welfare policy is family policy because it defines what is a "deviant" family, sanctions "inappropriate" adult gender and work roles, penalizes "undesirable" sexual relations, and regulates the family's responsibilities to its children. By constructing welfare recipients as deviant families, the state symbolically institutionalizes the image of the "good" family to the nonpoor and the poor alike.

As we shall see in the next chapter, poor women, including mothers, *always* had to work for income (Kessler-Harris, 1982). During the nineteenth century, distinctions were drawn between the values and behaviors of female wage work and those of women who did not work. The difference evolved into what was called the "domestic code." Fundamentally patriarchal, nineteenth-century industrial society constructed the home as sanctuary. Men worked in the paid labor force. Wives were home managers, child rearers, and sources of emotional support, valued for piety, purity, and submissiveness. Children became the center of women's activity, their calling. This was women's "separate sphere," part of the "natural" social order (Kessler-Harris, 1982, pp. 43–51).

The domestic code sharpened class, gender, race, and ethnic lines. In practical terms, the domestic code applied only to the middle and upper classes. It complemented capitalism and was seen as a symbol, a desired end and reward for those who worked hard and played by the rules. The symbolism of the domestic code was "shored up" precisely because lower-class women had to work. Wage-working women became the negative symbol, seen as selfish and neglectful of their families. Of course, those in extreme poverty had to work—especially free African-Americans and immigrants; the domestic code considered them all but outcasts (Kessler-Harris, 1982, pp. 70–71). At the same time, despite their exploitation in labor markets, wage-working women received little sympathy and support; instead they were condemned for working for frivolous reasons, for depressing wages, and for making working conditions worse for men. They were blamed for the decline of the family wage. The domestic code, fueled by male competition and hostility, as well as deteriorating working conditions, defined female wage labor as "without virtue" (p. 68). It is important to keep in mind that throughout history (including the present), poor women were never morally excused from paid labor. Not only did necessity drive these women into the paid labor force, they also performed the lowest-paid, unskilled, most menial kinds of work—working as laundresses, domestics, factory workers—as well as illegal activities (e.g., distilling and selling alcohol). These women were disproportionately immigrants and African-Americans. In an important sense, they were "degraded to begin with" (L. Gordon, 1988).

Thus poor mothers were caught in a central contradiction. Capitalists, largely indifferent to the ideology of the domestic code as far as the lower social orders were concerned, considered poor women to be part of the paid labor force. At the same time, poor mothers were declared deviant because they violated the domestic code. They were stigmatized because they had to work and because of the kinds of work they had to do. Because lower-class families could not fulfill the domestic code, they presumably also failed in their socialization functions, which were becoming increasingly important for the developing capitalist economy. Not surprisingly, the social reformers of that day became convinced that the traditional family had become a social problem (L. Gordon, 1988). In a related effort to shore up the traditional family, the social reformers "discovered" child abuse. Child protection, along with the wage-working mother, was part of the growing concern about social disorder (pp. 29–33).

The concept of child protection fit with prevailing ideas of the patriarchal family; indeed, the purpose of protection was to reconstitute the traditional family. The family as a whole became the object of ideology: Upper-class Protestant women were seeking to subordinate the immigrant poor; conservative feminists were seeking to enhance respect for women and children (L. Gordon, 1988, pp. 56–57). Child protection and, particularly, the definition of child cruelty changed, moving from concern with abuse to the more expansive "neglect." Mothers, and especially working mothers, were blamed for inadequate supervision and fathers for inadequate discipline. The shift from abuse to neglect was important. Men were blamed when abuse and individual vice were emphasized. When inadequate social conditioning was the fault, mothers were blamed; after all, they were in charge of the children (L. Gordon, 1988).

Single mothers were in the most difficult position. They were the poorest group. Between the demands of the domestic code and the child protection conception of proper child rearing, they faced impossible expectations. The very life-style of these single women was morally suspect. They had to work outside of the home to survive, but lack of supervision became one of the defining elements of child neglect. Almost by definition, they failed at mothering and at playing the proper feminine role.[3] And because they were very poor, they were also suspect as paupers (L. Gordon, 1988, p. 84). Because caseworkers generally saw these mothers as incapable of maintaining a home and earning a living, they frequently found neglect, and, rather than help the mothers maintain the home, they often recommended that the children be removed.

As will be discussed in the next chapter, the central contradictions facing poor women were always manifest in the rhetoric of the aid to dependent children program. When ADC was first proposed, during the second decade of this century, both proponents and opponents evoked the image of the traditional, patriarchal family. The proponents argued that men and women belonged in separate spheres; motherhood and the home were privileged, and should not be compromised by paid labor. Mothers' pensions, they said, removed the necessity for paid labor and would thereby reinforce patriarchy and domesticity. The opposition believed that pensions would weaken traditional family ties, the responsibility of the husband, and encourage single motherhood. That both sides thought that their respective positions privileged patriarchy should not be surprising. Political events and ideologies are always ambiguous. Each side constructed its own explanation of the social problem and argued for its own solutions. In addition, it is no accident that most professional social workers, and particularly those involved in child protection, would, at least initially, oppose a program that threatened their ideologies.

The moral ambiguity was resolved in terms that would prove to be paradigmatic in American welfare policy. In practice, at the field level, the programs were restricted. The "worthy" widows, those who in their race and behavior affirmed the domestic code, would be brought back into majoritarian society. They would still be single, but their homes would reflect the separate sphere. They would devote themselves to home management and child rearing. They would be morally excused from work. The value of both the non-working middle-class mother and the worthy widow would be affirmed by those who were denied entry; the unworthy mothers were cast out, and had to rely on degrading labor and male breadwinners. Both morality and local taxpayer costs would be saved. The mothers' pension movement served important symbolic purposes. In practice, the vast majority of poor mothers and their children remained the socially constructed enemy to be dealt with in the local communities where the contradictions and ambiguities of labor discipline, gender, class, race, and ethnicity had to be sorted out. The mothers' pension movement was symbolic and expressive—an exercise in status politics. For the vast majority of female-headed households in poverty, nothing had changed.

Similar patterns of myths and ceremonies periodically occurred throughout the history of AFDC.[4] For most of its history—until the 1960s—the mothers' pension pattern prevailed; the "degraded to begin with" were excluded and kept in the labor market. When African-American divorced, separated, and never-married women began to enter the program, deviant behavior social controls began to be enforced—"man-in-the-house" rules, "fit and proper homes," and so forth. In addition to local political campaigns, there were real victims—cases were terminated[5]—but these victims also served larger important symbolic roles. They reminded majoritarian society who welfare recipients were; as African-American unmarried women came into the program, they had to be restigmatized into welfare abusers, spawning generational dependency.

As we shall see, a similar analysis applies to the various AFDC work programs, including the Family Support Act of 1988. The new wave of reform will serve important symbolic functions. The presence of these programs, with their attendant publicity of both opportunities and obligations, will serve to remind the public of what is now expected of welfare recipients. Some will succeed; they will progress with education and training, obtain work, and leave welfare (whether as a result of the program is another matter), but most will fail. As with the worthy widow of the mothers' pensions days, those who succeed will validate the dominant ideology and condemn the failures. The great bulk of welfare recipients will still be excluded.

Race, Ethnicity, and Class

Throughout U.S. social history, racial discrimination and nativism have served to affirm dominant values, status, and power by defining people of color and immigrants as deviant and degraded. Women of color and immigrants have been disproportionately unable to conform to the domestic code. Not only did they have to work, they also had to work in the lowest, most "unfeminine" jobs. They were important economically (Kessler-Harris, 1982), but because they had to work for wages, they were further victimized.

Race has always had an independent effect on welfare policy; this was particularly true in the South, where, until the post-World War II period, most African-Americans lived. Southern African-Americans were excluded from the polity, from patriarchal construction, and from welfare. To include African-Americans in welfare was considered a threat to white southern hegemony. Programs in the South were deliberately discriminatory.[6] Although less obvious and direct, similar effects of race are also evident in welfare policy in other parts of the country. As southern African-Americans were recruited into jobs in other regions, often as strikebreakers, their fate became inextricably linked to the economies of the industries they worked in, and welfare served its regulatory functions.

As part of the dominant social and economic order, welfare policy has served the societal values of racial hostility, discrimination, subordination, and exclusion. For most of welfare history, African-Americans, regardless of their circumstances and needs, were simply excluded from welfare; they were considered the most unde-serving poor. As noted, since the 1960s, African-American single mothers have entered AFDC in large numbers; we argue that the entry of this undeserving class has resulted in the increased social control features in the program.

The new racial stigmatization is the "underclass" (Katz, 1989, chap. 5). Loosely defined, this is an umbrella label for a great many of the assorted tragedies of the African-American urban ghettos: crime, drugs, unemployment, poverty, wretched housing, failed schooling, poor health, and, of course, out-of-wedlock births. Despite the fact that only a very small proportion of African-Americans live in high-concentration, ghetto neighborhoods and could be considered part of the underclass, however defined (Ellwood, 1988; Ruggles, 1989), the contemporary stereotypical welfare recipient—the young African-American unmarried mother—is considered to be a major part of "the problem."

The young mother with a very young child is officially targeted as the potential long-term welfare recipient, and state "workfare" programs are required to give priority to this group. This is a laud-able objective; work and training programs are potentially most ef-ficient for those recipients least likely to get off of welfare on their own (see Chapter 4). There is no doubt that much help is needed—the prospects for independence for these mothers and their children are indeed dim (Garfinkel & McLanahan, 1986). But it is also true that this group is the most difficult to work with. In general, these young women lack education, skills, and work experience, and it is often hard to motivate teenagers. Further, because of their very young children, programs for these teenagers are especially expen-sive. If past experience is any guide, field-level agencies will find ways of deferring this group. The myth will be that we are provid-ing work and training opportunities; the ceremony will be the few who gain entry and succeed. But the vast majority of young Afri-can-American mothers, because they will remain on welfare, will continue to be morally degraded.

Threats to the Social Order

Much of welfare policy is driven by the belief that the poor pose silent, insidious threats to dominant ideologies and the social order. The poor have always been considered a major threat to the economic order (Himmelfarb, 1984). In the nineteenth century, the indiscriminate giving of aid was considered one of the prime causes of pauperism and social unrest. As we shall see, the relatively generous early New Deal work-relief programs were bitterly attacked and ultimately repealed on the grounds that they were undermining local labor markets. The AFDC program, from its earliest mothers' pension days through the present, has been attacked repeatedly on the grounds that it undermines family values. Today, the underclass is considered the new enemy. Welfare is blamed for contributing to the growth of permanent inner-city crime- and drug-infested communities posing serious threats to urban life in particular and the country in general (Katz, 1989).

Threats to the social order are not solely figments of the imaginations of the rich. There is always resistance on the part of the poor—they have to survive. They struggle to assert themselves, to claim benefits; they try to manipulate the system. Women, minorities, and their children experience in their daily lives the contradictions and injustices of the dominant discourse; they, and sometimes their neighbors and allies, know that they are not at fault, that they are victims of uncontrollable forces; they define their own needs (Fraser, 1989). Throughout welfare history, there have been varying degrees of resistance at the local level to the harshest programs—for example, the abolition of outdoor relief and the poorhouses. At times, more widespread social movement has developed, the most notable recent example being the campaigns of the National Welfare Rights Organization in the 1960s, largely spearheaded by African-American welfare recipients demanding the dignity and benefits of entitlements (Piven & Cloward, 1977). Today, feminists struggle against the dominant ideologies in welfare reform (Abramovitz, 1988; Fraser, 1989; White, 1990).

From time to time throughout history, threats have become violent. Food riots, crop burnings, rent strikes, and rural and urban riots and rebellions occur periodically. While there has been no satisfactory theory predicting violent collective behavior by the poor (Piven & Cloward, 1990), there is little doubt about the frequency and impact of such behavior on organized society. Responses to mass disorder varies—sometimes the poor are brutally repressed; at other times, demands are met, at least in part. The nineteenth-century Poor Law reforms in Great Britain were undermined, in part, by localized rural rioting. The social disorder in the late nineteenth century in the United States stimulated the campaigns to abolish outdoor relief. On the other hand, the urban riots and massive protest actions by welfare recipients in the United States in the 1960s contributed to the liberalization of welfare. Overt, collective protest by the poor produces public response, but whether that response is liberal or repressive is not predictable by the fact of protest alone. The most that can be said is that from time to time, welfare policy does respond to quell social disorder (Piven & Cloward, 1990).

Charity

Running counter to the efforts to frighten and punish the poor, is, of course, the charitable impulse, the moral injunction to help the poor and the stranger. This tradition remains a powerful force under liberal capitalism if for no other reason than that relief of the poor serves to legitimate the state. At times the charitable impulse seems to be overwhelmed by other forces, but it is never completely silent. Even during periods of stringent, harsh, and regulatory social control policies, the full rigor of the state has often been blunted by the desire of local people to help their unfortunate neighbors.

We tend to think that the liberal or charitable interpretation of welfare history is exaggerated, but we do not mean to make the opposite mistake. The charitable impulse is enduring. At times, it predominates, and liberal, generous programs are enacted, at least for some of the poor. Even when the liberal impulse seems to be overwhelmed, quite often there is enough strength to create bargains or compromise either at the policy level or at the local level. Nevertheless, while specific acts of charity provide real benefits to some, charity is, by and large, myth and ceremony. It does little to relieve poverty; at the same time, it confirms the status of the donor and the recipient.

THE SYSTEM OF SOCIAL REGULATION

The production of symbols is one thing; the actual separation of the worthy from the unworthy poor is quite another matter. Welfare policy creates symbols, but it also deals with the lives of people in concrete settings, and it is in concrete settings that competing and contradictory policies get sorted out.

To lend credence to the symbols, sufficient public resources must be committed to welfare policy. The poorhouse has to be built, relief has to be distributed, the poor have to selected and matched with various forms of relief, and then they have to be monitored. Hence a system of social regulation of the poor is established, representing a concrete manifestation that "something is being done about the problem." It is a system, an array of welfare programs, that regulates the lives of the poor and produces the myths and ceremonies to uphold the symbols. The ceremonies of welfare are the categorization and certification of the poor, enforcement of eligibility requirements, selection of candidates to work programs, and monitoring of behavior, especially potential fraud.

Yet, the moral ambiguity of poverty always threatens the integrity of welfare programs as a system of social regulation. Contending ideologies embedded in welfare policy itself create contradictory regulatory and ceremonial requirements. Moreover, once a class of "deviants" has been created, an enforcement system has to be established requiring the exercise of discretion. Therefore, a major concern in the administration of welfare policy is the allocation of *jurisdictional responsibility*. When there is a lack of consensus about the moral deservingness of a particular category of the poor, the jurisdiction for welfare programs is more likely to be local, letting the local community sort out the ambiguities.

The amount of resources committed to welfare policy and how they are distributed among the poor are influenced less by the needs of the poor themselves than by the wishes of the policymakers and their constituents to affirm the symbols. Yet, the commitment and distribution of public resources also entail other considerations having to do with the *political economy* of the state. Once categories of poor are defined, their numbers are affected by the political economy of the state, such as its economic wealth, patterns of immigration and migration, allocation of resources to human capital improvements (e.g., education and health), and the ideologies of its political elites. The resources committed to welfare, raised through tax revenues, as meager as they may be, do have an impact on the economy of the state, especially the costs of production. The poor themselves, particularly the able-bodied poor, are an important source of low-wage workers, especially in the secondary labor market.

To administer the welfare policy a *welfare bureaucracy* has to be created, and procedures must be developed to process, manage, and monitor the welfare clients. The bureaucracy, having its own needs to survive and manage its work, becomes a significant actor in shaping welfare policy, through both its day-to-day administration of welfare and its control over information about welfare recipients.

Thus welfare as a system of social regulation is embedded in three larger systems: legal jurisdiction, the political economy, and bureaucracy. Each of these systems shapes welfare and each of the other systems. The symbolic ambiguities become resolved and unresolved in each of the systems.

Federalism and State Discretion

The allocation of jurisdictional responsibility has always figured prominently in welfare history. In the earliest days, in medieval England, relief of the poor was a local responsibility. This meant that local authorities decided who was deserving, how much support they would receive, and under what conditions. Local communities decided who were "strangers." Conditions of relief and settlement and removal were part of the system of regulation and mobility of labor.

In the United States, the allocation of authority among the federal government, the states, and local governments (counties, municipalities) continues to serve important regulatory functions. In general, when issues of labor discipline and social control of deviant behavior are strongest, programs tend to be more locally administered. Conversely, when consensus forms, programs tend to be federally administered. An expanded federal social security system and old-age assistance program developed when agreement was reached on a retirement age and racial politics changed.

When programs are ambiguous and contradictory, local administrative officials respond to the needs and exigencies of the local economy and impose the community's definition of morality. This is an old tradition in welfare administration; it was the local officials who decided who had to break stones or chop wood, who would be excused from the poorhouse. State and local political economies vary considerably from each other; some are highly industrialized and unionized, resulting in more progressive welfare policies; others are more dependent on agriculture or single industries and suffer more from economic swings than diversified economies. Welfare programs that are concerned with labor and morality reflect these economic exigencies. General relief in West Virginia is different from that in New York.

State economies also influence patterns of migration and immigration, which bear on the supply of low-wage labor. Historically, welfare policies have been used to regulate this flow through residency requirements, benefit levels, and work requirements either to discourage the inflow of low-wage and potentially dependent populations or to attract industry on the basis of the availability of cheap labor and low taxes. Residency requirements are now illegal, but welfare benefits, work requirements, and low taxes remain important instruments of policy (Peterson & Rom, 1989).

As stated, labor discipline is never an unambiguous policy; deservingness is often contested terrain. In day-to-day operations, difficult judgments have to be made in individual cases. There are conflicting demands of generosity. Communities differ on the moral assessment of the poor and their attitudes toward race and gender. Economic and political pluralism allows these conflicts to be fought out at the local level. This is an effective strategy for sharply contested issues. The economic and moral conflicts are most keenly felt at the local level; local elites want to retain control over their labor supply; communities want to retain control over their social victims. Dominant local elements want to decide who is deserving and who is undeserving. Inevitably there is at least some degree of resistance on the part of the poor themselves at the local level. Whatever elites may think, women, minorities, and their children know differently and struggle to survive. At the same time, national leaders find it in their interests to delegate conflicts to low-visibility state and local decision makers. Delegation or diffusion of hot issues serves both levels of government; federalism is an effective strategy to manage welfare conflict.

While states want autonomy in administering welfare, they also want to shift the burden of welfare costs to the federal government. Hence, in shaping welfare policy, states and local governments act as important interest groups. States with high welfare expenditures push to shift the burden to the federal government, while states with low welfare expenditures resist federal efforts to impose uniform standards. States and local governments also exert important influence because of the categorization of programs: Cutbacks in higher-level programs (e.g., disability, Medicare) will result in increased state expenditures; cutbacks in state-funded programs (e.g., Medicaid, AFDC) will increase local expenditures. Thus federalism creates government groups pressing their own demands.

The Political Economy

At the macro level, the general level of the economy, both nationally and in the states, affects welfare allocations. In general, wealthier states have more generous programs than poorer states despite greater need in the latter. With rare exceptions (such as the Depression), tough times lead to tough welfare policies. During periods of state deficits, AFDC and general relief budget levels will remain frozen. There are, of course, differences in public support for social welfare expenditures depending on the "deservingness" of the client population and the form of the social benefit. The public is more inclined to support income maintenance for the aged, whereas programs for the undeserving poor are peculiarly vulnerable to the economic health of the states and the federal government.

At the micro level, welfare policy is driven by the economics of labor and gender, specifically those policies and institutions that determine the demand and supply of low-wage labor among men and women, the division of labor among men and women, and the distribution of income along race and gender lines. The changing structure of low-wage industries alters the demand for cheap labor among men and women, their employability, and the distribution of income among them.

There have been significant changes in female labor force participation in the United States. During the colonial and early republican periods, women were actively encouraged to seek paid labor. Between the 1840s and the 1960s (except for World War II), women were actively discouraged from paid labor; as previously discussed, this was the period of the ideological development of the patriarchal family, the domestic code, and the doctrine of separate spheres. Of course, poor women, including wives and mothers, and their children were excepted; they supplied an important pool of low-wage labor. Working men, unions, and many social reformers were interested in reducing the competition of women in the paid labor market and preserving patriarchal families; capitalists were not.

The South, during the century following the Civil War, was basically an agricultural, plantation economy. Buttressed by politics, law, and social practices, the economy was based on the subordination of rural African-Americans (Quadagno, 1988). As we shall see, southern race discrimination and economic subordination, combined with one-party political strength in the Congress, had an enormous impact on restricting the development of the American social welfare state at the national level during the Depression and the period immediately following World War II. The South was able to veto any national initiative that would send public dollars to African-American tenant farm families and thereby disturb existing patterns of racial subordination.

Race prejudice figured prominently in the development of welfare policies in the North as well. Persistent patterns of discrimination condemned African-Americans to low-wage jobs and poverty. The role of welfare was to reinforce race and gender prejudice and the segmented labor force. As stated, the guiding principle of welfare was the deserving/undeserving poor distinction. During this period, welfare policy sought to remove the deserving from the work force, primarily through old-age assistance and the gradual development of social security, but to maintain labor discipline and the subordination of African-Americans and women through a restrictive aid to dependent children program, the exclusion of agricultural and most service workers, and most women and their children. Welfare was primarily for whites who were aged, in male-headed families, and widows. Minorities, singles, and childless couples, and mothers who were single, divorced, or separated and their children were disproportionately excluded from income support. They had to work; they were the undeserving poor. Welfare reflected and supported existing patterns of labor, class, gender, race, and ethnicity.

The political economy changed significantly starting in the 1960s, but in contradictory directions. The civil rights movement, southern politics, and industrialization radically changed southern society. African-Americans voted, the South lost its veto power in Congress, and poor southern African-Americans became a poverty problem in the urbanizing South. Southern political and business leaders became much more receptive to the expansion of welfare. In the North, civil and legal rights movements, urban riots, and other forms of mass protest led to a significant expansion of welfare. There were huge transformations in the economic and social status of women. Massive numbers of women, including mothers of young children, entered the paid labor force; today, a majority of women work for wages. At the same time, there has also been a dramatic increase in the number of the poor living in female-headed households. For a variety of reasons, primarily the deteriorating labor market conditions for both men and women, women and children now constitute the largest number of poor in the United States (Bane, 1986).

These contradictory directions in the economy are reflected in the contradictory paths of welfare. A series of moves reflected generosity. Programs for the aged and the disabled—those who do not present a threat to the low-wage structure—expanded significantly. Large numbers of previously excluded nonwidowed single mothers, including African-Americans, were admitted to AFDC and, at least for a time, benefits rose. The welfare poor, along with many other deprived groups—for example, minorities, women, the handicapped, the mentally ill, children needing special education—benefited from the legal rights movement that developed during the 1960s out of civil rights campaigns. Many legal entitlements were created. Old programs were recast, new ones were created, and there was a considerable expansion in enrollments and benefits. Under the impetus of the legal rights movement, many of welfare's social control features were eliminated (e.g., residency requirements, man-in-the-house rules).

Later moves were restrictive. AFDC benefits levels were frozen, and, as a result of inflation, real benefits declined significantly, reducing competition with low-wage jobs. Stricter accountability rules and increased bureaucratization were imposed, resulting in greater sanctions against recipients. Work requirements were imposed at all levels. The disability programs were tightened, ostensibly to cut back on the incentives for early retirement. Work programs were introduced into AFDC; mothers of young children were now expected to work. And general relief programs became harsher and more exclusionary. Welfare recipients continued to be stigmatized and otherwise morally degraded. In sum, as more of the undeserving poor—those not morally excused from work—were let into the programs, the programs were recast to reflect greater efforts to impose labor discipline and social control.

The Bureaucracy

The bureaucracy of welfare plays an active role in shaping the operational characteristics of welfare policy (Lipsky, 1980). It determines which recipients will be admitted to programs, under what conditions, and who will be sanctioned (Hasenfeld, 1987). The conflicts and contradictions of the symbolic and regulatory systems, for the most part, are delegated to the bureaucracy; it is at the field level, in the day-to-day implementation decisions, that the vague, ambiguous, and contradictory demands of the law, competing systems, and the local political culture get sorted out. Clients have to be processed, money allocated, and real and symbolic demands reconciled.

The welfare bureaucracy, like all public bureaucracies, is primarily concerned with its own self-maintenance; accordingly, it will try to manage its environment to conserve its resources and maintain legitimacy. The bureaucracy does this by developing structures and processes that conform to the prevailing symbols of welfare, while partially decoupling the actual administration from such structures. In decoupling administration from policy, the bureaucracy organizes the processing of welfare recipients as a strategy to manage its relations with its political and economic environment (Hasenfeld, 1987). The ways the bureaucracy processes welfare applicants and recipients or manages its work requirements are influenced by its negotiations with key elements in its environment to maintain self-preservation and legitimacy. The bureaucracy will differentially interpret and enforce welfare policy to suit its own needs. As previously mentioned, and as will be discussed in detail in Chapters 4 and 5, key strategies in administering the work test are "creaming" the most employable and deferring, or putting on administrative "hold," cases considered to be "difficult," which turn out to be the great bulk of the welfare caseload.

Welfare bureaucracies—national, state, and local—represent important interest groups that influence the formulation and reformulation of welfare policies. By imposing a test of what is "do-able" from their perspective (i.e., what will enhance their own interests), they advocate for certain welfare policies. Especially, they strive to increase their autonomy and discretion in administering welfare.

THE WORK REQUIREMENTS: CONTRADICTION, RESOLUTION, AND AMBIGUITY

The major symbolic and regulatory systems interact in contradiction and ambiguity. The relief of misery is contradicted by the need to uphold the work ethic. Individual, moral responsibility for work must be tempered by blamelessness. The patriarchal domestic code is compromised by the need of capitalists for cheap labor and the need of poor wives, mothers, and children to earn income. Racial and ethnic discrimination, and its special form of labor discipline, conflict with the charitable impulse and the domestic code. The major symbolic and regulatory systems conflict with the ideologies and needs as defined by the poor themselves.

Throughout welfare history, the contradictions and ambiguities have reached different, but temporary, resolutions. We argue that the most persistent attempt at resolution is the effort to distinguish the deserving from the undeserving poor. The deserving poor possess attributes that could readily justify public protection and care without challenging dominant cultural, economic, and political norms. The undeserving poor, mostly the able-bodied, are those whose behavior and attributes challenge such norms. Much of the history of public relief and welfare can be seen as cyclical attempts to draw boundaries between the worthy poor and the pauper (Himmelfarb, 1984; Katz, 1986). These boundaries are redrawn as the social conditions producing poverty, and the number and characteristics of the poor change. Yet, there is a paramount need to maintain the deserving/undeserving distinction in order to preserve dominant cultural norms, protect the economic order, and punish fault, but show compassion for the blameless.

Thus the evolution of welfare policy is, in large part, the process of creating and revising the moral classifications of the poor. Sixteenth-century London classified the poor into three "degrees" (which were further subdivided): (a) the poor by impotency, (b) the poor by casualty, and (c) the thriftless poor. The last group, being "undeserving," was required to work for relief (Webb & Webb, 1927, vol. 7). The twentieth-century United States has evolved a complex classification of the poor, ranging from the disabled, blind, and elderly, who are deserving in that they are morally excused from work, to female heads of household, who, if their children are over the age of 3, or even 1 in some states, are considered able-bodied and are required to work.[7] Nonworking singles, mostly males, mostly African-American, are the "true paupers"; if they can get relief, it is usually only short term, and they must work. Most often, they are simply excluded.

There are two symbolic themes running throughout the deserving/undeserving poor distinction. Those who are deserving are morally excused from work—typically, the aged and the significantly disabled. For this group, moral ambiguity has been resolved; generosity is not constrained by the need for labor discipline, patriarchy, and child rearing. However, until recently, generosity, even for this group, was severely constrained by race discrimination. While overt racism has been largely eliminated in the actual administration of the programs that serve these groups, the effects of *societal* racism are still present—for example, African-Americans are disproportionately underrepresented in the social security system.

The undeserving are not morally excused from work, and it is among this diverse group that the contradictions and ambiguities are manifest. Here, one finds the clash between generosity and the symbols of work, responsibility, and proper family and personal behavior. The classic approach is deterrence. By making the conditions of relief sufficiently onerous for the "truly" needy, the able-bodied will be deterred from choosing welfare over work. Stiff work requirements for outdoor relief—the stone pile or the wood yard in a prior age, trash collection in our age—serve the same purpose as the nineteenth-century poorhouse. Nowhere are the contradictions, the moral ambiguities more apparent than in the work requirements for the welfare poor. The emphasis on work epitomizes the dilemma of granting relief and providing humane care while preserving the work ethic, controlling deviance, maintaining labor discipline, and regulating the labor market (Katz, 1986). The work requirement has both symbolic and social regulation functions. As a symbol, it reinforces for the poor and nonpoor alike the moral superiority of those who work, even if the work is menial, low paying, or degrading. The work requirement casts welfare recipients as morally depraved because it assumes that they lack the inner motivation to work, which must, therefore, be forced upon them. It is the secular affirmation of the work ethic. Full citizenship rights are granted to those who work and are denied to those who are on welfare.

Indeed, for some, such as Lawrence Mead (1989), acceptance of public assistance signals a voluntary act of nonwork and an abdication of the recipient's obligations to the state as a citizen. Therefore, Mead argues, the state is justified in imposing its authority by requiring the welfare recipient to work as a condition of accepting relief. That is, once welfare recipients are labeled deviants and deficient in their work ethic, it is easy to enunciate a moral position that they have lost the right to free exchange of their own labor. Although such a moral principle runs counter to the basic tenet of the capitalist market economy that work is a private commodity to be exchanged freely in the marketplace, it is justified by viewing welfare recipients as undeserving of economic citizenship rights.

As social regulation, the work requirement is meant to deter the working poor from disengaging from the labor market by imposing penalties on those who do. The enforcement of the work requirement also regulates the availability of a pool of low-wage workers. A more stringent enforcement of the requirement increases the size of the pool. These are regulatory justifications for work requirements. However, as we shall point out, the symbolic functions of the work requirements are far more salient than their effectiveness as a method of social regulation.

The work requirement is fraught with contradictions and uncertainties. First, it calls for a distinction between able-bodied and non-able-bodied poor. It tries to typify the poor into distinct social categories whose boundaries are blurred in real life. Second, it requires some sort of a work test to deter those who merely want to exploit the welfare system, yet it does not want to discourage the "truly needy" from seeking assistance. Third, the work requirement is expected to be "rehabilitative," so that the poor can become productive and self-sufficient. At the same time, it expects to bring a decline in the welfare rolls. Fourth, the work requirement should be imposed by the state but should not result in increased dependence on the state for employment. Fifth, the work requirement should be administered effectively and economically, without burdening the taxpayers. Sixth, the work requirement should not compete with the normal labor market dynamics, either by undermining current wage structures or by affecting the supply and demand of low-wage labor. Yet, it should provide for a sufficient level of subsistence. How these contradictions are handled by welfare administrators will depend on the constellation of economic and political forces they encounter, such as the nature of the local labor market, the characteristics of the poor themselves, the fiscal condition of the local government, and the amount of pressure from political elites to affirm their symbols.

The tumultuous history of welfare is partly a result of the struggle to cope with these issues (e.g., Katz, 1986; Mead, 1986; Rein, 1982; Webb & Webb, 1927). Both the English Poor Laws and the American welfare laws offer vivid testimony to this struggle (see, for example, Aaron, 1973; Bell, 1965; Brown, 1940; Leman, 1980; Lynn & Whitman, 1981; Moynihan, 1973). Remarkably, despite repeated failures and disappointments in organizing and structuring work-relief or work requirements for the poor, the institution of work requirements remains in one form or another.

Why does the institution of work requirements persist? Our argument is that the key purpose of the work requirements is not actually to set welfare recipients to work, but to reaffirm the work ethic; to confirm the importance of work in defining social, gender, and ethnic status; and to legitimate the morality of low-wage work. As regulation, the work requirement is used to enforce the compliance of the poor with the conditions of welfare, to remove from welfare recalcitrant recipients, to reduce welfare expenditures, and to lower the welfare rolls to meet rising demands for low-wage work. The contradictions inherent in setting the poor to work are manifested in the welfare policy itself. It embraces symbols and rhetoric that have ambiguous and contradictory meanings. The "success" of the policy is not necessarily measured by specific outputs, such as the number of able-bodied poor who work, but by its ability to express the values of its framers. What matters is the very existence of work program legislation, regardless of whether or not it can be implemented effectively and efficiently. The tensions and contradictions in the policy itself initiate periodic efforts at revisions either to relax or to tighten the work requirements as various political and ideological groups gain or lose political influence. Yet, there is always a significant disparity between the symbols and myths and the actual allocation of resources or use of sanctions. By circumscribing the allocation of resources or the imposition of sanctions, there is avoidance of confrontation with the moral and programmatic dilemmas that the work requirements generate. Finally, the policy grants local communities considerable discretion in implementation. Discretion provides for a decoupling between the policy and the administration of the program. It enables the program to weave its way through the contradictions of the policy and it permits the policymakers to retain the myths without having to be fully accountable for the consequences.

In sum, the contradictions in our cultural values and norms about welfare and work are reflected in the formulation of policies that themselves are ambiguous and mostly symbolic. The implementation of these policies by work programs is mediated by political and economic variables as these programs try to "make sense" of the policies. It is through these processes at the programmatic and organizational levels that the moral ambiguity of work programs becomes institutionalized. Indeed, they permit the creation of a chain of moral causality of "who is to blame" when work programs fail. This chain begins with the clients who are to blame for the lack of program success. It continues, as the failures persist, to administrative structures and procedures, and then to the external political economy (i.e., lack of funds and resources). Ultimately it proceeds to the policy-making level, but it seldom continues from there to challenge the cultural values and norms themselves.

CONCLUSION

While policies, as interpreted and applied, are often diverse, contradictory, and ambiguous, their *names*, as Murray Edelman (1988, p. 16) tells us, are something different. A policy's name allows us to ignore inconsistencies and ambiguities; the name reassures us that there is agreement on the dominant ideology and that change has come about; the name masks hesitations and contradictory actions that minimize or cancel accomplishment. This was true with the name "mothers' pensions." The name signified accomplishment for the reformers and their allies. But the nationwide campaign had been won for them alone; as we shall see, local administrators made sure that the vast bulk of single mothers in poverty were not to be removed from the labor force. So, too, with workers' compensation insurance and unemployment insurance, both of which were hardly insurance then or now. So, too, today with the Family Support Act of 1988, and the various names given to the required work programs that will be discussed in Chapters 4 and 5—WIN, Project Chance, GAIN, and so forth. These, too, are myth and ceremony, designed to affirm the modern, contemporary, middle-class employed mother by ensuring the failure and moral condemnation of the welfare mother.

While the programs themselves are myth and ceremony, the consequences for the undeserving poor are concrete and serious. Especially today, with the increase in eligibility requirements, verification, quality control, and work requirements, those who are admitted to welfare are subject to suspicion, humiliation, stigmatization, and various forms of harassment. Offices and programs vary, of course, but entry is nowhere easy, and often truly daunting.[8] Not surprisingly, many are deterred from applying, and in many programs enrollments are now quite low. Ceremony, too, can be costly, and there have been widespread cuts in real benefits. The results are evident. Whereas at one time food stamp programs were largely responsible for substantially reducing hunger in the United States, as a result of program cuts and low enrollments, hunger now is widespread (Lipsky & Thibodeau, 1990). Welfare families are increasingly becoming homeless (White, in press). The number of people below the poverty line and the depth of their poverty is increasing (Ruggles, 1989). Thus the dominant society is having its cake and eating it too. It has its symbols and ceremonies, and is saving money at the same time.

NOTES

1. "In an important sense, language constructs the people who use it rather than the commonsensical assumption that people construct the language they use" (Edelman, 1988, p. 112).

2. For example, there has always been a problem of take-up rate of the elderly in Supplemental Security Income. The fact that this is recognized as a problem, and efforts have been made to do something about it, demonstrates the character of the program. See Chapter 3.

3. The same views were also held of employed married mothers, since fathers in these families rarely earned a living wage (L. Gordon, 1988, p. 85).

4. In 1962, the program was changed to Aid to Families with Dependent Children.

5. Governor Jimmy Davis of Louisiana campaigned on terminating AFDC benefits for all mothers who conceived while on the program. He was elected, and he carried out the campaign promise; more than 20,000 cases were closed (Bell, 1965).

6. Old-age benefits for African-Americans were lower than for whites (Quadagno, 1988). In programs providing aid to dependent children, African-Americans were subject to far more social control rules, including forced agricultural work (Bell, 1965; Law, 1983).

7. Roughly half the states acknowledge needy two-parent families as deserving, but one of the parents, typically the father, is required to register for work. These programs, thus far, have been quite restricted. The Family Support Act mandates AFDC-UP by 1994, but there are many loopholes (see Chapter 6).

8. For a description of general relief in Los Angeles County, see Handler (1987–1988).

2

The Historical Development of Welfare Policy: To the New Deal

Studying the historical development of AFDC will serve two purposes. First, it will illustrate the moral ambiguities and central contradictions of welfare policy, contradictions that still remain unresolved today. In addition, the story of this pre-New Deal period demonstrates our basic thesis about the nature of welfare reform, namely, that because the underlying contradictions remain unresolved between the ideological and structural demands of the political economy, on the one hand, and patriarchy, child rearing, race, ethnicity, and relief, on the other, welfare policy and administration become decoupled from each other. In effect, welfare reform evolves as the organized production of symbols at the policy-making level while the underlying contradictions get sorted out in terms of contending interests and values of the political economy, federalism, and bureaucracy at the local level. This review of welfare's historical development will demonstrate continuities as well. Because dominant moral values toward most of the poor have not changed, the contradictions and ambiguities of welfare policy remain. The historical record will illuminate the symbolism behind the current welfare consensus and explain the most likely shape of both welfare policy and local bureaucratic behavior in the coming years.

This chapter and the next will present the long sweep of welfare policy, looking at the development of several different programs from the nineteenth century to the present. The following chapters will focus on the central, organizing principle of the development of welfare policy—the relation of welfare policy to the discipline of labor.

THE FORMATIVE YEARS

The roots of welfare policy have been tangled in the contradictions of preserving labor markets and controlling deviant behavior while at the same time relieving misery. In the nineteenth century, the great struggle was over outdoor relief—that is, relief given outside the confines of institutions. It was strongly felt by policymakers that relief officials had a particularly difficult time in separating the worthy from the unworthy poor in the local community, and that spreading pauperism was due, in large part, to lax administration. There were serious depressions in the second half of the nineteenth century that produced widespread unemployment and poverty. Bands of single men roved the country in search of work, raising fears of crime, delinquency, and the threat of social corruption. The attacks on outdoor relief coincided with these periods of great unemployment, poverty, unrest, and general social distress (Katz, 1986).

The remedy was disarmingly simple. Abolish outdoor relief—the cause of pauperism—and confine the poor to institutions—poorhouses. If the applicant and the family were willing to subject themselves to these onerous conditions, then they must be truly destitute. The instrument of relief would become the test of necessity. Thus the conditions of the poorhouse were deliberately harsh and stigmatic. The poorhouse reforms carried important symbolic messages. Society's outcasts were not only to be subjected to physical and social indignities, they were also to be deprived of their liberty—the basic rights of citizenship. As bad as poorhouse conditions were, they were no doubt better than what many suffered on the outside; but that was not the point. It was the deprivation of liberty that was the ultimate indignity. Those who presented themselves to the poorhouse were casting themselves outside of moral society. It was this loss of status, of citizenship, that fueled the liberal opposition to the poorhouses (Himmelfarb, 1984).

The poorhouses were never successful. As with many social welfare programs, their goals were contradictory. They provided shelter and relief for the truly destitute. It was claimed, by some reformers, that institutional confinement would extricate poor children from the baleful influence of the slum and they would learn good habits (Axinn & Levin, 1975, pp. 36–45). At the same time, the poorhouses had to deter those in danger of permanent dependency. In practice, the poorhouses were poorly administered, unhealthy, and miserable. They were more expensive than the dole. Although outdoor relief was abolished in some communities, it persisted overall and, at any one point in time, there were always more people on outdoor relief than in the poorhouses.[1] A compromise was struck in most communities. Outdoor relief would be given, but under very strict conditions, including a rigorous work test. As one local superintendent of the poor put it, "Especially for strangers, nothing would certify worthiness as well as the willingness to break stone" (Katz, 1986, p. 56).

For the general, undifferentiated mass of the poor, during this formative period, four features of poverty policy are worth emphasizing. Work—the ability and willingness to work and its moral importance—was the central theme. Work and welfare were inextricably joined. The undeserving poor were defined primarily in terms of work; *as a category*, they were not morally excused from work, although individual members of the class would be excused for short periods of time under limited conditions.

Second, there were two aspects to the work requirement; both have continuing importance even today. One was the *administrative* work test. As a condition of receiving relief, the recipient had to engage in some sort of work. In the nineteenth century, this was true whether the person was in or out of the poorhouse. With outdoor relief, the able-bodied recipient had to engage in hard manual labor, such as chopping wood or breaking stones. A work requirement was part of the welfare program, as in workfare today. But there was another work requirement that is often ignored. If we consider the category of potential applicants for relief, then a work requirement was also imposed on those who were *excluded* from the program. The moral claim for material support of those considered able-bodied by the state is to be found in the market. This is what we will call the *paid labor* work requirement. Entry to welfare is denied, and it is assumed that the rejected applicant will somehow get along, most probably by finding some sort of work. In any event, as far as society is concerned, it is the applicant's affair. By restricting entry, as social control welfare programs do, the market discipline is being applied to the unworthy poor. In fact, the market or paid labor work requirement is much more common than the administrative work test. Most of the poor throughout history, including the present, have received no cash assistance at all. But even many who are on the rolls are still subject to the paid labor market because benefits are so low that recipients have to seek work in order to survive.

The third point is that during the formative period, the great mass of the poor was the responsibility of local municipal administration under very broad discretionary powers. This is the principle of *local responsibility*. For example, the original Wisconsin statute, which borrowed heavily from Pennsylvania, the Northwest Territory, Ohio, and Michigan, simply stated: "Every town shall relieve and support all poor and indigent persons, lawfully settled therein, whenever they shall stand in need thereof" (Wisconsin Revised Statutes, 1849). Administration was in the hands of the town supervisors. Neither eligibility nor budget was prescribed; it was up to the local administrators to decide who was poor and indigent, and what, if anything, to do about it. This is where the moral determinations were made. Local decisions were not always harsh. Part of the reason for the persistence of outdoor relief was the refusal of communities to send the aged, widows, and families with husbands temporarily thrown out of work to the poorhouse. On the other hand, breaking stones was for strangers (Katz, 1986).

Fourth, as Michael Katz (1986) has shown, the administration of relief was built on a hostage theory: Those who were "truly" needy were given relief under such conditions as to deter those capable of work. During the nineteenth and early twentieth centuries, the vast majority of those who actually got relief, either outdoor or in the poorhouse, were desperate—widows, children, old people, the sick—in short, very few who were capable of work. Yet, the conditions of both forms of relief were deliberately made miserable to deter the able-bodied, to prevent them from becoming threats to the social order. The truly needy were segregated, stigmatized, and sanctioned. They were *morally degraded*.

The late nineteenth-century campaign to abolish outdoor relief highlights the basic characteristics of welfare policy. The leading reformers of that day constructed their belief as to the causes of poverty: The indiscriminate giving of aid encouraged permanent dependency or pauperism on the part of the able-bodied. Pauperism was a serious social menace; it was the enemy. The proposed remedy affirmed the moral values of work by stigmatizing as well as denying relief to those who did not conform. While outdoor relief was abolished in several cities and communities, the social reformers were ultimately unsuccessful. For some people, poorhouses were an intolerable remedy. Local people would not send their "deserving" poor to these harsh institutions. The relief of misery remained a contradictory goal. More important, poorhouses were more expensive than outdoor relief, and when symbols become burdensome to the local taxpayers, other, less expensive methods of satisfying the same goals will be used. In this instance, a tough work requirement—humiliating pauper labor—for the unworthy poor was combined with low levels of outdoor relief.

The failure of the poorhouse did not mean a rejection of the ideology of that reform period. Those who did manage to get relief—those who were truly destitute—were nevertheless stigmatized and sanctioned. Even though they could not find paid work, the conditions of relief deterred the able-bodied, thus affirming the dominant moral values of work. Tough, harsh, degrading work-relief, in addition to its other symbolic and instrumental purposes, distinguished independent "regular" market labor from pauper labor. In addition, harsh, miserly relief saved taxes, never a minor concern at the local level. Symbolically, the values of the social reformers were adopted at the local level even though the local level worked out its own solutions to meet local needs. We will see this basic pattern of symbolic production and local accommodation to the ambiguous demands of labor markets, social control, and charity throughout social welfare history.

The Rise of the Categories

While the general mass of the poor were to be handled at the local (municipal and county) level, the states, starting in about the 1830s, began to distinguish classes of poor in terms of moral blameworthiness, those for whom work was not an issue. As part of the more general institutional movement of that century, separate state institutions were created for the blind, the deaf and mute, and the insane. Eventually children were removed from the poorhouses and placed in orphanages. This was the start of categorizing the poor, a basic characteristic of our social welfare policy that continues today. The morally blameless poor, the deserving poor, were to be separated from the general mass of unworthy poor.

Separate state institutions were not created primarily for custodial efficiency. There was clear recognition of the fact that these unfortunates were to be separated from the baleful influence of the general mass of the poor, from the paupers. In Wisconsin, for example, initially there was a means test for residency in the state institutions; the law was quickly repealed on the grounds that this category of the poor should not have to obtain "certificates of pauperism." Other examples of separation grew out of the Civil War: State orphanages were created for children of deceased veterans and relief programs were authorized for indigent veterans and their families (needy soldiers are not a "class of professional paupers, but are poor by misfortune"). While outdoor relief for poor veterans and their families was locally administered, a separate administration, composed in part of veterans, was created to avoid the pauper stigma (Handler & Hollingsworth, 1971, pp. 17–19).

The Civil War veterans' pension program, which began in 1862, grew into a massive income-maintenance program. In 1890, eligibility was expanded to cover any veteran or his dependents. The only other eligibility criterion was inability to perform manual labor. Thus, in addition to patriotic service, this group was morally excused from work. By the end of the century, approximately half of all native-born whites in the North and many of their widows received pensions. "In effect, the veterans' pensions formed a rudimentary system of old-age assistance for the respectable working class" (Katz, 1986, pp. 200–201). Caught in late nineteenth-century partisan politics, the program came to be criticized as being overly generous and corrupt. When the veterans began to die off, after 1910, working-class groups and unions tried unsuccessfully to continue the noncontributory pensions (Orloff, 1988a; Skocpol & Ikenberry, 1983, pp. 95–98). As discussed in Chapter 3, the experience of this massive program figured prominently in the construction of the New Deal income-support programs.

The Progressive Era

The next big step in categorization occurred in the Progressive Era (1890–1920). Among other things, this reform period was concerned with the treatment of children; two of its accomplishments were the initial aid to dependent children programs, or mothers' pensions, and the juvenile court. At this point, the various reform strands become much more complex. The Progressive reformers emphasized the patriarchal conception of women's place in the home. This ideology, in turn, strongly influenced the Progressive concepts of child abuse and neglect. What was considered the "proper" role of women served to define the deviant mother and those children in need of protection. Child protection reformers in this era saw close connections between poverty, crime, and the sordid breeding grounds of the urban slum and the impact of these conditions on the traditional family. They were particularly concerned about "predelinquent" children—children growing up in ignorance and vice, who would become paupers and criminals. They argued, ultimately successfully, that the state had the right and the duty to intervene in a bad environment to save a child from delinquency. Initially, these social reformers were in favor of breaking up homes and separating impressionable children from wicked parents, but as the harsh realities of reformatories, other kinds of institutions, and shipping children off to midwestern farms set in, they switched their emphasis to family preservation. The child protectors pushed for reforms in education, the abolition of child labor, programs for child and maternal health, and establishment of juvenile delinquency courts and mothers' pensions (Katz, 1986).

Two themes are connected here. First, the patriarchal family itself was considered by the Progressive reformers to be in danger; women in the paid labor force posed a particular threat. Second, child abuse and neglect emerged as a social problem. Both themes

defined deviant behavior and ultimately justified public intervention. Both themes played a significant role in the construction of the
early ADC programs; and, as we shall see, these ideologies continue to have importance in today's welfare context. We will first
discuss gender roles and women in the paid labor force, and then
child abuse and neglect.

Patriarchy and Working Women

Alice Kessler-Harris, in her book *Out to Work* (1982), traces the
emerging attitudes toward women and work. The colonial period
was concerned with both idleness and poverty, and there is no indication that exceptions were made for women. All citizens were expected to work; those who could not, including widows with small
children, were expelled from towns. As the number of single mothers began to multiply, towns began to combat rising relief costs
more vigorously. Rhode Island, Massachusetts, and Connecticut allowed single mothers to settle only after they had been "warned
out"—that is, they were told they could stay as long as they did not
apply for relief. But since these women had few work options, they
were forced to move from town to town. At various times, communities tried to set up work sites, such as woolen mills, or bound out
poor women to factory owners. These measures were never sufficient to relieve poverty.[2] The important general point is that from
the earliest days, women, and especially women in poverty, were in
no sense morally excused from work. Indeed, quite the opposite
was true: Poor women and mothers were both expected and required to work (Kessler-Harris, 1982, pp. 16–18).

More complex and contradictory attitudes toward women and
paid labor started with the beginning of the early national period
and the rise of manufacturing. While the home and the family were
exalted as the central focus of women's lives, there were also growing labor shortages, and single women and children were viewed
as surplus agricultural workers. The development of factories has-
tened the call for female employees; it became the responsibility of
available women to support their communities and their families
by taking wage work in the mills.

But almost immediately, class lines were drawn. Distinctions
were made between those women who could afford to cultivate
domestic skills without pay while awaiting marriage, and those
women, whether married or single, who needed income either for

themselves or their families. These distinctions sharpened during the 1830s and 1840s, as working conditions worsened in the mills— wages declined but hours and work discipline increased. When wage-working women protested and struck, they were ridiculed and attacked on the grounds that their behavior conflicted with dominant attitudes toward female delicacy (Kessler-Harris, 1982, pp. 23–43).

By the 1830s, public consciousness was beginning to draw comparisons between the values and behaviors of wage workers and those of women who did not work. The difference evolved into what was called the "domestic code." Fundamentally patriarchal, nineteenth-century industrial society constructed the home as sanctuary. Men, increasingly subject to the rigors of industrialized laissez-faire, needed wives as home managers, child rearers, and sources of emotional support. The wife and mother in the home was to be the source of higher moral and ethical values than were found in the business world. Women were valued for piety, purity, and submissiveness. Children now became the center of women's activity. The home and children constituted women's "separate sphere," which was seen as part of the "natural" social order (Kessler-Harris, 1982, pp. 43–51).

The domestic code sharpened class, race, and ethnic lines. Women who confined themselves to their separate sphere were defined as respectable, fulfilling their true calling. Those who worked demonstrated that their husbands were failing. Instead of the earlier conception of wage-working women as helping their communities and their families, such women were now defined as selfish and neglectful of their families. Never mind that those in extreme poverty had to work—especially free African-Americans and immigrants—the domestic code considered them all but outcasts. It was not that this was a small group. One study of a working-class district in New York City conducted in 1855 found that between one-fourth and one-third of married immigrant women participated in wage work. By the time of the Civil War, about half of the women had at least some experience in wage work. About two-thirds of this group left the labor force upon marriage, but the other third, married or not, continually sought to scratch out a living from wage labor. Increasingly this group tended to be immigrants and urban dwellers, who were often considered "degraded" even before they started work (Kessler-Harris, 1982, pp. 70–71).

Writing about women in the labor force, Alice Kessler-Harris (1982) says:

Everywhere the industrial process contributed its own pressures on women to enter the labor market. To the widows produced by [the Civil] war and the women who supported diseased and crippled men, it added an increasing toll of industrial victims. Workers died in mines, in steel factories, and on railroads. They died young of consumption, pneumonia, and industrial diseases. Urban working-class families had few resources to fall back on when disaster struck. High unemployment rates, seasonal work, technological dislocation, and real wages that barely kept pace with rising living costs all encouraged women to seek jobs. The result was a steadily rising number of women, married and unmarried, who felt impelled to contribute to their families' economic sustenance. . . . Women who headed families . . . found the push into the work force even greater. . . . Black women, released to an uncertain freedom by the Civil War, had the least choice. . . . economic circumstances forced married women and their daughters from low-income families to seek paid work. (pp. 122–123; see also Stansell, 1987, pp. 11–17, 115–129, 217–218; L. Gordon, 1988, pp. 95–99)

The domestic code pitted men against women. Wives and daughters at home contributed to men's self-respect and comfort. Wage-working women were exploited, but instead of receiving sympathy and support, they were condemned by male workers for making working conditions worse for men (Kessler-Harris, 1982, p. 68).

In sum, by the middle of the century, the domestic code, male competition and hostility, and deteriorating working conditions defined female wage labor as "without virtue." Those who were forced to earn a living were socially isolated from "good" women. "Wage work became the refuge of immigrants, the desperately poor, and those without male support" (Kessler-Harris, 1982, p. 72). By stigmatizing working women, and especially those at the bottom of the labor force, it was hoped that women who did not need work would not be tempted.

Views as to what to do about the deplorable conditions of female wage labor also divided along class lines. From time to time, working women engaged in labor militancy to improve their lot. Some middle-class women reformers believed that married working women neglected their families and that single working women were in danger of vice. In their view, most female wage work was caused by either bad luck or irresponsible husbands. They opposed women who agitated for improved working conditions on the grounds that this would make jobs more attractive. Instead, they sought to lessen the harsh impact of wage work. Home-based work would be provided to worthy widows and poor married women, and boardinghouses, clubs, and discussion groups to single women. The idea was to preserve women's sensibilities and to encourage them to return to the home (Kessler-Harris, 1982, p. 90).

The ambiguities and contradictions between the domestic code and economic necessity are illustrated by attempts to deal with child care during this period. The "charitable nursery"—the first institution organized solely for the purpose of child care—dates from the closing years of the eighteenth century. Female Quaker philanthropists, the Friendly Circle, set up a nursery to allow the employment of widows of the 1793 yellow fever epidemic. The spinning room, a central location, was considered more economically efficient than the prior practice of outdoor relief and "given-out" work to be done in individual homes. The Friendly Circle became the Female Society of Philadelphia for the Relief and Employment of the Poor, and its primary institution was the House of Industry (Michel, 1988, p. 6).

The goals of this group of reformers were, first, the productive employment of these poor widows; the House of Industry and its successor institutions were primarily concerned with finding ways for poor mothers to work, to prevent dependency. Second, these reformers were concerned about the moral education of the children; they wanted to provide proper role models and education that "would prevent them from following their parents down the path to poverty" (Michel, 1988, p. 7). Thus the House of Industry was both a charity and a business; the word *industry* in the name was intended in both its business and moral senses. While wages were very low (below subsistence) and working conditions strict, the House of Industry was certainly preferable to the almshouse (pp. 12–13).

This example is significant for several reasons. As Sonya Michel (1988) points out, the Female Society recognized the specific problems of poor women, especially when children are involved. The Female Society confronted the fact these women had to take care of their children as well as work; the House of Industry was their attempt to harmonize both obligations. By accepting the necessity of work, the Society recognized the class lines in the domestic code: "In the lives of poor women there was no place for the conceit of the non-working wife as a symbol of the husband's ability to maintain his 'angel in the house' " (pp. 14–15). However, by making it clear that *these* women had to work, the female philanthropists were able to affirm *their* ideological construction of motherhood (p. 15). Many of these reformers believed that the necessity for work was only a temporary phenomenon for these mothers; they would not recognize the fact that for both married and single mothers wage work was a "normal," permanent need (p. 20).

The believed negative impact of female wage work on mothering was the subject of increased attention during the closing decades of the century. Many public and private studies investigated the working conditions of women wage earners. They found that while most of the female workers were both poor and single, an increasing proportion were unmarried mothers. Working women were considered to be a threat to the traditional family. Their associations with men, impulsive spending, immodest dress, and profane language inevitably led to moral laxity. Working women depressed wages, depriving men of the ability to marry, thus perpetuating the problem (Kessler-Harris, 1982, pp. 97–98). Despite the strong evidence of need, despite widowhood and poverty, male workers as well as employers continued to blame women for low wages; it was charged that most women were willing to work for such wages because the money was needed only for dress and pleasure. Running through all of the debates was deep concern about the effects of women's working on morality. Leaving the protected home and being exposed to the temptations of work "seemed to threaten all women and thus all of society" (p. 105). Women would become discontented; they would be overworked and their maternal functions would be impaired; subjected to these physical effects, they would produce "stunted and dwarfed children." The deepest fear, according to Kessler-Harris, was that low-wage women would slip into prostitution (pp. 99–103).

Necessity was common. At the turn of the century, in major cities such as Baltimore, Philadelphia, Chicago, and Boston, between one-third and one-half of the population consisted of immigrant families living in squalid, crowded conditions. Most dwellings lacked indoor running water. Doing laundry for pay, as well as daily chores, was sheer drudgery. As Kessler-Harris (1982) describes it: "To gather sufficient water for a day's washing, drinking, and cooking, housewives had to get up early, fill huge tubs, and haul them indoors, sometimes up several flights of stairs. Few had indoor toilets, central heating or refrigeration" (p. 121). But unskilled male workers did not earn wages that could support a family. Families with members working in the textile mills needed the incomes of three wage earners to survive. Married women took in boarders and sent their children to the mills, or left their babies with siblings and went to work themselves. Nearly a third of the women who worked in the mills were married (p. 120). Industrial accidents also contributed to the push to drive women into the labor force. From a variety of sources, more and more poor single and married women had to contribute to the family income. Necessity was even greater for female heads; everywhere, reports Kessler-Harris, these women were disproportionately represented in the labor force. Because of their poverty, African-American women were much more likely than white women to work for wages (p. 123).

The separate sphere ideology was not restricted to the nonwage social life; *everywhere*, including the workplace, marriage and the patriarchal family were the predominant values. Jobs themselves were valued in terms of patriarchal appropriateness. Gentility, morality, and cleanliness were valued over the male values of competition, aggressiveness, and ambition. The categorization of jobs in terms of feminine qualities served to stabilize labor markets and reduce competition. Within those jobs reserved for women, hierarchies were defined according to the domestic code; as ever, values reflected class, ethnicity, and race. Those occupations that coincided with the feminine role, such as nursing and teaching, were privileged. Some occupations, such as buyer or manager, and some fields, such as medicine, were considered incompatible with marriage, and women who worked in these areas generally did not marry. The status hierarchy of jobs, defined in terms of domestic respectability, depressed working conditions; women would take less money to work in department stores rather than work in factories, and they would work in factories if they could rather than go into domestic service (Kessler-Harris, 1982, pp. 128–138).

Social reformers were divided in their approach to working women. While many sought to improve the working conditions of women, others supported the domestic code, which tended to reduce women to the poorest levels. By the turn of the century, the prevailing view of a wide variety of individuals, groups, and interests was that working women threatened the home and that women should be encouraged to remain at home or to return there. Wage-working women were generally unskilled and unorganized, and they competed for few occupations, characterized by the worst wages and working conditions (Kessler-Harris, 1982, p. 142). Developing unions incorporated the patriarchal values of the day and, in the main, sought to exclude women from the paid labor force (pp. 153–154). The movement for protective labor legislation caused divisions among feminists, as well as labor, but in general, both labor and the largest women's organization supported the legislation. As with most major reforms, protective labor legislation was claimed to serve a number of goals: improving the working conditions of women and establishing the first step for broader, protective regulatory programs. An important rationale was the separate sphere: Women who worked had to be protected in order to protect motherhood and family life. Special laws were needed "to permit efficient motherhood and healthy children"; the legislation, in a sense, "institutionalized social reproduction as women's primary role. It thus extended a version of the ideology of domesticity to working-class people" (pp. 205–206, 212–213).

This was the general ideological structure of the family at the turn of the century. Preserving the traditional family had become a social problem. The domestic code had defined both the proper family—the male breadwinner and the nurturing wife and mother—and the enemy—the wage-working mother. The proper place for a woman was in the home; her central calling was child rearing and providing a nurturing, caring atmosphere for her husband. Women who worked threatened the traditional family; they were morally suspect; they challenged the dominant conception of domesticity; they were independent. Moreover, within female occupations, the domestic code sorted out women, again in terms of moral conformity; those at the bottom who had to work from brute necessity had the most morally suspect jobs. These were immigrants, African-Americans, widows, and female heads of households, often considered "degraded" to begin with.

Child Protection: Abuse, Neglect, and Delinquency

The dominant interests in nineteenth-century society constructed explanations and proposed solutions for the "degraded" part of the population. One set of solutions involved children. For a long time, upper-class reformers were concerned with humanizing child rearing. According to Linda Gordon (1988), these reformers "discovered" child abuse in the 1870s. The discovery of this social problem emerged out of the romanticization of home life, the growing sensibility toward children, and revulsion to interpersonal violence, especially with regard to children. The existence of street children, who were exposed to violence and depravity, was not only a moral wrong, but a threat to society; it was "a kind of pollution, poisoning the stock of future citizens." Interest in child protection, as with the wage-working mother, was part of the growing concern about social disorder (pp. 29–33).

The concept of child protection fit with prevailing ideas of the patriarchal family; indeed, the purpose of protection was to reconstitute the traditional family. In terms familiar to the domestic code, the family as a whole became the object of ideology: Upper-class Protestant women were seeking to subordinate the immigrant poor; conservative feminists were seeking to enhance respect for women and children (L. Gordon, 1988, pp. 56–57).

Family and child protection policies were also influenced by the organization and professionalization of private charity and social work. During the Gilded Age (1870s-1890s), a growing class consciousness, increasing poverty and social unrest, and heightened fear of threats to the social order stimulated a change in the conception of charity from individualized acts to organized professional activity. The upper class began to think more in terms of entire social groups rather than of deviant individuals. The most important organizational development was the appearance of Charitable Organization Societies (COSs), which spread throughout the country and became very influential in campaigns to abolish outdoor relief and in opposing the mothers' pension movement (L. Gordon, 1988; Katz, 1986).

Professional social reformers started with a critique of indiscriminate outdoor relief. Outdoor relief became the constructed explanation for continued dependency, or pauperism; it was socially harmful and wasteful; it dealt only with symptoms rather than underlying causes. The explanation provided the solution—abolish public outdoor relief and replace it with "scientific charity," which, in addition to helping the poor through more systematic analysis and help, would upgrade the status of, initially, the volunteers and then the professional social workers. From scientific charity developed the first methodology of professional social work—casework. The goal of casework was long-term independence rather than temporary help; it involved careful fact investigation and individualized treatment. Casework fit with the changing convictions of the child protection reformers—individual acts of neglect or delinquency must be considered reflections of more basic family functioning (L. Gordon, 1988, pp. 62–63). The reformers and emerging professional social workers firmly believed that outdoor relief was dangerous and counterproductive in that it would undermine longterm independence and a sense of responsibility. By the 1880s, the prime solution was to try to separate the deserving from the undeserving in order to exclude the latter from aid (p. 63).

The COSs spread and became an important voice in welfare organization and policy. Local agencies gradually became professionalized; volunteers were either eliminated or reduced to lower-level tasks. Charitable fund-raising began to be organized in most major cities. A national organization was formed in 1874. In several major communities, the COSs were able to abolish outdoor relief (L. Gordon, 1988, p. 63). It was from the New York Charity Organization Society that Carl C. Carstens came to lead the Massachusetts Society for the Prevention of Cruelty to Children (MSPCC), which became the single most influential child protection organization in the country (Anderson, 1978, p. 225; L. Gordon, 1988, p. 63).

It was through the professionalization of the MSPCC and child protection that the definition of child cruelty changed from abuse to the more expansive "neglect." Neglect came to be diagnosed as the result of family pathology. The child protectors were particularly concerned about "individualistic tendencies" in family life. By this they meant divorce and increasing numbers of single-mother households. These concepts were inextricably linked to gender roles as defined by the domestic code. COS and MSPCC caseworkers condemned women who worked outside the home. In their campaigns against juvenile delinquency, mothers, and especially working mothers, were blamed for inadequate supervision and fathers for inadequate discipline. The shift from abuse to neglect was important. Men were blamed when abuse and individual vice were emphasized. When social conditions or neglect were at fault, the mothers were blamed; after all, they were in charge of the children (L. Gordon, 1988). By the turn of the century, the Progressives, according to Gordon (1988), "were in a panic about the erosion of 'traditional' values." The Progressive Era child protectors feared the erosion of parental authority and domesticity. They broadened the definition of *cruelty* to include all sorts of neglect. Child protection intervention was broadly conceived; not only was it to be used negatively to control harmful acts, but also positively to promote healthy family relationships. Expert supervision, through casework, was necessary to strengthen family authority (p. 76). The explanation for child neglect and the proposed solutions enhanced the prestige, authority, and resources of the child protectors.

In Linda Gordon's (1988) review of MSPCC neglect case records, the poor, in general, were overrepresented; they lived in crowded, wretched housing. People were coming and going during this period of rapid immigration and migration, and the poor often had no extended family to fall back on. As discussed in Chapter 1, single mothers, who formed the poorest group, were in the most difficult position. The demands of the domestic code and the child protection conception of proper child rearing resulted in impossible expectations for these women. They had to work outside of the home to survive, but their lack of supervision of their children became one of the defining elements of neglect. These women were viewed as depriving their daughters of proper role models and their sons of true fathers.

Single mothers were not a rare phenomenon. In 1900, for example, they accounted for 20% of Boston's families. There were increases in rates of both divorce and desertion (May, 1986). It was about this time that single mothers were "discovered" as a "social problem" (L. Gordon, 1988); desertion had become "a great evil" and an "unnatural and awful crime" (May, 1986, p. 12). Because caseworkers usually saw these mothers as incapable of maintaining a home and earning a living, they often recommended that the children be removed from the home. Not surprisingly, single mothers constituted a fourth of Gordon's study of child abuse and neglect cases, a higher proportion by far than any other group. In part, this was due to the great hardships that these women faced trying to earn enough income at miserable jobs to keep their households together. But a large part, Gordon argues, was due to professional labeling. While the social workers believed the worst of working-class men—they were considered to be depraved and degenerate—and the best of women—they were morally pure, blameless victims—at any moment, they believed, these women were likely to fall into sin. The women were held to high standards, and were much more likely than men to be condemned as immoral by the social workers. And single mothers suffered the most. In Gordon's (1988) records, they were more likely to be judged intemperate and sexually immoral (p. 92). Gordon states: "Only one variable other than single motherhood was a better predictor of child removal: poverty. But this was just another aspect of the same phenomenon, for single mothers were poorer than other parents" (p. 94). The MSPCC maintained that it never removed children from the home solely because of poverty, but

> poverty was never alone. The characteristics of child neglect in this period—dirty clothing, soiled linen, lice and worms, crowded sleeping conditions, lack of attention and supervision, untreated infections and running sores, rickets and other malformations, truancy, malnutrition, overwork—were often direct results of poverty. (p. 95)

Gordon argues that agency discrimination against single mothers was based primarily on concern for their children. The difficulties that these women faced were apparent, but the social workers were primarily concerned about the impact of pauperism on the children as well as the threat to the children posed by the mothers' demands for both independence and custody. More often than not, contradictions and doubts were resolved by the children's removal from the home. Between 1880 and 1920, almost three-fourths of the neglected children removed by the MSPCC were children of single mothers. At the turn of the century, the majority of children in institutions were "half-orphans" (L. Gordon, 1988, p. 107).

Single mothers had few options. There were no public or private aid programs of any size or scope; with luck, some might scrounge small amounts of temporary aid from private agencies or public relief. Few (in Gordon's case records) were able to live with others. Almost 70% tried to survive on their own earnings, but jobs were hard to come by, and wages were low. There was some domestic service work available, but live-in requirements meant finding day care, which was generally lacking. By the turn of the century, night work in office buildings began to increase. Other women took in boarders, or did laundry, baby-sitting, or piecework. Caseworkers discouraged boarders; they were considered a threat to the moral character of the house. Having sex with a boarder automatically labeled a mother "unfit." There was also illegal home work, such as prostitution and bootlegging; the manufacture of home brew was common, even before Prohibition, and also brought an automatic "neglect" charge (L. Gordon, 1988, pp. 96–97).

The Progressive Era child protectors focused on four main areas confronting the single mother: desertion, illegitimacy, employment, and pensions. In each area the goal was to "condemn immorality, protect children, and encourage the construction of the proper family" (L. Gordon, 1988, p. 99). Desertion was considered a major form of child cruelty. Deserted women frequently sought agency help. However, since deserting fathers were considered weak and cowardly, it was thought that giving the deserted mothers aid would undermine the men's duty to support and further weaken their authority; such requests for support had to be resisted. Instead, the agencies tried to force the deserters to pay and, if possible, to return to the home (L. Gordon, 1988, p. 100; May, 1986).

Illegitimacy, too, caused conflicts in social work policy. Keeping the child in the home increased the risk of bad mothering; removal would reward bad behavior and punish the child. Some agencies believed that the unwed mother herself was a child in need of help (L. Gordon, 1988, p. 101).

One of the significant reforms accomplished by the child protectors was the establishment of the juvenile court. As discussed above, the child protectors were particularly concerned about "predelinquent" children—children growing up in ignorance and vice, who would become paupers and criminals. They argued that the state had the right and the duty to intervene in a bad environment to save the child from delinquency. As part of their reform program, the child protectors pushed for the establishment of separate juvenile courts (Katz, 1986).

By the end of the century, juvenile courts (or county courts with juvenile court jurisdiction) were created with jurisdiction over delinquent, dependent, and neglected children. *Delinquent* meant committing acts that would be criminal if done by an adult. *Neglected* meant abandoned, either in fact or by poor parental caretaking. *Dependent* meant poverty that was inflicted or caused by misconduct. Neglected and dependent children were considered predelinquent; the court could intervene to prevent pauperism and crime. It was taken for granted that poverty, drunkenness, and a poor home were causes of delinquency; this was not a distinctive theoretical invention of the juvenile court reform—rather, as noted, it reflected the broad ideologies of the time (Sutton, 1985).

In the juvenile court, guilt or innocence was not the issue; rather, the judge, as a "kindly father," would inquire as to what the child and the family were like, and what was needed to help them. Two categories of state institutions were created—reformatories and industrial schools for delinquents, and state schools for dependents—but the judge could order any child to any of the institutions, in addition to imposing various forms of probation (Handler & Hollingsworth, 1971; Katz, 1986; Sutton, 1985). The juvenile court was a major accomplishment of the Progressive child protection reformers in their efforts to control immorality, protect children, and reconstitute deviant family structures.

However, at the same time that neglected and dependent children were being removed, either through child protection or the juvenile court, some in the social work profession began to question this policy. They began to argue that even without marriage, mothers and children ought to be kept together. But what options were there? The mothers wanted jobs, but this conflicted with the domestic code; it would weaken the father's responsibility and encourage the temptation of the mother. A good mother was supported by her husband. Of course, this made women dependent on men, even if, as social workers well knew, this meant abusive relationships. By the turn of the century, many reformers began to believe that some form of public aid for single mothers was the solution (L. Gordon, 1988, p. 104). This brings us to another major reform of the Progressives—aid to dependent children, or mothers' pensions, as it was popularly known.

Aid to Dependent Children

By the turn of the century, family policy was at an ideological and structural impasse; it was caught between the fear of pauperism and the demands of the domestic code, between the ideology of patriarchy and the inescapable material needs of women and children in poverty. Child protection required the loving, pure mother devoting her full time in the home. Societal norms of economic independence opposed outdoor relief, which would also undermine the responsibility and authority of the husband. Paid work for the mother would increase the danger of bad mothering. Above all, single motherhood, by itself, was a morally suspect position. The moral, gender, class, race, and ethnic bases for these ideas cannot be overemphasized. Those mothers who could not conform, whatever the reason, those who had to earn money, were condemned and degraded; even within their own sphere of work, invidious distinctions were drawn in terms of dominant values of middle-class motherhood. It was in the context of these contradictions that the idea of pensions for mothers and their dependent children was born. The idea of supporting single mothers and their children in their homes was considered to be a sharp break from previous policy. The new policy was spearheaded by the child protectors; their goal was to save children, and their program—aid to dependent children—became known as "the children's program."

However, before proceeding to an analysis of this reform effort, it is important to understand the distinctive moral conception of poor children in families. As noted, the "deserving" poor, those who were morally blameless, were extricated from the general mass of poverty. They were treated separately either in state institutions or, in the case of Civil War veterans and their families, in separate programs. This was also the situation for children who were blind, deaf and mute, or mentally ill, and those who were orphans. *But this was not true for the general mass of poor children in families.* Despite the rhetoric of many of the reformers, these children and their parents were still part of the general mass of poverty, the category that was undeserving. The vast majority of these families survived, as best they could and by whatever means, as most of the rest of the poor did. The mothers worked where they could—in the sweatshops and the mills, taking in laundry or boarders, working as domestics—and their children worked. The child protection reformers failed to abolish child labor. In other words—and this is the key point—these families, both adults and children, as a category, were in no sense excused from work. From time to time, in periods of unusual hardship, and if they were lucky, they received small amounts of public or private relief. Sometimes they showed up in the poorhouses. As noted above, a common practice was for parents to place children in orphanages—on a temporary basis, they hoped. But homes were also permanently broken up (L. Gordon, 1988).

In addition to the actual economic and social plight of poor children, we must also not forget their deviant status. Throughout this period, the reformers were strongly concerned about deviant behavior, and especially the transmission of the wrong values and habits from the parent to the child (L. Gordon, 1988, pp. 461–462, 466–467). While the juvenile court was not considered punitive in the adult criminal law sense, it certainly was intended to be a strong and effective form of social control. Thus it is clear that dependent children in families were not considered as part of the deserving poor. While these children might still be blameless, they were predelinquent—if not controlled, they were likely to become paupers and criminals. It was the ascribed reason for poverty for the category that determined the applicable program. As distinguished from the deserving poor, children in poor families had no moral claim on the state for material well-being.

This was the ideological context within which the mothers' pension movement was born. Given the moral and gender constraints, as well as the intense contradictions in family policy, it is no surprise that the consensus of the reformers was, in Mark Leff's words, "startlingly narrow" (1983, p. 397). The proposed reform, in words that will continue to ring familiar, promised to be cheap and morally uplifting, while "raising no specter of dissolute male misfits lining up for their monthly liquor money" (p. 397).

Disenchantment with orphanages and other institutions led child protectors to argue that even a poor home was better than a good institution. There was sympathy for the widow, for her impaired ability to be a good mother, which threatened the well-being of the child. There developed among reformers what Gordon (1988) calls the "sentimental cult of motherhood"—childbirth and infant care would create a sense of love that would help reform the mother (p. 104).

In addition to social work reformers, a major supporting group was the Chicago-based National Probation League. This was a recently formed organization whose mission was the promotion of probation as an alternative to prison or reformatories for both child and adult offenders. Along with the juvenile court judges, the National Probation League believed that delinquent children went "bad" because their working mothers could not take care of them.

They, along with other reformers, argued that administration of this new relief program should be in the juvenile courts; not only were the juvenile courts an existing bureaucracy that had responsibility for dependent children, but this would disassociate the new program from both private charity and outdoor relief (Leff, 1983, pp. 400–401).

There was substantial opposition to mothers' pensions, and this included most of the professional social workers. While their arguments tended to focus on the relative merits of public relief versus private charity, outdoor versus indoor relief, and the fears of pauperism, the most salient agenda concerned patriarchal family relations and the preservation of the domestic code. Gordon (1988) reports that C. C. Carstens, at that time the most influential person in the child-saving movement, opposed mothers' pensions on the grounds that they would weaken the traditional family; public policy, in his view, should abolish single motherhood, not encourage it. It was firmly believed that mothers' pensions constituted an attack on the family (p. 104).

The catalyst for the program is usually attributed to the first White House Conference, called by President Theodore Roosevelt in 1909 (Bell, 1965; Leff, 1983). The conferees condemned existing arrangements for children in poverty. They now declared that "home life is the highest and finest product of civilization," and that "no child should be deprived of his family by reason of poverty alone" (Bell, 1965, p. 4). Institutions were condemned as failures, and the conferees concluded that public programs should be established to provide financial assistance to children in their own homes. On the other hand, the conferees were not in favor of weakening the responsibility of the father by giving public aid. Accordingly, their famous recommendation read:

> Children of parents of worthy character, suffering from temporary misfortune, and children of reasonably efficient and deserving mothers who are without the support of the normal breadwinner should, as a rule be kept with their parents, such aid being given as may be necessary to maintain suitable homes for the rearing of children. (Bell, 1965, p. 4)

It is claimed that the principles elaborated by the White House Conference became the guidelines for the aid to dependent children or mothers' pension programs, as they were more popularly known (Bell, 1965, p. 4; Katz, 1986, pp. 127–129). Illinois enacted the first statewide statute, the Fund to Parents Act, in 1911; within 2 years, 20 states had similar legislation, and within 10 years, 40 states. Michael Katz (1986) calls the White House Conference a remarkable flip in public policy. Previously, poverty was considered a prime contributor to deviance; now, the poor but virtuous mother was to be supported by public funds. The home was to be preserved, not broken. Irwin Garfinkel and Sara McLanahan (1986) state: "In principle, the mothers' pension movement represents a clear reversal of previous expectations that poor mothers should work" (p. 99). This is the test of the deserving/undeserving poor distinction. Were poor single mothers now to be extricated from the general mass of poverty and placed in the deserving poor class?

When one examines closely what actually happened in the states, nothing could be further from the truth. The White House Conference recommendation and the publicity surrounding the enactment of the legislation was symbolic generation, the construction of a "solution" that salved the consciences of the reformers but did little to disturb underlying contradictions between the control of pauperism and the domestic code.

The Illinois Fund to Parents Act was an amendment to the juvenile court act. Recall that juvenile court jurisdiction was over "delinquent," "neglected," and "dependent" children. The Fund to Parents Act provided:

> If the parent or parents of such *dependent* child or *neglected* child are poor and unable to properly care for the said child, but are otherwise proper guardians and it is for the welfare of such child to remain at home, the court may enter an order finding such facts and fixing the amount of money necessary to enable the parent or parents to properly care for such child, and thereupon it shall be the duty of the County Board . . . to pay to such parent or parents, at such times as said order may designate, the amount so specified for the care of such dependent or neglected child until the further order of the court. (Illinois Statutes, 1911; emphasis added)

In other words, the juvenile court, as part of its jurisdiction over "predelinquent" children, now had an additional remedy. Or, to state the matter another way, if the parent was found suitable in the sense that poverty was unaccompanied by the usual vices (e.g., drunkenness, bad moral habits, a poor environment), she could now be an alternative probation officer. Recall the support of the National Probation League. In modern terms, this was a form of privatization of probation. Incorporating the statute in the Juvenile Court Act was not accidental. For a long time, the Illinois State Charities Commission had been arguing for much stronger public intervention with dependent children on delinquency prevention grounds (Handler & Hollingsworth, 1971, p. 21). As Gordon has demonstrated, during this time, the close connection between poverty and deviance was an unquestioned assumption. The child protection reformers argued that neglected children almost invariably became delinquent children, and neglect resulted from mothers' working; thus mothers' pensions constituted an anticrime measure (Leff, 1983, p. 413).

The Illinois act was not restricted to widows; children of divorced, deserted, and even unwed mothers were potentially eligible. While the Illinois act was influential, many other states parted company on the potential breadth of coverage. Nevertheless, substantial numbers of states did potentially cover children of divorced and deserted mothers; in almost a third of the states, unwed mothers were also included (Garfinkel & McLanahan, 1986, p. 98).

Of course, statutory coverage was only potential. After all, general welfare statutes also covered all the poor and the indigent. It was up to the judge or the county administrators to decide who among the *category* was worthy of receiving assistance (Bell, 1965, pp. 6–7). Mothers could be referred by county superintendents of the poor, or superintendents of any city or village, town officials, friends or relatives, or the local courts. The judge could give aid or not, or put the child on probation, or remove the child from the home and place him or her with another family, or commit the child to a state institution. The judge could also require the mother to work as a condition of receiving aid (p. 7).

The statutes, then, were very broad; potentially large classes of single mothers could be included. But implementation was placed in the hands of local officials, mostly juvenile court judges. Was moral ambiguity resolved? If not, how were the programs to be administered?

The apparent change in principle announced by the White House Conference reformers and the breadth of these early statutes did not escape the attention of those who opposed relief for single mothers. The Charitable Organization Society, which, it will be recalled, led the attack on public outdoor relief and was a major proponent of the juvenile court (Sutton, 1985), vigorously condemned the new program. So, too, did some of the most prominent social reformers of the day. Their characterization of poor mothers and their children sharply conflicted with the sentimental cult of motherhood. Mary Richmond, in 1912, called the mothers' pension schemes "backward." "Public funds not to widows only, mark you, but . . . funds to the families of those who have deserted and are going to desert!" (quoted in Bell, 1965, p. 6). Two years later, Homer Folks stated:

> To pension desertion or illegitimacy would, undoubtedly, have the effect of a premium upon these crimes against society. . . . It is a great deal more difficult to determine the worthiness of such mothers than of the widow, and a great deal more dangerous for the state to attempt relief on any large scale. (quoted in Bell, 1965, pp. 6–7).

One of the strongest statements was made by Florence Nesbit in arguing that these programs could not

> possibly be considered worth the expenditure of public funds unless there can be reasonable assurance that children will have a home which will provide at least the conditions necessary to make possible a moral, physical and mental development. Ill-trained, ill-nourished children, predisposed to crime and disease, growing into a stunted, ineffective adulthood, are a serious liability, not an asset to society. Perpetuating homes which produce such results would be both uncharitable and unwise. (quoted in Bell, 1965, pp. 6–8; see also Abbott, 1938, p. 232)

As with the general, undifferentiated mass of poverty, these social reformers warned of the historically difficult task of separating "fit" from "unfit" mothers, the worthy poor from the unworthy (Abbott, 1938; Bell, 1965, pp. 6–8).[3]

In fact, the opponents had little to fear. The programs turned out to be neither expensive nor disruptive of the existing social order (Leff, 1983). The burst of legislative activity masked the essential shallowness of the support for reform. Many opponents, including juvenile court judges, chose a strategy of nonenforcement rather than public confrontation. Leff (1983) reports that mothers' pensions were never a central political concern, and although supported by Progressive newspapers and magazines, the issue was never high on the agenda of most politicians, including organized labor. Women were the principal support, although those in the more militant wing of the suffragists were uneasy about the glorification of women's place in the home. Leff argues that no single group or individual was that influential in the movement; rather, it caught on legislatively because it fit with current social attitudes of the time (p. 410).

It was up to the line officials (judges as well as county agencies) to make the day-to-day distinctions, to separate the worthy mothers from the unworthy. In the early years, most counties refused to implement the law at all; officials claimed either that there were no cases or that local poor-relief officials were doing an adequate job (Leff, 1983, p. 413). Significantly, in many other jurisdictions, the programs were turned over to the local Charitable Organization Societies and similar-minded social workers, even though they had vigorously opposed the laws in the first place. These administrators, deeply suspicious of the single mother to begin with, were delegated the authority to decide who was fit and proper (Nelson, 1988; Orloff, 1988a).

Practice, of course, varied, but a few solid generalizations emerge. First, the program, as administered, was overwhelming for white widows. Winifred Bell (1965) reports that nationwide, widows constituted 82% of the program. In a 1931 survey, 96% of the families were white, 3% African-American, and 1% other. Moreover, about half of the African-American recipients lived in Ohio and Pennsylvania. In North Carolina, there was only one African-American family enrolled. Houston, Texas, had none, even though African-Americans constituted 21% of the population. In Marion County, Indiana (Indianapolis), with an 11% African-American population, there were no African-American families on the program; there was one family in Gary, Indiana; and so forth (p. 10).

Echoing the Poor Law commissioners of England (recommending the substitution of poorhouses for outdoor relief), local administrators complained of the difficulties in administering the vague test. Ultimately, they had to rely on judgment, prejudice, and gossip. Once a family was on the program, continuing supervision was called for to make sure that the home remained fit and proper. Workers were supposed to supervise home management, diet, cleanliness, school attendance, and, of course, moral behavior. As in the administration of child protection, sex was a particularly serious offense. Practice varied depending on the availability of staff, their particular moral views, and local community attitudes, but Bell (1965) reports more or less continuous regulatory control and terminations during this period (pp. 11–13).

The programs remained small. In 1930, there were 3,792,902 female-headed households. The Children's Bureau conducted a survey in 1931, and reported that 93,620 families were aided in that year, less than 3% of the pool. Tight eligibility and public budgets combined to reduce the size of the caseload (Bell, 1965, p. 14). According to a 1928 federal survey, more than half of the recipients reported working during the month that they received the grant; Garfinkel and McLanahan (1986, p. 99) say that this is an underestimation.

In summing up this early period, Leff (1983) notes that "nothing receded like the mothers'-pension movement after its legislative success. Like most Progressive reformers, mothers'-pension advocates proved more vigilant in promoting passage of the law than in monitoring its administration and assuring its adequate financial support" (p. 414).

What, then, can we say about female-headed households in poverty *as a category*? As a category, they were still part of the general mass of poor; the vast majority were not excused from work. For some, but for only a very small number, ADC was available. But even this program was a highly structured form of social control (Nelson, 1988). It was conditional (including a work test) on moral behavior. The excluded were forced to get along as best they could—they worked, their children worked, they were hungry and miserable along with the rest of the poor. The White House Conferees and the elite participants in the mothers' pension movement may have hailed a dramatic change in social attitudes toward the poor female-headed household, but in the states and local communities, this class was still clearly in the undifferentiated mass of unworthy poor. Margaret Rosenheim (1966) sums up this early period as follows:

We may mislead ourselves by speaking of the history of AFDC as though the original impetus was to provide a choice between employment and unemployment. It might better be characterized as offering mothers an alternative to institutionalization of their children or to starvation where employment was not a live possibility or brought insufficient income for the entire family. The latter possibility is supported by our knowledge that working women do not represent a new phenomenon, though undeniably our attitudes toward the acceptable reasons for women seeking employment have broadened. Lower-class women generally have been expected to work when the possibility was open to them. (p. 187)

The disjuncture between the rhetoric of the mothers' pension movement and the practice is instructive. The controversy over the wisdom of outdoor relief for dependent children necessarily involved ideological positions as to family and gender roles. The proponents and opponents both evoked the image of the traditional, patriarchal family, but differed sharply as to the impact of ADC. The proponents argued for the domestic code—men and women belonged in separate spheres; motherhood and the home were privileged, and should not be compromised by paid labor. Mothers' pensions, they said, removed the necessity for paid labor and would thereby reinforce patriarchy and domesticity. The opposition believed that pensions would weaken traditional family ties, weaken family (husband) responsibility, and encourage single motherhood. That each side thought its position privileged patriarchy should not be surprising. Each side constructed its own explanations of the social problem and argued for its own solutions. In addition, it is not surprising that most professional social workers—especially those involved in child protection—would, at least initially, oppose a program that threatened their ideologies, special competence, and authority.

The deep ambivalence in social attitudes toward motherhood was resolved in familiar terms. As discussed in Chapter 1, in practice the programs were restricted. "Worthy" widows, those who affirmed the domestic code, were admitted; they were brought back into majoritarian society. Although they were unmarried, their homes reflected women's separate sphere. They devoted themselves to their role of home management and child rearing. They were morally excused from work. The value of the nonworking mother and the worthy widow was affirmed by those who were denied entry—the unworthy mothers. These women were cast out; they had to rely on degrading labor and male breadwinners. Morality was served, and local taxpayer costs were saved.

The mothers' pension movement served important symbolic purposes. To whom were the arguments of both the reformers and the opponents addressed, and for what purposes? The importance of women and children in the paid labor force at this time was far from trivial. Brenner and Ramas (1984) argue that we should not confuse middle-class reformers with the actual representation of the capitalist class. The latter have always resisted expanding state responsibility for dependents. Enough benefits would be provided to maintain legitimacy and order, but not enough to undercut work incentives (see also Quadagno, 1988). As far as the dominant business interests were concerned, work incentives (restricted eligibility and low benefits) were more important than patriarchy in the lower social classes (Piven & Cloward, 1988b, p. 639).

To whom, then, were the arguments of reformers and their opponents addressed? While the rhetoric of reform was the preservation of traditional patriarchy, with the wife and mother at home caring for the family full-time, the reality for the vast majority of poor women and mothers was work. For many intact working-class families, the family wage was insufficient, and the vast majority of single mothers had to scramble in a variety of paid jobs. So the reformers and their opponents were addressing themselves—Protestant, white, middle-class—and "Others." For themselves, they were defining the norm, the acceptable standards of behavior; in so doing, they were separating themselves from the others, those families where the mothers *had* to engage in paid labor, the lower social classes, the deviants. The vast majority of poor mothers and their children remained the socially constructed enemy, to be dealt with in the local communities caught in the contradictions and ambiguities of the specter of pauperism and the tangled web of gender, class, race, and ethnicity. The mothers' pension movement was symbolic and expressive, an exercise in status politics. For the vast majority of female-headed households in poverty, nothing had changed.

Policies, as interpreted and applied, are often diverse, contradictory, and ambiguous; they reflect the spectrum of political interests.

But, as pointed out in Chapter 1, the name of a policy can allow us to ignore inconsistencies and ambiguities; the name reassures us that there is agreement on the dominant ideology and that change has come about; the name masks hesitations and contradictory actions that minimize or cancel claims of accomplishment (Edelman, 1988, p. 16). The name "mothers' pension movement" did all these things. Despite the fact that more than four-fifths of the state statutes never used the term *mothers' pensions*, instead reflecting the child protection basis of the reform, referring to the programs as "aid to dependent children" or "aid to mothers of dependent children" (U.S. Department of Labor, 1934, Chart 3), the name of the reform effort was "mothers' pensions." The name signified accomplishment for the White House Conference reformers and their allies—for them alone a nationwide change in policy had occurred.

The Adult Programs

Aid to the blind. Programs to provide aid to the blind were enacted in the states contemporaneously with ADC, but the contrast between the two types of programs could not have been more clear. By the time of the New Deal, 27 states had programs to aid the blind. The theory behind these programs was that blindness itself was a "sufficiently well-defined cause of poverty" as to merit special relief, that is, relief that would be "deserving."

> The blind people themselves have been especially active in initiating and promoting such legislation since they feel that a special allowance, made in consideration of their handicap, is free from the stigma commonly attached to "poor relief," and moreover that, by the setting up of special administrative provisions, they are spared the humiliation of investigation by the poor relief authorities who, they feel, do not understand the special needs and problems of blind people. (Irwin & McKay, 1936)

In addition to blindness, eligibility was based on age, residence, and need. The only conditions were usually that the recipient not be an inmate of a state institution or receiving other public aid; the only moral condition was usually that the applicant not be publicly soliciting alms (10 states). The blind were morally excused from work.

During this period, there were a variety of programs, often with the active support of the blind, designed to increase their self-sufficiency; however, only one state required participation in such a program as a condition of aid (U.S. Committee on Economic Security, 1937).[4] Aid to the blind statutes have always been part of the welfare codes; in almost all of the states, administration has been the responsibility of welfare agencies (U.S. Committee on Economic Security, 1937, pp. 306–307).[5]

Old-age assistance. In contrast to aid to the blind, in its initial period old-age assistance resembled ADC. In view of the fact that today the elderly are so firmly entrenched in the deserving poor category, it may come as a surprise to learn how different the early approach was. Public old-age pensions came late to the United States, compared with Europe. There is much dispute about the reasons for American exceptionalism—for example, fear of another corrupt public program (such as the Civil War pensions), southern political resistance, or a divided and generally weak labor movement. But one strong source of opposition, at the state level, was employers. In addition to opposing increased state taxation, which would make their products less competitive in interstate markets, they were concerned about the labor supply. At this time, there was no agreed-upon retirement age, and people over 65 were still considered part of the labor force (Quadagno, 1988, p. 70).

In contrast with ADC, which swept the country, old-age programs proved very difficult to enact. Programs began to be enacted in the 1920s, and at that time, the aged poor were viewed with as much suspicion as the rest of the poverty population. Most Americans believed that if a person worked hard and saved, he or she would not be destitute in old age; therefore, outdoor relief would reward the shiftless and lazy. There was also the view that it was the duty of children to support their parents in old age, and that to relieve this duty would loosen family ties (U.S. Committee on Economic Security, 1937, p. 158).

About 30 states had old-age assistance programs prior to the New Deal, and, although they varied, they were small, uneven in coverage, and virtually bristled with moral conditions. In addition to citizenship, there were long residency requirements and strict financial eligibility requirements. Many states required the transfer of assets to the welfare agency; almost all provided for liens on recipients' estates; and most prohibited aid if property was transferred in order to qualify. In many states, aid would be denied to persons who had deserted their spouses or failed to support their wives, or had been convicted of crimes, or were "habitual tramps, vagrants, or beggars" (U.S. Committee on Economic Security, 1937, pp. 160–163). The old-age statutes, more than any of the others, sought to exclude the "morally unfit." Relief for the aged, at this time, raised questions about pauperism, work, saving, and family responsibility. As distinguished from the blind, the category was suspicious; administrators had to pick and choose the morally deserving.

Workers' Compensation

During this period, another important social reform was established, but it had a legal and administrative structure very different from that of the contemporaneous relief programs. Workers' compensation shows that the respective structures of the various relief and social insurance programs were not accidental; they reflected different strategies to deal with different substantive conceptions of causes and cures of poverty.

Until the New Deal, workers' compensation was the only social insurance program in the United States. However, despite the expectations of Progressive social reformers, it did not herald the start of social insurance in the United States during this period; it was designed and supported to meet only one specific problem—industrial accidents (Lubove, 1967).

By the turn of the century, several prominent capitalists, organized labor, and social reformers had become concerned about industrial accidents. An influential report on the accident rate in Allegheny County, Pennsylvania, in 1907–1908 dramatized the scope of these tragedies. During this period, out of 250,000 workers, mostly in steel, railroads, and mines, 526 died and another 509 were injured. Most of those killed or maimed were young. The report investigated the causes of the accidents and disproved the current ideology that employee carelessness was primarily to blame; most accidents were the result of the nature of the work. Even those attributed to employee carelessness were ambiguous—employees were "green," or pressured to work fast and to take chances. Speed, noise, long hours, and monotony took their toll on attentiveness and safety. In short, it was unfair to hold the worker primarily responsible for the accident.

The Allegheny report then went on to document how few workers or their families received any substantial compensation from their employers. The loss fell on the injured worker and his dependents, producing poverty, widows seeking paid work, and neglected children. A social insurance scheme, argued the report, would spread the loss, compensate the victims, and encourage employers to institute preventive safety measures (Lubove, 1967, pp. 255–258). There were numerous other reports, legislative hearings, and commission studies of industrial accidents. Most recommended some form of workers' compensation (Friedman & Ladinsky, 1988, p. 278; Weinstein, 1968, p. 40). There was little doubt that the industrial accident rate in America was appalling (Tishler, 1971, p. 112).

Employers came to support workers' compensation in order to control costs, stabilize labor relations, and deflect the increasing negative publicity and public outrage over industrial accidents. The traditional common law defenses against worker claims had become unreliable. The common law required employers to use reasonable care to safeguard employees. However, in order to prevail in a suit for damages, an injured workman had to show that the employer failed to exercise reasonable care in providing a safe workplace and that the employer's negligence was the proximate cause of the injury. The employer had three potentially very effective defenses. He would still not be liable if (a) the employee assumed the risk of a dangerous condition, (b) a coworker contributed to the injury (the "fellow servant" rule), or (c) the employee was in any way contributorily negligent. These defenses were gradually eroded, mostly by legislatures growing increasingly hostile to railroads (Asher, 1983, pp. 198–202; Friedman & Ladinsky, 1988, p. 274). By the turn of the century, there was sufficient uncertainty in the law that increasing numbers of employee claims were made and tried; juries, employers felt, favored plaintiffs. In complaints familiar today, the system, it was charged, encouraged fraudulent plaintiffs and their lawyers. Settlements were on the rise, along with liability insurance premiums, reflecting the increased uncertainty of losses (Nelson, 1988). Employers began to suffer larger costs of settlements, insurance, administration, legal fees, and staff lawyers (Friedman & Ladinsky, 1988, p. 276). Besides, some studies showed, most of the recovered money went to the lawyers and the insurance companies, and not the victims and their families (Tishler, 1971, pp. 115–117). Employers and insurance companies thus saw an advantage in a compensation scheme that would replace an uncertain liability with a fixed, but limited, cost; eliminate sensational and often bitter litigation; help stabilize labor relations; and lessen public outrage over the treatment of injured workers (Lubove, 1967, pp. 261–262; Weinstein, 1968, pp. 44–45).

Labor's position was different. It was now beginning to reap the fruits of its long campaign against the common law defenses. It rightly feared that a compensation system of fixed costs would mean low costs to employers and low benefits to injured workers (Weinstein, 1968, p. 43). Accordingly, it favored the English system, where the injured employee had a choice—to opt for the certainty of a low, but fixed, compensation or to sue in tort for greater damages. The right to sue, labor thought, in addition to providing more compensation for plaintiffs, would exert upward pressure on compensation scales. For these same reasons, employers staunchly opposed the right to sue for damages; they considered the elimination of litigation to be the key element in the package (Lubove, 1967, pp. 263–268).

Labor was weak and divided. Not surprisingly, the employers proved to be the decisive force; they got their fixed costs, and at a low level. Rejecting the recommendations of the Progressive reforms for full coverage of health care costs and two-thirds of an employee's wages, the schemes adopted in the states provided low compensation along with meager medical benefits. For less serious accidents, claimants, after a waiting period, would receive a small percentage of their wages. Long-term disability was compensated according to schedules—for example, a flat sum for the loss of an arm or a leg. By departing from disability insurance principles, employers had every incentive to keep the compensation schedules low (Skocpol & Ikenberry, 1983, p. 109). The injured worker still bore most of the costs of industrial accidents. Decisions were routinized. There were tables for calculating wage replacement, the extent of disability, and medical expenses (Nelson, 1988). There was virtually no retraining or rehabilitation for crippled workers. With rare exceptions, the right to sue was not allowed. In most states, the programs were administered by industrial accident boards or commissions, promoted and staffed by employers and their lawyers (Nelson, 1988; Skocpol & Ikenberry, 1983, p. 108).

CONCLUSION: THE STRUCTURE OF SOCIAL WELFARE PROGRAMS

Prior to the New Deal, a variety of social welfare programs existed, each designed to meet a particular problem. The varying structures of these programs reflected the different social constructions of their clientele and intended remedies.

General relief, the basic, bottom-line program inherited from England, was the main bulwark against pauperism, the main defender of labor discipline. Its clientele consisted of people from the general, undifferentiated mass of poverty. General relief was the most decentralized program; during this period, and still largely today, general relief was administered at the municipal level. There, local officials separated, on a case-by-case basis, the worthy from the unworthy. This is the program that is the most discretionary and the most miserly in benefits, and that has the harshest conditions—workhouses, poorhouses, and other kinds of menial, grueling labor. General relief operates on the assumption that most applicants are potentially undeserving; the conditions and administration of relief constitute the test of necessity, and the function of the program, while grudgingly relieving misery, is primarily deterrence. The able-bodied must earn their support, and not seek relief.

The public response was different when the category of the poor to be served was considered worthy, when they were morally excused from work. Separate state institutions were created for the blind, the deaf, the insane, and orphans. While these unfortunates were dependent, they were not paupers; their poverty was not due to moral fault. Separate administrative institutions were also created for Civil War veterans; this was outdoor relief, but veterans were not to be stigmatized by applying at the same door as the pauper. Bureaucrats were more sympathetic to that category of the poor that had already demonstrated a worthy character.

The three categorical programs—aid to dependent children, aid to the blind, and old-age assistance—also differed in structure. The origins of ADC are deeply interwoven with the control of deviant behavior—working women, single mothers, and child protection—all threats to the ideology of the patriarchal family and the domestic code, the sentimental cult of motherhood, and white Protestant morality. The potential clientele of this program, as a category, was morally suspect. The vast majority were considered part of the labor force. The conditions of relief reflected the historic moral concerns about the indiscriminate giving of outdoor relief to the unworthy. The ADC programs were strongly exclusionary, miserly, highly discretionary, and, for the most part, administered by the juvenile courts.

Aid to the blind was different. Here, there was consensus that the cause of poverty was faultless. The rules were simple and easily administered. There was separate administration so that these applicants would not suffer investigative humiliations at the hands of local poor-relief administrators.

Old-age assistance, in many respects, resembled aid to dependent children; at this period in our history, the category of potential applicants was morally suspect. Would relief discourage hard work and saving, and family responsibility? There was no agreed-upon retirement age; hence the aged were still part of the work force, and employers feared a decrease in labor supply. Here, there was no consensus as to the cause of poverty. Accordingly, because moral issues had to be determined, old-age assistance, too, was miserly, and full of conditions designed to weed out the unworthy on a case-by-case basis. Administration was in the hands of the local relief officials.

Workers' compensation took another distinct turn. Despite its categorization as a "social insurance" program, it was hardly that, at least in its formative period. Here, too, a consensus formed as to the nature of industrial accidents. The older, competing moral values embodied in the common law defenses became vulnerable to legislative repeal. The "consensus" was dominated by employers; accordingly, the thrust of this program was to regularize and reduce the costs of industrial accidents for employers. After the change, the victims still bore most of the costs. Decision rules were routinized, field-level discretion was sharply reduced, and administration was lodged in separate specialized agencies.

Looking at this array of programs, during the formative period, we can make the following generalizations. When consensus forms as to the nature of a social problem and its solutions, then program design is transparent and congruent with ideology. This is true whether programs are benign—separate state institutions, veterans' pensions, aid to the blind—or repressive, such as workers' compensation. With the relief of poverty, there is agreement only when the moral basis for dependency is not at issue. When moral responsibility is at issue, there is ambiguity and conflict in ideology and program, resulting in disjunctures or decoupling between symbolic production and implementation. The conflicts are delegated to the field level, where they are fought out on a case-by-case basis, largely hidden from view. General relief, aid to dependent children, and old-age assistance raise issues of work, responsibility, pauperism, race, gender roles, the construction of the family, moral behavior, and child protection.

NOTES

1. See, generally, Katz (1986, chap. 1) for an excellent account of the rise and decline of the poorhouse in the United States. See also Nash (1976) for an account of poor relief and the failed attempts at institutionalization in Philadelphia.

2. For an excellent account of a failed attempt in colonial Boston to require poor widows and children to engage in factory labor, see Nash (1979).

3. Part of the reason for preferring the juvenile courts or special administrative agencies may have been to blunt this criticism. In urging these administrative arrangements, the new programs were to be "utterly segregated from public poor law outdoor relief," which was criticized by some for failure to stress the "obligations" of proper child rearing (Leff, 1983, p. 412).

4. Missouri denied benefits to persons who refused training to make them self-sufficient (Irwin & McKay, 1936, pp. 272-273; U.S. Committee on Economic Security, 1937, p. 308).

5. In Idaho, the probate court was the administrative agency. In a few other states, courts administered the program, but under the supervision of welfare agencies.

3

From the New Deal to the Present

The American welfare state is usually dated from the New Deal, and, indeed, major changes were made during that period. Moreover, the patterns set by the New Deal are with us today. Nevertheless, while innovative in some respects, in many others New Deal programs reflected existing ideologies and structural patterns. The grip of the past was loosened, but only somewhat. What is striking are the continuities in social welfare policy solidified by the Social Security Act of 1935.

The Social Security Act and the New Deal period reaffirmed the moral categorization of the poor in terms of the work ethic, gender, and race. Initially, in response to the widespread unemployment caused by massive structural dislocations in the national and international economy, there was a brief, national response of meeting the needs of the unemployed; but this was then replaced by enforcing the work ethic for those considered to be in paid labor market—at that time, primarily males. The exclusion of the vast majority of the able-bodied poor continues to the present. Poor single mothers and African-Americans were excluded from the major reforms of this period; they were still defined as the Other, thus affirming patriarchy and racial subordination. This pattern continued until the welfare gates were forced open by massive economic and social changes starting in the postwar period: the civil rights movement, the urban riots and welfare rights protests of the 1960s, changing electoral politics, and the dramatic changes in legal culture.

We discuss this period—from the New Deal to the present—in terms of four groups of the poor: unemployed males, the aged, single mothers and their children, and African-Americans. The policy responses to these groups varied, illustrating the ideological importance of welfare policy in terms of work, gender, and race and how these ideologies mediated the changing economic, political, and social conditions of the poor. In this section, we summarize the major arguments.

Prior to the New Deal—indeed, throughout welfare history—the unemployed male was the paradigmatic undeserving poor; he is the one category unambiguously in the paid labor market, and therefore giving aid to this group above all imperils the work ethic. This normative position was severely challenged by the massive unemployment of the Depression and the fear of social disorder. In response to great pressures, the Roosevelt administration launched massive public work-relief projects. Nevertheless, despite the overwhelming evidence of the structural causes of unemployment and the considerable success and popularity of the programs themselves, work-relief for this group was still a reluctant, morally ambiguous antipoverty strategy, sharply resisted by the business community. Rather quickly, the norms of preserving the work ethic and denouncing dependency prevailed. The national work-relief programs were crushed and the relief of the able-bodied poor was returned to the states to "preserve local labor markets."

The experience of work-relief set the pattern for the Social Security Act reforms. Despite the obvious national implications of unemployment, unemployment insurance (UI) was state and locally based. For much of its history, UI has been essentially for white males, but even so, benefits are meager and most unemployed workers are excluded. Most unemployed males, then and now, get no relief or only temporary, miserly benefits from locally administered general relief. Welfare policy most stringently enforces the work ethic for this group.

The story of the dependent aged is the one counterexample. Here, there occurred a dramatic change in the ideological construction of the moral basis of poverty. Put simply, with the onset of the

Depression, the aged were morally excused from work; they were now considered to be the deserving poor. Accordingly, there was strong, popular pressure to provide the dependent aged with simplified flat-grant "pensions." However, for a variety of reasons that will be discussed, the Roosevelt administration tenaciously opposed a "relief" program for the dependent aged and preferred instead a contributory, insurance-based retirement program for workers. The struggle between the two approaches lasted until well into the post-World War II period. Who won? We argue that the dependent aged won. While the form is a that of a social security retirement program with the *symbols* of contribution and insurance, the fact is that in response to continuous pressure on behalf of the dependent aged, social security retirement benefits have been raised and greatly expanded, taking in huge numbers of the elderly despite their lack of contributions; in short, social security has become redistributive. In classic political terms, the Social Security Administration co-opted its opponents, but in so doing, transformed its program into a broadly based, redistributive, nationally administered, nonintrusive, relatively generous program dramatically reflecting the moral transformation of this category of the poor. Here is the one example of a case where the myths remained, but the ceremonies gave way to real, substantive change.

The opposite story applies to single mothers and African-Americans. During the New Deal period, these were the excluded groups. The state aid to dependent children programs became one of the social security grant-in-aid programs, but ADC remained the stepchild. Benefits were lower than in programs for the aged and the blind. The programs remained under local control. They still were highly exclusionary. ADC was "welfare." It was the kind of relief that the Roosevelt administration opposed in pressing its case for contributory insurance. Single mothers (along with unemployed males and the dependent aged) were made the enemy in the struggle to establish the image of prudent, actuarially sound, insurance programs. Single mothers in poverty, those who had to try to find work, thus suffered terribly during the Depression. "Proper" women were not considered part of the paid labor force; the New Deal concentrated on their husbands.

Racial discrimination was severe during this period. Most African-Americans lived in the South on the land as tenant farmers. Southern political power was sufficient to block provisions in all programs—unemployment insurance, social security retirement, food programs, and the grants-in-aid—that would disturb existing patterns of racial subordination. African-Americans were simply excluded. They were largely excluded in the North as well. Despite commendable efforts on the part of the Roosevelt administration, African-Americans were discriminated against in work-relief, and very few were eligible for social security. These patterns changed only as a result of irresistible pressures on state and local welfare bureaucracies: the massive migrations of African-Americans off the land and out of the South, civil rights campaigns, the urban riots of the 1960s, pressure from the federal government, welfare rights protests, and the legal rights revolution. Starting in the 1960s, large numbers of previously excluded African-American single mothers streamed into AFDC. The transformation of AFDC produced new tensions. The *demography* of the program changed from white widows to large numbers of women of color and out-of-wedlock children, but, we argue, the *moral* categorization remained; recipients still formed a stigmatized category. As a result, the long struggle to assert social control over this deviant group started during this period and continues today through the Family Support Act. This story we describe in the next three chapters.

In sum, the moral categorization of the poor—the ideological construction of the particular "problem" that each category presents and the "solution"—is reflected in the structural characteristics of the particular programs. Each program, though its own system of myth and ceremony, mediates societal norms and the demands of the political economy.

THE NEW DEAL REFORMS

Work-Relief

The Social Security Act's enduring accomplishments were unemployment compensation, national old-age pensions, and grants-in-aid for the so-called categorical programs (aid to dependent children, aid to the blind, and old-age assistance). But before these programs could be addressed, the Roosevelt administration had to deal with the unemployed. For several years, the country experienced massive unemployment, unprecedented widespread poverty and hardship, and serious threats of social disorder (Katz, 1986, p. 207). The first task the new administration undertook was the direct, immediate relief of the unemployed. While these programs turned out to be temporary, that brief history will explain much about the ultimate shape of the Social Security Act and the future course of the American welfare state.

It is hard to exaggerate the extent of the unemployment confronting the Roosevelt administration. Between 1929 and 1933, the overall, official rate rose from 3.2% to almost a quarter of the working population. In some major cities, more than half the work force was unemployed (Katz, 1986, p. 207). The existing structure of state, local, and private relief was overwhelmed, and by 1933, when the new administration took office, large numbers of local governments were in default. Moreover, those who finally did apply for relief, now in huge numbers, no longer fit the stereotype of the dependent poor; the new supplicants were respectable, hardworking family men. Overwhelmingly, they were experienced white male workers. While spells of unemployment were endemic in the working population, there had never been anything to compare with this seemingly endless disaster in size and scope. Disorder increased. There were food riots and looting, demonstrations, rent strikes, the seizure and occupation of vacant buildings, and rallies and marches. The U.S. military was called in to rout unemployed veterans and their families demonstrating at the Capitol. Prominent businessmen, politicians, and journalists warned of revolution (Katz, 1986, pp. 214–216).

The country demanded action—in addition to massive unemployment, poverty, and hunger, the bank system was about to collapse, agriculture was in ruins, state and local officials were pleading for help. But there were (or seemed to be) constraints on what the federal government could do at that time. Aside from the lack of a national administrative capacity, certainly in the social welfare field, there was federalism. The national government was one of limited powers, which did not include, at least specifically, social welfare; legally, it was quite uncertain what kind of federal activity would survive constitutional challenges. Federalism was more than a matter of constitutional law. States' rights was an important ideology protecting a number of interests—local labor practices, political arrangements, low taxes, the control of relief, and, especially in the South, existing agriculture and race relations (Katz, 1986, p. 218).

Despite these limitations, the Roosevelt administration acted decisively, and with amazing results. The Federal Emergency Relief Administration (FERA) was established within two months of Roosevelt's inauguration, and within a year was providing relief for 4.5 million families and single people. The money was allocated to the states through the grant-in-aid system, which proved to be an effective device; states found the match and the federal funds flowed. There was an enormous expansion of staff at all levels of government (Katz, 1986, pp. 219–221).

Even though the states administered the funds, with varying benefits, the federal government asserted administrative controls; for example, practically all the states were required to set up separate emergency relief agencies rather than use existing welfare departments. The aim of the federal government was to create a single, coordinated administrative unit spanning the three levels of government. FERA set uniform minimum benefits (wages); prohibited racial, religious, and political discrimination; and insisted on public accountability. Militant groups of unemployed pressured states that were reluctant to agree to the national terms (Katz, 1986, pp. 221–223).

FERA provided both work-relief and direct relief.[1] Between 1.4 and 2.4 million people per month worked at wages that were higher than direct relief, and, at times, higher than prevailing market wages as well. Among the unskilled, white males received the most and the best assignments; among white-collar workers, both white males and females were favored; the "undeserving" included transients and homeless people, women in low-skilled jobs, and African-Americans. White males were also favored in two additional programs: the Civilian Conservation Corps and the Public Works Administration (Rose, 1989, p. 67).

Despite the great need, and despite the apparent success in meeting this need, the federal work-relief programs were immediately and vehemently attacked by the business community on the grounds that the programs abandoned traditional welfare work requirements and thus, in addition to wasting money, compromised labor discipline. The work ethic of the most menial laborer is enforced, they argued, by separating "regular" employees from work-relief recipients and instilling in the former the fear of being laid off if they are not sufficiently productive. FERA, it was charged, compromised work requirements by making work purely voluntary for the work-relief recipient and providing payment in cash rather than in kind. In response to this criticism, FERA drew a distinction between white- and blue-collar workers. A great many projects for the former were created with a simplified application process administered by professionals in separate offices.[2] This contrasted sharply with the process blue-collar applicants endured; in an effort to discourage permanent dependency, they were subjected to thorough financial investigations, personal contacts with previous employers, home visits, and contacts with family, friends, and churches to see about alternative support. The intention of these differing administrative arrangements was to separate white-collar workers from the stigma of the blue-collar, "ordinary relief applicants" (Rose, 1989, p. 69).

A great deal of controversy focused on the wage levels, which were considered too high by the business community. High work-relief wages propped up the wage structure and provided too much of a cushion for the low-wage worker to fall back on, thus compromising labor discipline. Organized labor and most federal officials tried to maintain high, mandated minimum wages on the grounds that this would raise the very lowest wages and increase purchasing power. Perhaps most controversial was the 30-cents-per-hour minimum, which was considerably above a significant number of private sector wages, especially in the rural South. In November 1934, under great pressure, the FERA minimum wage was rescinded (Rose, 1989, pp. 70–71).

In anticipation of the winter of 1933–1934, the administration launched the Civil Works Administration (CWA) to supplement FERA's work-relief programs. CWA was unique. Its aim was to provide public jobs rather than relief; wages were negotiated through collective bargaining agreements; and it assumed complete administrative responsibility for its projects. There was no means test. Relatively high minimum wages were established according to skill and geographical area (Rose, 1989, p. 72). CWA's accomplishments were "heroic" (Katz, 1986, p. 225). By January 1934, it employed 4.26 million people. At this time, CWA, along with FERA and the Civilian Conservation Corps, "assisted about 8 million households with 28 million people or 22.2 percent of the American population" (p. 226).

The CWA also provoked immediate reactions. CWA avoided using a means test because it did not want the unemployed to suffer the stigma of relief. Yet, within two months, a means test was forced upon it by Congress (Rose, 1989, p. 68). While federal and state officials, workers, and small merchants were enthusiastic, most of the business community voiced the same complaints, and in January 1934 CWA was cut back (Rose, 1989, p. 74).

President Roosevelt regarded both FERA and CWA as temporary; he feared a permanent, entrenched bureaucracy of thousands in public jobs. He worried about the effect of relief on work incentives and initiative, and warned that "continued dependence on relief induces a spiritual and moral disintegration fundamentally destructive to the national fibre. To dole out relief in this way is to administer a narcotic, a subtle destroyer of the human spirit" (quoted in Katz, 1986, p. 226). There was fierce opposition to FERA and CWA, regarding both their size and their wage rates; the South especially feared that continued federal intervention in the labor market would disrupt traditional race relations and threaten the supply of low-wage African-America labor (Rose, 1989, p. 64). At the end of the winter, despite their popularity, both were terminated by Congress (Katz, 1986, p. 227).

There were those in the administration who argued that the states lacked the capacity to handle all those who had been aided by FERA and that a national relief program was needed, but they were overruled. The new strategy was to provide jobs, not a dole, through a national work-relief program only for "employable" people who could not find jobs in the private sector, with the states providing relief for the "unemployables." Within a year, the newly created Works Progress Administration (WPA) employed more than 3 million people. With few exceptions, WPA was a grant-in-aid program; the funds went to the state and local governments, which planned and sponsored projects. Traditional relief practices—a means test and investigation to determine eligibility—were required (Bremer, 1975). In line with the emergent conservative position that government was not to interfere with private business, wages were targeted to fall between private sector rates and public relief, projects that would compete with local businesses and employers were banned, and federally sponsored projects were restricted to work that "would not otherwise be done" (Bremer, 1975, p. 644). The program enrolled only a fraction of the unemployed (Katz, 1986, pp. 228–229). The smaller size and administrative practices of WPA reflected administration sensitivity to the business community. Throughout the Depression, Congress cut and re-stricted WPA (except just before elections), always trying to force WPA workers to seek private employment (Katz, 1986, p. 229). The return of a strict means test, locally administered, and the abandon-ment of a national minimum meant, as one official put it, "a satis-factory adjustment to the customs and requirements of the commu-nities" (Rose, 1989, p. 75).

In 1934, many government officials and other reformers tried to press for work-relief as a permanent federal program. The Presi-dent's Committee on Economic Security (CES) floated an employ-ment assurance component on the grounds that work is preferable to relief. Again, there was strong opposition from business leaders. Their position was that the federal government should return all relief programs to the states, abolish work-relief, and lower direct relief payments to balance the federal budget (Rose, 1989, p. 82). In the end, the business community prevailed. The Social Security Act eliminated employment assurance. WPA continued as a relatively small, temporary program providing work-relief. Usually never more than a third of the jobless were employed; most (75–80%) worked as unskilled laborers at the lowest wage levels (Bremer, 1975, p. 648). Direct relief was returned to the states and local gov-ernments, which reimposed their traditional work tests. WPA kept adjusting its wage rates to avoid local criticism, and monthly in-come fell to about the same level as direct relief (Bremer, 1975). The historic role of work-relief is to shore up the economic order rather than to meet the needs of the poor, and this became the program of the New Dealers as well (Bremer, 1975).

This was the context within which the Social Security Act was formulated, debated, and enacted. Despite massive unemployment and impressive work and relief measures, traditional attitudes to-ward relief policy and labor discipline prevailed. It mattered not that the vast number of the unemployed were in no sense marginal members of society and that they were out of work due to global structural dislocations. The failure to support oneself and one's family through work was still considered to be fundamentally an individual moral problem. Those who had to seek relief were mor-ally degraded by intrusive welfare administration, menial jobs, and relief wages (Bremer, 1975). Labor markets were not to be tampered with. Regulating employment was more a matter of industrial dis-cipline and the prevention of dependency than of meeting need, and the administration of social control was best left in state and local hands. The federal government was not to be trusted, as the national work and relief programs well demonstrated. This dominant attitude toward work and relief of the undeserving poor and the jurisdictional allocation of authority explains the first major task of the social security reformers: unemployment insurance.

Unemployment Insurance

The social security planners had two models to reflect upon: one historical—the Civil War pensions—and the other contemporary—the European welfare state. The Civil War pension system was enacted in 1862. Initially, benefits were tied to service-connected injuries or death, but as a result of political party competition, patronage, and corruption, by the turn of the century it had become an enormous social welfare program.[3] The program was for the favored white middle class and more privileged members of the working class; while it met the needs of many of the aged and widows, it excluded African-Americans, southerners, and immigrants (Skocpol & Ikenberry, 1983, pp. 97–98).

The corruption and political patronage of the pension program offended Progressive Era social reformers (and, later, the New Dealers), who were pushing for insurance for all members of society who were at risk of loss of earnings due to accident, disease, old age, or unemployment (Orloff, 1988b, pp. 45–50). These reformers were deeply ambivalent about a national public program. They did not want to create another free-spending, patronage-based public distribution system (Orloff, 1988b, pp. 50–53; Skocpol & Ikenberry, 1983, pp. 104–113).

These fears were fueled by the experience of Europe in the post-World War I period. In response to widespread, persistent unemployment in Britain, the contributory unemployment insurance system gradually yielded to an open-ended system of relief for the unemployed. The system produced "horror, not only among strict fiscal conservatives, but also among reformist businessmen and politicians. . . . Social welfare in the United States was not to be provided through 'government doles,' declared the establishment figures of the 1920s" (Skocpol & Ikenberry, 1983, p. 114).

Accordingly, the initial approaches adhered closely to private market concepts as an alternative to national social insurance. Under "welfare capitalism" (the 1920s), enlightened companies would provide pension programs for loyal workers; safety and health plans would lead to improved working conditions while compensating accidents; and guarantees of stable employment and unemployment compensation would ameliorate the problems of temporary layoffs. In practical terms, of course, very few companies actually instituted such policies, but during this period the ideology of welfare capitalism reinforced the political mood that opposed new government taxing and spending initiatives (Orloff, 1988b, pp. 62–63; Skocpol & Ikenberry, 1983, pp. 114–115).

Other reformers concentrated their efforts at the state level. The "Wisconsin plan," developed by John Commons and tested by the Wisconsin State Industrial Commission, stressed the "preventive approach" to the vicissitudes of industrial employment—through adjustable tax rates, employers were encouraged to stabilize employment and prevent accidents. Employer taxes would go into individual company reserve funds. Companies that had stable employment records would have lower taxes; companies that laid off workers would be taxed to replenish their funds. Unemployed workers would receive benefits, however, only until their companies' reserves were exhausted. This perspective fit well with welfare capitalism, in that loss of earnings due to accidents or layoffs was viewed as an individual (corporate) responsibility rather than a structural problem (Patterson, 1981, pp. 26–27). The preventive approach would prod capitalists toward more enlightened employment policies (Amenta & Carruthers, 1986, p. 150). The Wisconsin system, argued Commons, would avoid the "socialistic and paternalistic schemes of Europe" (Skocpol & Ikenberry, 1983, p. 118).

The massive unemployment of the Depression sank both welfare capitalism and the Wisconsin plan. Relying on individual companies to meet the unemployment crisis was out of the question; state and local officials and private relief organizations clamored for national action. By 1932, organized labor—that is, the national American Federation of Labor—finally reversed course and endorsed public unemployment insurance. There had to be fixed taxes and a statewide insurance pool to provide uniform benefits to all workers regardless of their companies' previous records and tax payments. This latter alternative became known as the "Ohio plan."

Nevertheless, many New Deal officials, including the president, were reluctant to establish large federal programs for fear that they would become expansionary, uncontrollable, and therefore, in a short time, permanent. The principal actors in the administration, all from state government, including the president, favored sound administration and balanced budgets (Orloff, 1988b, p. 71). Roosevelt insisted that relief, including work-relief, should be separated from the more permanent insurance programs, and that unemployment insurance had to be actuarially sound, financed by contributions and taxes. Unemployment insurance, in his view, was not to become a dole for the able-bodied, as was happening in Europe (Skocpol & Ikenberry, 1983, pp. 124–125). When the administration went forward with its unemployment and retirement insurance provisions, they were clearly designed to avoid giving the impression that they were meeting the needs of all the unemployed or the aged. As Skocpol and Ikenberry (1983) point out, in this initial period, the major impact of the social security insurance programs was to put the payroll taxes in place rather than to distribute benefits (p. 126). As far as the federal government was concerned, once the threat of social disorder began to subside, shoring up capitalism took priority over meeting need.

An actuarially sound program could be national or state. The federal government could collect the payroll taxes and provide uniform benefits or could finance state plans that would distribute benefits with or without national standards. The plan finally recommended by Roosevelt's Committee on Economic Security allowed for maximum state control. There would be a federal offset tax plan, in which the federal government would collect the payroll tax but forgive 90% to employers who contributed to approved state plans.[4] The states would set benefit levels, conditions, and administrative practices; they could choose between the Wisconsin or Ohio plans or establish merit ratings for individual employers.

Those who favored a more national approach were, in general, the CES and other professional experts and business and labor advisers; they favored an Ohio plan at the national level or at least national standards and opposed state control over benefits or taxes on business—the fear was that progressive employers would be undercut by low-cost competitors. In the end, however, the president, who favored the tax-offset scheme, prevailed. There were two compelling reasons: First, it was felt that only a tax-offset plan could survive the Supreme Court; second, Congress insisted on a state-dominated scheme (Skocpol & Ikenberry, 1983, pp. 127–129).

By this time, several states had enacted unemployment programs, and Congress could be relied on to defend local administrative arrangements (Orloff, 1988b, p. 70; Patterson, 1981, p. 71).

Significantly, the dispute over the administrative form of the unemployment insurance program was the dominant issue in 1934 (Skocpol & Ikenberry, 1983, p. 130). Why was the states' interest in unemployment insurance predominant? It was at the state level where the conflicts between capital and labor were fought out (Amenta & Carruthers, 1986, p. 140). The South was able to make sure that all of the Social Security Act provisions, not only unemployment insurance, left its agricultural economy and race relations undisturbed. However, the insistence on state control of unemployment insurance was broader than southern interests. Unemployment insurance was an intense, prolonged political struggle between capital and labor over the fundamental issues of welfare versus labor discipline. "Sensitivity" or "control over local labor markets" was the code for the social control of marginal workers; the capitalists insisted that the price and availability of local labor were not to be disturbed (Weir, 1988, p. 152).

In the end, the state unemployment compensation laws reflected the outcome of these battles: Unemployment compensation was handled as a local, rather than a national, matter; at the local level, the programs failed to reached those in most need—employees of small firms, agricultural workers, women, African-Americans, and migrants. State benefits varied widely, but the most common standard was 16 weeks of benefits at half pay, but usually with a maximum of $15 per week. (In England, the rate was 75% of weekly pay.) Significantly, this maximum was about the average WPA rate. Once benefits were exhausted, there was no other relief for the unemployed worker unless he got onto WPA, which was difficult (Patterson, 1981, p. 72). As with work-relief, unemployment insurance was more concerned with bolstering capitalism than with meeting need. Compensation was more in the nature of temporary, emergency relief; there were various eligibility provisions in the state laws to make sure that benefits were paid only to deserving workers, that is, workers who had been steady and reliable in covered employment. As noted, marginal workers were excluded altogether. Subject to the maximums, compensation was calibrated in terms of length of employment and rate of pay. There were various waiting periods before benefits would come due. In general, employees would not be eligible or waiting periods would be lengthened if they quit voluntarily or were discharged for cause or because of a labor dispute, or failed to register at a public employment office and be available for suitable alternative work (Stewart, 1938, pp. 34–35, 36, 41, 47, 55, 59).

Two other defeats suffered by the Committee on Economic Security underscore the influence of decentralization. Even though the CES recommended the tax-offset plan, its proposals for establishing minimum national standards and centralized administration within the Department of Labor were rejected. Perhaps more significantly, the CES recognized that without the guarantee of a public job—employment assurance—unemployment insurance would not be able to provide for economic well-being, since it was, after all, only a temporary income support for certain categories of workers. The CES had in mind the New Deal public employment programs (Orloff, 1988b, pp. 77–78). As we have seen, these programs were cut or sharply reduced; work-relief was returned to the states and employment assurance was never even proposed by the administration. In sum: "The great leeway left to the states . . . ensured that conservative or racist interests would be able to control welfare coverage, benefit-levels, and administration in large stretches of the nation" (Skocpol & Ikenberry, 1983, p. 137).

The three approaches to the unemployed male—state initiatives, federal work-relief programs, and the Social Security Act unemployment insurance program—were all of a piece. The central contradiction between relieving misery and a disciplined work force was joined; once the threat of social disorder subsided, the ideology of labor discipline prevailed. This was the business-corporatist period of the New Deal; appeasing business and rural interests was a major consideration of the Roosevelt administration (Weir, 1988, pp. 156–158). The federal work-relief programs were sharply cut back; strict eligibility, a means test, and, most significantly, low benefits sensitive to local wages were reintroduced, all designed to make the relief worker "less eligible." Direct relief was returned to the states. At the state level, capital again prevailed. Unemployment compensation programs drew lines between deserving and undeserving workers. The steady, reliable, compliant industrial worker would receive some benefits; looking over his shoulder, he saw those below—the undeserving, without benefits, with no relief except perhaps traditional local work-relief. Gone were large numbers of federal public jobs with an adequate minimum wage. Moreover, unemployment benefits were short-term. Even for the deserving worker, unemployment compensation was carefully designed to discourage any thought of lingering; there were requirements for being available for alternative suitable work. For the undeserving unemployed, if they were lucky, there was some work-relief; otherwise, there was great hardship. Later, we will describe what we know about general relief during this period.

This was the states' position. Why did the federal government go along with it? Why were the Social Security Act unemployment insurance provisions, in essence, a massive delegation to the states? Unemployment insurance is a major example of how federalism is used to manage conflicts over the relief of the able-bodied poor. The social problem of the unemployed was constructed in terms of controlling deviant behavior. The symbols of "insurance" and "compensation" were evoked to pacify reform impulses; as with mothers' pensions, the name—here, insurance—reassured the reformers that there was agreement, that contradictions had been resolved, and that change had or was soon to come about. The ceremonies were the fairly meager, conditioned, short-term benefits. The national-minded reformers hoped that the social security unemployment program would be the start of an eventual national program, a hope, as we shall see, that was in vain.

The task of applying the program, of working out the conflicts between capital and relief, was delegated to the local level. The delegation allowed politicians at the higher levels to avoid tough decisions. The major unemployment insurance issues were very controversial politically; with the tax offset plan, the administration and the Committee on Economic Security could avoid taking stands (Orloff, 1988b, p. 72). At the same time, the delegation allowed those at the local level—those with the most at stake—to control the actual operations of the programs. We have seen this arrangement before. The unemployment insurance story mirrors the story of aid to dependent children at the state level prior to the New Deal. The reformers got the "mothers' pension" symbol while the local judges, welfare administrators, and Charitable Organizations Society workers made sure that their conception of gender and family roles would not be compromised by aiding the unworthy. The social control of the undeserving—whether workers or single mothers—is too important to entrust to reformers or upper-level politicians.

Work-relief and unemployment insurance were the New Deal response to the unemployed white male. We turn now to the aged.

Old-Age Insurance

The centerpiece of the Social Security Act—indeed, of the New Deal—was the establishment of a contributory national pension program for the aged. In fact, old-age insurance (OAI) has become synonymous with the term *social security*. As we have seen, prior to the New Deal, public assistance for the aged was controversial, states were slow in enacting the programs, and the programs were crabbed. One reason for the ambivalence was that there was no settled retirement age at the time; people in their 60s were still considered part of the labor force. Accordingly, the business community opposed public pensions on the grounds that they would interfere with the wage structure and different state taxes would adversely affect competition. In addition, southern planters considered old-age pensions to be a family grant, which would weaken their control over their African-American farm tenants (Quadagno, 1988, p. 100).

By 1935, however, the political climate outside of the South had changed. The elderly, along with the working population, were politically active and demanding radical action. In addition to Senator Huey Long's "Share-the-Wealth Movement," the Townsend Plan called for a flat federal pension of $200 per month for everyone over 60 on condition that they would stop working and spend the entire amount each month. The Townsend movement was well organized and exerted a lot of pressure on Congress (Katz, 1986, p. 235; Quadagno, 1988, p. 108). However, despite popular pressure, even on behalf of the elderly, Roosevelt was firmly committed to contributory insurance and opposed to anything that resembled the dole, even for the aged. He believed that the threat to the development of a national contributory insurance scheme for the aged came primarily from the proponents of public assistance and redistribution. In his view, "social security" would attain political legitimacy to the extent that it was "earned" and that it benefited primarily blue-collar and middle-class workers rather than the poor (Katz, 1986, pp. 238–239).

Contributory insurance meant protection for clearly defined "risks," such as unemployment, widowhood, a fixed retirement age, and industrial accidents. There would be no means test, so beneficiaries would not have the stigma of the dependent poor. The program would be financed by contributions, in part from workers; in addition to saving public money, contributions from workers would mitigate the pressure for increasing benefits. In general, benefits should reflect wages. This would strengthen incentives by not redistributing income (Quadagno, 1988, p. 110).

Unlike the English system, which provided equal pensions for all the aged at subsistence levels, the social security scheme, as finally enacted, linked pensions to past earnings. Pensions were to be 50% of average wages, with a minimum of $10 per month to a maximum of $85. This provision was similar to those in corporate pension plans that were tried in the 1920s (Patterson, 1981, p. 73). Even though demographic projections indicated that contributions would not be sufficient, Roosevelt refused to consider any supplementation through general tax revenues. He insisted on preserving the appearance that the fund would be sufficient to meet all expenses (Katz, 1986, pp. 236–237).

The program was sold on the insurance ideology despite the fact that it contained a number of noninsurancelike features. For example, workers were taxed and not making "contributions," and early retirees would not have made sufficient contributions to match their benefits. Nevertheless, the public relations strongly emphasized the insurance features of the pension scheme. Reflecting the deserving/undeserving poor distinction, OAI was a dignified program paying individually earned benefits to most citizens as of right; relief was for people who had to demonstrate need (Patterson, 1981, pp. 74, 76; Skocpol & Ikenberry, 1983, p. 137).

Social attitudes (outside of the South) toward the elderly had changed; now there was a strong desire to get older workers out of the labor market to make way for the young, who, it was argued, would be more productive. As a further incentive to retire, the administration proposed, and Congress accepted, a limitation on the amount of income a worker over 65 could earn without losing benefits (Patterson, 1981, p. 74). Changing American mores also favored OAI. During the 1920s, the family changed; there were fewer children, and more couples lived apart from their parents. The young adults did not want the old folks moving back in with them, and an old-age insurance scheme would help maintain the separate households (Patterson, 1981, pp. 74–75).

In contrast to unemployment insurance, here, there were strong arguments in favor of a uniform, national scheme. During the welfare capitalism of the 1920s, large companies tried to establish voluntary contributory pension programs, but as the Depression deepened, it became clear that the voluntary approach would not meet the need; on the other hand, state programs, with differential taxes, would hurt competition. These difficulties stimulated big business support for national pension legislation. Big business leaders had a large and significant impact on the conception and construction of the legislation; they were consulted early and frequently, and were on important committees. They favored as much national control as possible in order to minimize competitive advantages. In the end, they were quite satisfied with OAI; there was complete federal control over employer-employee contributions. The fact that there was little redistribution because of contributions and the general relationship between wages and benefits meant that wage structures and regional variations would not be disturbed. Small businesses were opposed, but they were ineffective (Quadagno, 1988, pp. 100–113).

As with old-age assistance, the South was also opposed to OAI, but the exclusion of agriculture and domestic workers, at its insistence, ensured that the planter control over African-American labor would not be disturbed. The exclusion of these workers, plus the elimination of national standards in the grant-in-aid program for state old-age assistance, discussed below, meant that the vast majority of elderly African-Americans were just about completely excluded from federal protection (Quadagno, 1988, pp. 113–116).

Old-age insurance was an income-maintenance program for the deserving worker, the citizen (white male) who had made his contribution to society and was now morally excused from work. The architects of the Social Security Act considered it vitally important to establish the symbolic difference between this category of claimants and the undeserving poor—the unemployed, the dependent aged, and single mothers and their children (Cates, 1983). The deserving retirees were in a *contributory insurance scheme*; this was not redistribution; it was not welfare. And OAI has always been sold on this basis, despite the increasing tenuousness of its insurance characteristics. The unemployed, in contrast, were central components of the labor market; they would be helped, but not all of them—only the deserving workers—and then only temporarily. Labor markets had to be preserved, and, as we shall see, the administration was not interested in helping poor single mothers.

But why was OAI national and not unemployment insurance? The arguments in favor of a national OAI applied as well to UI—the mobility of labor and a uniform tax rate were necessary to avoid competitive advantages. The reason for the different jurisdictional location of the programs lies in the differential effects on labor markets. OAI wanted its beneficiaries out of the labor market; UI wanted to make sure that its beneficiaries stayed in. And in the United States, the regulation of work tests is invariably at the local level. Work is both an economic and a moral issue. Local businesses want to keep close control over the economic issues (and avoid taxes); the local community wants to keep control over moral behavior. OAI, as originally conceived, touched on these issues in the South, but the exclusion of agricultural and domestic workers left race relations undisturbed. A consensus was reached on who was included in the "deserving" category; the program could be nationalized.

The importance of maintaining local control over moral behavior is illustrated by the following discussion of the third part of the Social Security Act—the grant-in-aid programs.

The Grant-in-Aid Programs

Old-Age Assistance

The division between OAI and old-age assistance (OAA) was not a foregone conclusion prior to the enactment of the Social Security Act. As evidenced by the Townsend movement, there was strong support for a universal, national, flat pension for the aged. With the onset of the Depression, the aged were excused from work. Why, then, did the country separate deserving retirees from the dependent aged?

A large part of the answer undoubtedly lies in the political structure of the United States at that time. The Congress was dominated by southerners who controlled the committees. While the South

desperately needed federal money to relieve distress, southern legislators strongly resisted any federal controls that would disturb
their existing economy and race relations (Quadagno, 1988, p. 127;
Skocpol & Ikenberry, 1983, pp. 131–132). Many southern tenants
were on the work-relief rolls, but local relief offices were responsive
to the demands of labor discipline. In many areas, the offices would
close when crops came in. Relief was kept below the subsistence
that landlords provided their tenants. African-Americans were
greatly underrepresented on the relief rolls and received lower
benefits than whites (Quadagno, 1988, pp. 131–132).

Roosevelt needed southern support to get the Social Security Act
enacted, but the South exacted its price. While it was a consistent
principle of the administration that relief properly belonged in the
states and the funding mechanism would be the grant-in-aid, the
issue was what national standards would be required of the states
as a condition of their participation. The original grant-in-aid proposal for old-age assistance specified that state benefits levels had
to provide "a reasonable subsistence compatible with decency and
health." In order to make the states accountable for the standards,
the proposed legislation also provided that there had to be "a single state authority to administer or supervise the administration of
the plan and insure methods of administration which are approved
by the Administrator" (Quadagno, 1988, p. 115). Both clauses were
strongly and successfully opposed by southern congressmen on the
grounds that they threatened control over African-American labor
and race relations (Patterson, 1981, p. 68; Quadagno, 1988, p. 116).
The federal government agreed to pay 50% of the costs of the program, but the states could set their own eligibility requirements and
benefit levels and have an administration independent of the federal government (Quadagno, 1988, p. 116; Skocpol & Ikenberry,
1983, pp. 131–132).

Southern intentions were carried out. None of the southern states
had previously enacted old-age assistance, and they were the slow-
est to respond to the Social Security Act. When they did enact their
programs, eligibility was more stringent than required. Characteristic of traditional poor law, administration was at the local level,
with very broad powers in determining need; there were strict residency requirements and the power of removal. In contrast to the
aged industrial worker in the North, the aged agricultural tenant

worker in the South was considered part of the labor force. Raising old-age assistance benefit levels was resisted on the same grounds as OAI, namely, greater benefits would tend to subsidize the whole tenant family and make them less dependent on the landlord. Despite provisions against discrimination, benefits for African-Americans were substantially lower than for whites. Local officials used different criteria of need, and southern states were permitted to give aged veterans maximum grants. In sum, "cash grants to blacks were carefully monitored so as not to undermine prevailing wage rates and so as to intrude as little as possible on the planter-tenant relationship" (Quadagno, 1988, pp. 134–136).

Elsewhere in the country, the aged were viewed differently. OAA was strongly supported, especially since substantial numbers of the insurance retirees would not begin to receive OAI benefits for some time (1942). Within a year of the enactment of the Social Security Act, 36 states and the District of Columbia enacted programs; in many of these states, existing pension programs were converted to meet federal guidelines (Quadagno, 1988, p. 242). The federal subsidy for OAA was substantially higher than for ADC (Orloff, 1988, p. 75). OAA, by now, was a popular program. In fact, there was strong political support favoring old-age assistance over the slowly starting retirement program, creating a national program of flat grants with simplified or no means tests. These moves were vigorously resisted by the administration and the Social Security Board, which, among other things, insisted that state programs require a means test as a way of distinguishing the deserving retirees from the dependent aged (Cates, 1983).

At this time, there was a sharp conflict in the country over the moral basis of poverty among the elderly. Substantial parts of the country considered the elderly morally excused from the work ethic and thus deserving of dignified relief in the form of a pension. The administration, however, still clung to the view that the dependent aged were morally problematic and that including them in OAI would ultimately delegitimate the retirement program and the work ethic. The national pension system had to be reserved for the deserving retired worker. The conflict over the moral characterization of the dependent elderly, which will be discussed shortly, was not resolved until the 1970s.

Aid to Dependent Children

In important respects, the female household in poverty differed from the dependent elderly and the unemployed. The former category of the poor, as we have seen, had been the subject of considerable public attention for about 50 years—the controversial working mother, especially the single mother; the child protection movement; the juvenile court reform; and mothers' pensions. There were programs, at least on the books, in almost all of the states; and there was a special federal agency—the Children's Bureau—that was to monitor developments and encourage states to pursue policies. This was a category that had claimed considerable political, social, and professional attention.

On the other hand, there were important similarities among the female-headed household in poverty, the dependent elderly, and the unemployed. The Depression seriously worsened the plight of this category. Poor single mothers and their children were already at the bottom of the labor market. Divorce and desertion increased, as well as joblessness and homelessness (Abramovitz, 1988, p. 315). There were virtually no relief programs for the vast majority of these families. Only a small number were enrolled in the state ADC programs, and, given the conditions of ADC and the meager benefits, many mothers had to supplement their grants with low-paying jobs (Patterson, 1981, p. 69; Piven & Cloward, 1988a, 1988b). The social control features of ADC were manifest, and that meant a strong interest in maintaining local control. As with the unemployed, the Roosevelt administration confronted developed state and local interests and programs.

And the administration was perfectly content to let ADC remain at the state level. The old problems continued to dog this category—the stigma of poor single mothers, labor supply issues, and race. "No one in 1935 imagined throwing millions of dollars into broken homes" (Patterson, 1981, p. 68). The Children's Bureau lobbied the Committee on Economic Security, but neither Congress nor the administration had much interest in this program (Katz, 1986, p. 237). The basic thinking of the social security reformers was that as OAI took hold, more and more elderly and widows would be covered, and all public assistance would wither (Patterson, 1981, p. 70; Steiner, 1981, pp. 18–26). By conceptualizing ADC as a problem to be solved eventually by the retirement program—white widows of working men who would eventually be covered—the administration reflected both the thinking and the realities of that period: Divorced, deserted, and never-married women and women of color were simply not considered to be part of organized public welfare; rather, they and their children were lumped with the general mass of undifferentiated undeserving poor.

At the same time, federal funds were sorely needed merely to keep the state ADC programs afloat. The decision to include the state programs in a grant-in-aid program did involve some important reforms. Funds were to be granted to states, rather than to localities; ADC had to be implemented statewide (several states had no programs in heavily minority counties); the definitions of "lack of parental support" and "eligible caretakers" were broadened; benefits had to be paid in cash; and there were rights to fair hearings. In general, access for this category was increased, at least formally (Abramovitz, 1988, pp. 315–316).

On the other hand, the major characteristics of the state ADC programs were preserved. The disjuncture between the successful symbolic reform effort at the state level and the actual miserly operation of these programs at the local level countered the federal move to expand coverage. In contrast to OAA, where there was strong political pressure, most states delayed implementing the ADC grant-in-aid program; by the end of 1936, OAA was in 42 states and ADC was in only 26 (Abramovitz, 1988). As late as 1939, 10 states still had not signed on with ADC. Even the states that enacted the program did little to encourage enrollments (Patterson, 1981, p. 68). Congress did not encourage the states to move on ADC. The federal match and reimbursement rates were lower for this program than for the other programs.[5] There was no grant for the mother.[6] The difference between OAA and ADC was noticed during the deliberations on the Social Security Act, but there was little interest in Congress and the CES did not want to press the matter (Abramovitz, 1988, pp. 315–317; Orloff, 1988b, p. 75). The initial pattern of treating the adult programs—OAA and aid to the blind—more generously than ADC turned out not to be a mere oversight; higher appropriations, matching formulas, and benefit levels for the former two were retained by Congress and continue to the present; the beneficiaries of the adult programs are not in the labor market (Abramovitz, 1988, p. 317).[7]

There were other features of the new ADC program that preserved state and local practices. The southern resistance to national minimum subsistence standards in OAA was also successful in ADC; "states' rights" was the code for preserving local labor markets and racial discrimination (Abramovitz, 1988, pp. 317–318). States were still permitted to use their "suitable home" and "employable mother" policies to deny eligibility (Patterson, 1981, pp. 68–69).[8] Even under the Social Security Act, ADC continued to be primarily for white widows (Abramovitz, 1988, pp. 318–319).

In sum, in two important directions, the Social Security Act strengthened the categorization process. It created a new category of the deserving poor—working-class retirees and their survivors (OASI)—and this category was to be supported by pensions nationally administered under uniform standards, symbolically sold as "contributory insurance" to distinguish this category deliberately from the stigmatized public assistance poor. There was no means test; there were no class lines; there was almost no redistribution. The other direction was to reinforce locally controlled social regulation of the undeserving poor—those who were not legislatively declared to be excused from work: the unemployed male, the dependent aged, and poor single mothers.[9]

Categorization is the process of morally distinguishing the poor and then selecting eligibles from the particular categories. What happened to those who were not selected—the unemployed who did not qualify for unemployment insurance or used up their benefits, the dependent aged in states with meager programs, and the vast majority of single mothers and their children? What happened to those who were left behind, the general mass of the poor, those who did not fit into any category?

General Relief

During the 1920s, at the state level, two seemingly contradictory paths were followed. At one level, there seemed to be a professionalization and rationalization of social welfare. There was a great deal of statutory activity—Michael Katz (1986) says that between 1917 and 1920, some 400 public welfare laws were enacted (p. 208)—state and local expenditures increased and public social workers began to become professionalized specialists. Yet public relief still remained, in practice, at the local level—counties, districts, municipalities, towns. Some programs were quite large; others were tiny. In Ohio, for example, more than 1,500 local governmental units administered relief (Katz, 1986, pp. 209–210).

The Depression, of course, overwhelmed these agencies. Despite the fact that the newly unemployed often turned to public relief as a desperate last resort, neither local or state governments nor private charities could meet the need. Most people could expect only small amounts of food. Cash payments were pitifully small—for example, in Detroit, $3.60 a week for a family of two adults; in Baltimore, an average of $.80 a week in commodities; in New York City, $2.97 a week, and then only for a quarter of the unemployed (Katz, 1986, p. 213). Public relief for the undifferentiated poor was always miserly by public choice; in the Depression, there simply was no money left for the excluded.

THE POST-NEW DEAL PERIOD

The distinction drawn in the Social Security Act between the deserving and undeserving poor remained. The contributory retirement and survivors' insurance program—OASI—became the dominant program in terms of beneficiaries, revenues, and benefits, dwarfing all the other programs by far. Unemployment insurance retained its basic characteristics, a limited program for the deserving worker. Great changes occurred in the social characteristics of the clientele of aid to dependent children—now Aid to Families with Dependent Children—but its social control features were even more pronounced. The significant ideological change occurred with the dependent elderly. Their increasingly insistent demands for deserving poor treatment eventually produced two major programmatic changes. The social security retirement program was expanded to take in most of this group, and the categorical adult programs—old-age assistance, aid to the blind, and aid to the disabled (aid to the permanently and totally disabled was enacted in 1954)—were changed to the nationally administered Supplemental Security Income (SSI) program in 1974. During the 1970s, the great bulk of the aged poor became the deserving poor both morally and practically. We start with a discussion of the elderly, and then move to the undeserving poor.

The Elderly: OASI and OAA

While usually analyzed and discussed separately, OASI and OAA have always had an intimate relationship (Coll, 1988, p. 221). The architects of the Social Security Act intended public assistance to wither away, but that result was certainly not apparent in 1936. OASI (then OAI) was not scheduled to begin paying benefits until 1942. In the meantime, there was great pressure to do something about relieving distress. In contrast to the reluctance to enact old-age assistance prior to the New Deal, by June 1937, 44 states and the District of Columbia enacted the new grant-in-aid program; the rolls rapidly grew to a total of 1.2 million (Coll, 1988, p. 226).

Even though it was the firm intent of Roosevelt and the Social Security Administration to distinguish the contributory retirees and the dependent elderly, this distinction, as applied to this category of the poor, was strongly contested from the very beginning. Some states wanted to use the term *pension* and to dispense with a means test for OAA. The Social Security Administration insisted on need, being afraid that OAA would swallow up OAI (Cates, 1983; Quadagno, 1988, p. 126; Skocpol & Ikenberry, 1983, p. 133). The threat posed by OAA continued until the 1950s, since more people were on the public assistance rolls and benefits were higher than in the slowly maturing insurance program (Myles, 1988, p. 272; Skocpol & Ikenberry, 1983, pp. 136–137). The Social Security Administration responded in two ways. First, it insisted that state OAA plans consider income and resources in determining need; this made clear that public assistance was for needy individuals. In the administrators' view, this would mean that OAA would remain a demeaning welfare program, whereas OASI would be a dignified program for citizens who had made their insurance contributions to an "actuarially sound" insurance program (Cates, 1983; Skocpol & Ikenberry, 1983, p. 137). Second, on the administrators' recommendation, OAI was amended in 1939 (becoming OASI for survivors), to allow for benefits to be paid in 1940 instead of 1942; in addition, benefits were raised, and provisions for elderly wives of beneficiaries and survivor benefits were liberalized (including widows with dependent children).

Still, the country was divided. Congress raised the federal match for OAA, but refused to extend OASI to agricultural workers and domestic workers; the South would not allow interference with its economy or race relations (Coll, 1988, p. 230). As noted, the South maintained the most restrictive, locally administered OAA programs, benefiting whites and largely excluding blacks (Quadagno, 1988, pp. 131–133).

Over the next couple of decades, the South experienced enormous changes—the mechanization of agriculture, vast migrations of African-Americans from farm to city and from South to North, the decline of power in Congress, and the civil rights movement. One result was an increase in the poor, aged population, especially in rural areas, with an increasing welfare burden. These factors changed southern political opposition to liberalization of both OAA and OASI. In time, after much struggle, OASI was gradually, although grudgingly, extended to cover many agricultural workers (Quadagno, 1988, pp. 147–149).

In 1969, President Nixon introduced the Family Assistance Act, which proposed sweeping changes in all of the categorical programs.[10] The part of the bill that proposed changes in AFDC was strongly resisted, and, as a result, the entire measure was defeated. But there was strong support for the reform of the adult programs. In 1974, the Supplementary Security Income bill was enacted. The adult programs were federalized. They were completely federally funded and administered (by the Social Security Administration); there were uniform national eligibility standards and a basic federal income grant (with optional state supplementation). SSI was noncontroversial. The great bulk of the dependent aged were no longer part of the labor force; they were now full members of the deserving poor (Quadagno, 1988, pp. 150–151).[11]

In its early years, OASI, along with OAA, stagnated. After the 1939 amendments, Congress refused any liberalizations until 1950, when the program began its journey of slow incremental change. Gradually new groups were included, retirement ages were lowered for women, and benefits increased. However, until the late 1960s, it was still a low-level income-maintenance program. The big changes came in 1968 and again in 1974, when benefits were raised substantially and indexed to the cost of living, coinciding with the liberalization of OAA and the enactment of SSI (Quadagno, 1988, pp. 152–153). By about 1980, the average social security retirement benefit had increased by 44% in real terms (earnings from wages and salaries for the nonelderly had decreased during this period by 7%) (Zedlewski & Meyer, 1989, p. 19). Today, social security is a major source of income for the vast majority of the aged in America. It has become not only a retirement wage, but a "citizen's wage," an entitlement that has significant redistribution effects. It is comparable to the most advanced systems in Western Europe (Myles, 1988, p. 268).

In short, OASI changed from "equity" to "adequacy" (Ball, 1988), even though it is still sold on its insurance/contribution rhetoric. The distinction so long fought for by the Social Security Administration, between the contributory retirees and the dependent aged—the former had *contract rights* and the latter had *needs*—ultimately failed. The arguments in favor of the dependent aged were also based on rights—on social or citizenship rights—and in the world of politics, with enough power and pressure, social rights easily become legal rights. In order to meet the OAA challenge, the Social Security Administration expanded OASI by further attenuating its insurance principles; it shifted the balance to "adequacy," from giving benefits based on individual tax payments to giving benefits based on need (Derthick, 1979). The OAA campaigns were sufficiently powerful that the Social Security Administration, in violation of its principles, had to co-opt the flat pension movement.[12] One of the characteristics of co-optation is the adoption of the rival's program. Despite the distinctions between needs and rights that the Social Security Administration tried to maintain, it was the changes in societal attitudes and social construction that overlapped the two groups. For both groups of elderly, there was pressure to remove them from the labor force (Myles, 1988, pp. 271–272). When this ideological transformation was finally completed in the South, all of the dependent aged were treated as the deserving poor; labor force participation was no longer a concern. The deserving poor are "rights-bearing" citizens.

This does not mean that all income-maintenance problems among the elderly have been solved. Some 12.4% (3.5 million) of the elderly have incomes below the poverty line. There are gaps and deficiencies in both programs. In OASI, for example, the widow's benefit is two-thirds that of the married couple's, even though the widow's need is generally greater, and women constitute a larger share of the elderly poor and near poor (Zedlewski & Meyer, 1989, p. 21). There are serious problems with SSI. About 30% of the elderly poor receive SSI benefits, but it is the sole support of only 5%. SSI eligibility and benefits are both national and uniform, but states may supplement the basic federal grant. The federal grant is indexed, but the state supplements have declined in real terms since 1975. On average, the benefit is about 76% of the poverty line (for the aged) for a single person and 90% for married couples. In 27 states, there is supplementation (41% of SSI recipients). From its inception, participation in SSI has been low (between 50% and 60%), and the reasons for this are not well understood. But the fact that this is a matter of official concern, and outreach has been conducted (Zedlewski & Meyer, 1989, pp. 25–33), demonstrates that SSI is an *inclusive* program, one of the major characteristics of programs for the deserving poor. Programs for the undeserving poor are *exclusive*.

Unemployment Insurance

As set up by the Social Security Act, there were incentives to the states to provide temporary unemployment benefits for those who were eligible, less generous transfer payments for those deemed unemployable (the aged and the blind), and no benefits for those who were employable but ineligible for unemployment benefits (Weir, 1988, pp. 149–150). Several features combined to maintain these basic characteristics. Southern opposition remained steadfast during the 1930s; this would defeat any attempt to impose federal substantive or regulatory powers in unemployment insurance (pp. 157–158). The basic feature of state control of unemployment insurance remained in place (Becker, 1960).

But the problem was broader than southern agriculture and race relations; throughout the country, the unemployed differed from the aged in that the former were inextricably involved in the labor market. Helping the unemployed affects the bargaining of power of labor, since unemployment compensation is intended to diminish the pressure to take less desirable jobs and it lessens the pressure to limit strikes. Unemployment benefits thus affect wages, labor discipline, and productivity. It is for these broader reasons that UI has remained under state control and continues to use experience rating (Becker, 1960, pp. 484–485).

Over the years, there have been attempts to assert more national control over the program. These have taken two principal forms— supplementing state benefits (during particularly hard times) and establishing benefit standards. The most that came of these efforts were loans to the states to allow them to extend the duration of benefits. Significantly, the loans carried no federal standards and were optional. Still, only some states took up the option, and some of those only partially participated; some declined altogether. Proposals for equalizing state benefits or for establishing federal standards have been repeatedly rejected. This does not mean that the federal government has been entirely without influence. It does administer the tax; it decides how much each state will receive back; and it can declare a state program out of conformity (Becker, 1960, pp. 491–492). But, overall, federal influence is slight. Surveying the state programs, as of 1960, Becker concluded that while these programs have improved over the years, benefits varied considerably among the states, and, in general, they were quite low: The single worker could meet daily subsistence expenses (food, housing, clothing, medical care), but the unemployed worker with a family—probably the most important segment of the labor force—received only about two-thirds of need (p. 490).

Both the tax and experience rating features of UI—which are unique in the industrialized world—are evidence of the central relation of this program to the market. UI is entirely funded through the payroll tax; there are no funds from general revenues. Experience rating is based on the unemployment history of individual employers. It was originally advanced as an incentive for employers to stabilize employment. It is still considered important to police improper claims and to prevent collusion between employer and employee; without significant employer participation, government would have to maintain program integrity. Whatever the merits of these claims, even though very controversial, experience rating is firmly established (Becker, 1960, pp. 496–498).

In the meantime, UI continues to be a seriously inadequate program. Its original distinction between the deserving and undeserving worker remains in place; benefits are temporary and are only for people who have involuntarily lost their jobs. Excluded are those who quit, those fired for misconduct, new entrants or reentrants, those who refuse alternative suitable employment, and those who cannot find a job after 26 weeks. However, even for those who have involuntarily lost their jobs, coverage has declined sharply. Since 1955, the proportion of unemployed workers covered has fluctuated from about 40% to 50%, occasionally reaching 60% or even 70% in selected years. However, since 1985, coverage has been less than a third of the unemployed; 1988 was the record low of 31.5%. This meant that in an average month in 1988, 4.6 million jobless workers did not receive any unemployment insurance benefits. Coverage was even worse for African-Americans (21%) and Hispanics (14%). There continues to be great variation among the states (Shapiro & Nichols, 1989, pp. 1–5).

As will be pointed out, there are very few alternative income supports for the able-bodied unemployed who are not covered by UI. Aid to Families with Dependent Children with an Unemployed Parent (AFDC-UP) was been adopted in 28 states, but the programs are very restrictive and benefits are low.[13] General relief, if available for the able-bodied, is also very restrictive. Not surprisingly, poverty rates among the long-term unemployed are very high (Danziger & Gottschalk, 1990; Shapiro & Nichols, 1989, pp. 13–15).

A number of factors have resulted in the decline of UI coverage. During the Reagan administration, there were federal and state cutbacks: frozen or reduced benefit levels, increased waiting periods (the time between application and when benefits are awarded), reduced duration of benefits, increased criteria to meet in qualifying for benefits, and increased severity of disqualification criteria (Danziger & Gottschalk, 1990; Shapiro & Nichols, 1989). Misconduct denial rates have gone up (U.S. Department of Labor, 1988, pp. 118–137). As a result, it is "harder to qualify for benefits, easier to be disqualified, and less generous benefits [are] available for potentially shorter periods of time" (Shapiro & Nichols, 1989, p. 19).

Thus, despite its insurancelike features and symbols, unemployment insurance is a regulatory program for morally problematic unemployed workers (mostly males). It is a decentralized state-run program that leaves a large amount of discretion to local offices. Because of the flexibility in the statutes, rights are not clear-cut, as they are in OASI. To some extent, benefits are conditioned on an official's assessment of character and behavior. Benefits are for those who have a good work record, who diligently try to find work, and who, if necessary, are willing to accept lower-skilled, lower-paying jobs—in short, the deserving worker. When benefits are denied or terminated, the unemployed are basically thrown back into the market with the general undifferentiated poor.

Aid to Families With Dependent Children

From the New Deal to after World War II, ADC continued the patterns set during the mothers' pensions era. Although under the federal grant-in-aid requirements the programs were technically open to all children in single-parent households deprived of parental support, in all the states the program enrolled only small proportions of the potentially eligible, and these were overwhelmingly white widows. The states used a variety of techniques to exclude the undeserving: "suitable home" or "fit parent" requirements; work tests for employable mothers, especially African-American women; or simply not making the program available for particular categories of mothers or during certain times of the year (Abramovitz, 1988, pp. 318–319).

In the post-World War II period, the program experienced enormous changes. In 1940 there were slightly over 1 million AFDC recipients. In 1950, there were 2 million, and in 1960, 3 million recipients. By 1970 the number jumped to 9 million and continued to increase to 11 million in 1975. It has since leveled off and has remained at approximately 11 million. The expenditures also rose dramatically, from $550 million in 1950 to $4.8 billion in 1970, reaching a peak of $9.2 billion in 1975. Since then the expenditures have risen more moderately; in 1987 they stood at $16.3 billion (*Social Security Bulletin, Annual Statistical Supplement*, 1989). The characteristics of AFDC recipients also changed radically. No longer mostly white widows, the recipients over the years changed to the divorced or never married, and an increasing proportion of them were nonwhite. By 1975, 40% of AFDC parents were white, 44% African-American, and 12% Hispanic.

What caused this massive explosion in the welfare rolls, and why did the system of exclusion collapse? The answers seem to lie in the turbulent demographic, economic, and political conditions of the 1960s—the entry of women into the labor force; the massive migrations of African-Americans off of the land and out of the South; severe unemployment and underemployment in the inner cities, and the resulting increase in poverty; rising social unrest, disorder, crime, and riots in the cities; the changing politics of the Democratic party; and the pressure exerted on local governments by the War on Poverty, the welfare rights movement, and the legal rights movement (Piven & Cloward, 1971).

A major cause of the change was demographic, namely, a dramatic increase in the potential pool of eligible welfare recipients. Garfinkel and McLanahan (1986) show that for whites the number of mother-only families grew 37% between 1960 and 1970, and 40% between 1970 and 1980 (p. 49). For African-Americans the proportions were 37% and 35%, respectively. The rise in mother-only families was due to changing marital patterns. For whites, much of the growth was due to an increase in formerly married mothers. For African-Americans, since the 1960s, it was due primarily to an increase in the number of never-married mothers. Garfinkel and McLanahan further conclude that for whites the major cause of the increase in the divorce rate was the increase in women's labor force participation; for blacks the major factor was the decline in employment opportunities among males (p. 45).

The mechanization of agriculture, especially in the South, the demand for skilled labor, and eventual application and enforcement of the minimum wage law were devastating to the unskilled African-American farm family. In response to the increase in demand, southern relief practices tightened—there was more harassment and intimidation, and there were frequent efforts to purge the rolls by using charges of lack of suitable homes and illegitimacy. With no employment or relief, some 20 million people, including 4 million African-Americans, migrated from farms to cities. Within the space of a few decades, the African-American population changed from largely southern and rural to northern and urban (Piven & Cloward, 1971, pp. 201–212).

However, in the northern inner cities, jobs were changing, there was slow growth, and the newcomers lacked skills and suffered from discrimination. There was severe unemployment and underemployment. Although welfare was more generous in the North, it was still quite restrictive, and the response nowhere met the need; poverty increased substantially (Piven & Cloward, 1971, pp. 215–220). In the 1970s, the plight of poor African-Americans continued to worsen. Wilson (1987) has shown that the decline of manufacturing jobs in the urban industrial centers in the North, the suburbanization of blue-collar jobs, and the rise of the service sector eliminated many decent-paying jobs for unskilled minorities, resulting in high unemployment rates, especially among the males, in the inner cities. Consequently, there has been a sharp decline in the proportion of young African-American males who are in a position to support a family.

However, as we have seen, need does not necessarily lead to an increase in relief. Piven and Cloward (1971) argue that the rapid rise in AFDC caseloads, especially after 1964, was due to a combination of urban disorders and changes in electoral politics. The seeds of social disorder were sown through the loosening of traditional forms of social control; the massive influx of newcomers from the South; severe economic and social discrimination; the rise of single parenthood; very high youth unemployment; the rise of delinquency, vandalism, serious crime, and drug addiction; and the inability and unwillingness on the part of traditional white officials and bureaucrats to respond to these changes. In the 1960s, African-American disorder began to turn against whites; teachers, social workers, and the police were assaulted; riots began to target white establishments. More than 20 cities experienced widespread, destructive riots between 1964 and 1968 (pp. 220–239).

In Piven and Cloward's view, the turning of social disorder against whites, rather than being random or internal, meant that African-American urban disorder had become politicized, a change these authors attribute to the civil rights campaigns of the previous 10 years, during which racism, as well as poverty, was vigorously condemned by a wide range of groups (Katz, 1986). By attacking racism in voting, employment, housing, and education, these campaigns both politicized and alienated large numbers of poor urban African-Americans.

At the same time, this was also a period of growing liberalism—the Civil Rights Act was passed in 1964 and the Voting Rights Act in 1965—and corporate, foundation, and political elites were becoming more responsive to African-American demands, including antipoverty measures. African-American voting also began to increase, and northern politicians began to respond. However, it turned out to be far easier to loosen relief than to integrate schools, neighborhoods, and jobs, and welfare rolls began to swell. Similar changes were also occurring in some southern cities. In both North and South, however, there were still significant eligibility restrictions. By now, the federal government was also exerting pressure on the cities to make concessions to African-Americans. National electoral politics had changed; the Democratic party was cutting its losses in the South and trying to solidify its hold on northern African-Americans. The new political strategy was to "reach, placate, and integrate a turbulent black constituency" (Piven & Cloward, 1971, p. 281); translated, this meant that African-American unrest was to be directed against local government through demands for services.

The Kennedy and Johnson administrations courted northern urban African-Americans through inner-city service initiatives. This was the era of the Great Society. A wide variety of activist groups began attacking the welfare system, which now emerged as a national issue. A whole array of federally sponsored local initiatives was directed at the inner city—delinquency prevention, community mental health, community action, Model Cities, legal services. These federally sponsored services were intentionally designed to bypass traditional political structures, and a direct relationship was forged between the federal government and the ghettos. New inner-city, storefront centers were developed to help residents find jobs, organize, and secure access to public services, including welfare. Citywide and regional organizations in turn were formed. In all these organizations, the federal government insisted that there be "maximum feasible participation" on the part of the ghetto residents themselves. These new organizations, headed by community leaders, social workers, and lawyers, began to pressure, badger, and sue local agencies. In the meantime, federal funds were also being used to finance voter registration drives that further threatened the existing political order. Local African-American political leaders used the War on Poverty agencies to great advantage in organizing their communities and launching their careers. Eventually, local politicians were able to assert control over these agencies, but not before accommodations had been made to the new movements.

Local community groups, through a combination of community action neighborhood service centers, OEO (Office of Economic Opportunity) legal services, and grass-roots pressure groups, pressured city government on a broad range of issues. Local residents were encouraged to bring their problems to the neighborhood service centers, which were staffed by community leaders, VISTA (Volunteers in Service to America) volunteers, and activist professionals. Since the overwhelming problem for the vast majority of people was lack of sufficient income, the service center workers became both skilled and aggressive in dealing with the local welfare offices. Complaints were aggregated, groups were formed, and collective demands were made at local offices, often in a confrontational manner. In cities already shaken by urban riots, large numbers of angry, vocal African-American women flooded welfare offices and demanded relief from often sympathetic social workers and intimidated officials. This was a period of great social activism, and all manner of professionals who came in contact with the poor—social workers, teachers, health professionals, and lawyers—helped families get on welfare, which was the only source of additional income.

The moves from below coincided with dramatic changes in the legal profession and legal culture. The 1960s were a period of significant legal activism based on the stunning successes of the NAACP and the Legal Defense Fund (LDF) in the U.S. Supreme Court, as well as in lower federal courts. This was the Warren Court era. Starting with *Brown v. Board of Education* (1954), there were successes in cases involving segregation on buses, on golf courses, in bath houses, in courtrooms, and in voting, marriage, public accommodations, housing, and other areas of state activity. It seemed as if every year one could count on court decisions vindicating the rights of the disenfranchised in American society. These cases, and the law-reform class-action litigation model, had an enormous influence on young activist members of the legal profession (Handler, Hollingsworth, & Erlanger, 1978).

LDF provided the role model for a wide variety of public interest law organizations. Young militant professionals volunteered for campaigns in the South; committees and supporting organizations were formed. Eventually, a number of strands came together in the 1960s—civil rights, civil liberties, poverty law, environmental protection, and consumerism. It was in this milieu that a program for lawyers was added to the War on Poverty in 1965. This fit with the spirit of the Kennedy administration, which encouraged the use of law on behalf of the unrepresented and the belief that government institutions could be changed by citizens acting as advocates. "Poverty law" quickly caught on; by 1967, it replaced civil rights in attracting reform-oriented lawyers. While there was a conflict with traditional legal services, sponsored by the American Bar Association, the dominant model for OEO legal services came from two sources: One was the LDF's aggressive, class-action, law-reform approach; the other was storefront advocacy, working in close cooperation with community leaders, organizers, and local residents out of the community action neighborhood service centers. It was an aggressive, people-oriented style of legal practice. Legal services for the poor grew rapidly. Within two years (by 1967), there were nearly 1,200 lawyers working in approximately 250 projects with 850 offices. By 1972, there were 2,000 lawyers and 280 projects. Regional offices and backup centers were established to engage in research and appellate litigation.

Several welfare exclusionary practices were declared illegal, such as residency requirements, man-in-the-house rules, and employable-mother rules. In addition, due-process hearings were required to check arbitrary administrative terminations. During this period, HHS issued many regulations implementing court decisions. There is no way of knowing the direct impact of these decisions on the welfare rolls (Patterson, 1981, p. 179; Piven & Cloward, 1971), but it seems reasonable to conclude that the combination of favorable court decisions, federal administrative regulations, and large numbers of activist, aggressive lawyers both representing and helping organize clients had a significant influence in increasing enrollments. The storefront legal service lawyers, working with organizers and groups, represented countless citizens in their confrontations with welfare offices. From many sources, there developed the climate of legal rights and entitlements on behalf of a wide range of people dealing with public bureaucracies—patients, consumers, students, prisoners, employees, minorities, and women. There was a profound change in our legal culture (Handler et al., 1978).

The National Welfare Rights Organization (NWRO) developed out of the activities in the neighborhood service centers: groups of African-American welfare recipients meeting in the service centers, helping each other, working with the activist workers and professionals, strategizing, and engaging in direct action. Local "chapters" sprang up in many parts of the country, distributing welfare manuals and demanding entitlements. The neighborhood service centers were natural places for these groups to come together, and, in 1966, links among the local organizations were forged throughout the country. While NWRO attracted civil rights activists, professionals, religious leaders, and middle-class organizers, its core strength and driving energy came from African-American welfare recipients; this was a poor minority women's campaign (Katz, 1986, p. 253).

NWRO and local chapters conducted marches, demonstrations, pickets, and sit-ins; many were highly publicized and several were violent. They lobbied in Washington and various state capitals. On a day-to-day basis, the local chapters engaged in individual services—distributing simplified handbooks, assisting applicants and recipients, and providing advocacy. In certain parts of the country, the campaigns for enrollments and discretionary special benefits were extremely successful. In New York, for example, the average cost of discretionary grants per recipient rose from $40 in 1965 to $100 in 1968, with aggregate costs in that year of $100 million. As word spread of the success of NWRO in extracting benefits for its members, there were spontaneous demands by groups of poor women in several parts of the country, both for enrollments and for discretionary benefits. It is claimed that NWRO significantly influenced the reform of food stamps and other nutritional and health programs for poor families (Katz, 1986, p. 254). In 1969, NWRO claimed some 100,000 dues-paying members from 350 local groups (Piven & Cloward, 1971, p. 322).

The federal government contributed to the welfare explosion by encouraging the rise of NWRO through the neighborhood service centers and legal services. Subsequently, more direct links were forged when the U.S. Department of Labor gave NWRO a $400,000 grant (roughly equal to its privately raised budget), ostensibly to monitor local employment programs for AFDC mothers but mostly to support local groups in their campaigns against local welfare departments. In sum, during this period, the service centers, legal services, and organized recipients contributed to the explosion of welfare (Katz, 1986; Piven & Cloward, 1971). The proportion of potential eligibles rose from about a third, in the early 1960s, to over 90% in the early 1970s (Patterson, 1981, p. 171).

The liberalization of AFDC was strongly contested from the very beginning. Congress and the states tried to increase support from absent fathers; states cut benefits and tried to tighten eligibility requirements and administrative controls; and, as noted, many enacted or strengthened "suitable home" requirements and "man-in-the-house" and "substitute father" rules. This was the period of midnight raids (Abramovitz, 1988, pp. 321–328). However, as noted, many of the overt social control features, such as the man-in-the-house rules, were invalidated either judicially or administratively (Katz, 1986, p. 267). States eliminated or sharply reduced discretionary special grants, one of the principal organizing tools of NWRO, which proved to be a fatal blow. By 1976, NWRO ceased to exist. Considerable effort was made to reduce the discretion of local welfare agencies and their staffs. The Department of Health, Education and Welfare issued a great many regulations on areas formerly left to state discretion, and the federal courts invalidated state rules that were inconsistent with either federal statutes or federal regulations (Katz, 1986, p. 267). Nonetheless, costs and numbers rose steadily. The program appeared out of control, especially in terms of integrity—the popular phrase used was "administrative nightmare" (Galm, 1972). Popular attention, with implicit racial overtones, focused on rising costs, the large number of African-Americans, out-of-wedlock births, the moral consequences of marital disruption, single parenthood, and generational dependency (Abramovitz, 1988, pp. 321–322).

There were three major responses on the part of the federal government. The first, by the Kennedy administration, was to use social services. Rolls and costs were to be reduced by strengthening AFDC families and helping them toward self-support; indeed, the 1962 "social service amendments" renamed the program, making it Aid to Families with Dependent Children. This effort was substantially abandoned by 1967 (Abramovitz, 1988, pp. 329–332). Second, in that year, Congress changed directions and instituted the first federally imposed work requirements—the Work Incentive Program (WIN)—which will be discussed in the next chapter.

The third response was the reassertion of quality control. Ostensibly designed to address the validity of welfare determinations and the integrity of the system, quality control quickly concentrated on erroneous overpayments. Programs became computerized; clerical and intake workers replaced social workers. Workers were closely supervised under strict rules. Cases were monitored by both federal and state governments for errors. States were to be penalized if their caseloads exceeded a certain error rate; individual workers and supervisors were also subject to sanction (Brodkin & Lipsky, 1983; Kramer, 1988).

The vigorous pursuit of overpayments produced great distortions; quality control, along with monthly reporting requirements, resulted in a sharp increase in procedural denials. In time, AFDC no longer resembled the discretionary, chaotic, arbitrary program of the 1960s. Many of the financial and household composition rules were, in effect, federalized. There was a dramatic tightening of administrative practices. In short, the program became much more bureaucratic and rule-bound (Brodkin & Lipsky, 1983; Simon, 1985). The result of quality control has been what Michael Lipsky (1984) calls "bureaucratic disentitlement"—controlling welfare costs through the hidden, obscure decisions of the bureaucracy, such as increasing the verification requirements, closing cases for paper errors (e.g., missing social security numbers, birth certificates, and other required documentation), and closely checking work requirements (p. 109). There were also many more client redeterminations. One of the important consequences of this effort has been the transformation of the staff. With staff under great pressure to get the work out correctly, clients with problems became problems; many staff no longer offered assistance or gave full information. Instead, they cut corners to manage the work load and to avoid tasks that would create delays. Clients were placed under greater burdens to produce documentation and to correct errors on their own; they had to get back on welfare, but with less assistance from the workers. Error rates (defined as overpayments) have been sharply reduced. Many of the errors were on paper only, and some proportion of clients have been restored to the rolls; however, there are no reliable figures on the more permanent casualties (Brodkin & Lipsky, 1983; Chassman, 1987; Dehavenon, 1987–1988; Kramer, 1988; Lipsky, 1984).[14]

The importance of the administrative change in AFDC cannot be exaggerated. To a large extent—never completely—management gained control over the line staff by routinizing large parts of the program and asserting strict monitoring controls. Previously, AFDC administration had been characterized as discretionary, if not chaotic, at the field level; there were ample opportunities for the line staff to bend or ignore the rules (Handler & Hollingsworth, 1971; Sheehan, 1976). The program now is much more rule-bound and supervised. A large issue is whether this administrative capacity can be effective in administering the work requirements.

The states also responded with the most effective tool at their disposal—freezing welfare payments. This was done in two ways. First, increases in the AFDC need standard, which determines whether or not a family is deemed to be in need, fell far behind the increases in the cost of living. From 1970 to 1980, the increase in the median state need standard was 38%, while the Consumer Price Index increased by 212%. From 1980 to 1990 the increase in the median state need standard was 68%, while the CPI increased by 150%. Second, the benefit levels failed to keep up with inflation (with the exception of those in California and Maine). From 1970 to 1990 the median state maximum benefit for a three-person family, in constant dollars, declined by 39% (U.S. Congress, 1990).

In effect, what the states have done is to reduce both the income level at which a family becomes eligible for AFDC and the amount of support it will receive once on AFDC. More than any other strategy, the reduction in the need standard served to exclude many poor single mothers from welfare; the decline in benefits pushed recipients into greater poverty, thus forcing them to fend for themselves in order to support their families. Thus the states used their control over benefits to check the growth of welfare. They resorted to the time-honored approach of reducing relief to deter the poor from applying and to force those on relief to find other means, especially work, to support themselves.

In sum, AFDC has changed, but hardly in the direction of the programs for the dependent aged. An important part—the definition of financial elements—has become federalized, but, in contrast to the aged programs, where federalization has meant uniformity in favor of liberalizing benefits, in AFDC it has been used to clamp down on and control portions of benefits (e.g., work expenses, income-deeming rules) in the more liberal states. But in the main, AFDC is still primarily state and local in terms of basic benefit levels, administration, and, as we shall see in the next chapter, work requirements. The administrative changes at both federal and state levels were designed to tighten eligibility and benefits, to regulate clients rather than to help them.

Our argument is that in contrast to the elderly poor, social attitudes toward the female-headed household in poverty—the category of AFDC eligibles—have not changed. Despite all of the structural changes in AFDC, it is still a grant-in-aid program. The basic methods of *excluding* or *controlling* the undeserving are categorical eligibility, financial eligibility, benefit levels, and work requirements. The states, to a large extent, have lost control over categorical eligibility, but they still set financial eligibility and benefit levels and thus can still exclude many poor families. As we shall show in the chapters that follow, they also now have substantial control over the work requirements. The states control administration. In short, important, restrictive, substantive conditions continue to be administered at the state and local levels.

What explains first the continuation and now the increase in state and local control? Prior to the late 1950s, state and local administrators were able to exclude the vast majority of poor mothers and their families and subject them to the paid labor market along with the rest of the undeserving poor. In the 1960s, state and local administrators lost their ability to pick and choose; the formerly excluded now entered the program, which became more clearly dominated by the undeserving poor—primarily the single African-American mother and her children. Societal attitudes toward this category have remained the same; *what is now happening is that the program is in the process of being restructured to conform more nearly to social attitudes.* Poor female-headed households—especially African-American ones—continue to be considered deviant; as more have entered AFDC, that program is taking on more social control characteristics to conform to the normative view of its new clientele.

The contemporary unfolding of AFDC policy is repeating the mothers' pensions history. During the 1960s, liberal reformers were able to achieve some important changes in the laws, primarily opening the gates by changes in legal ideology, but their constructions and solutions were not widespread. While the liberal changes were being enacted, other constructions and solutions were also being forged—primarily the attack on "waste, fraud, and abuse," with its thinly disguised racial overtones, and work requirements. The struggle over the implementation of AFDC at the local level continued and, gradually, social control is prevailing. In the next chapter, where we analyze the development of the work programs, we demonstrate that the liberal rhetoric is giving way to the long-standing central idea that single mothers are part of the paid labor force.

However, before we turn to analysis of the work requirements, we need to complete our survey of the current income-maintenance programs. This will better enable us to place the moral position of the AFDC family.

Food Stamps

Food stamps would appear to be an exception to the above analysis. It is a major needs-based program (some 19 million recipients) that is noncategorical; it applies to all who are poor, whether working or not, whether two-parent or single-parent families, or singles; recipients do not have to be aged or disabled. While administered by local departments of welfare, food stamp distribution is fully financed by the federal government and operates under federal rules.[15] The food stamp program is the closest the United States comes to a national income-maintenance program. Since we argue that the structure of welfare programs follows the moral categorization of the poor, the food stamp program seems to represent a single national program that encompasses both the deserving and the undeserving poor.

In fact, however, the history and development of food stamps validate our thesis concerning the moral categorization of the poor. Although the initial program was part of the New Deal, its origins lie in agricultural rather than welfare policy. It started as a surplus commodity distribution program (Finegold, 1988). The first stamp program (1939), while directed at ending hunger, was still primarily designed to dispose of agricultural surplus: recipients would purchase their average monthly food requirement, and then receive "bonus" stamps, which were intended to give them incentive to increase their total food consumption. The plan was abandoned during World War II because, while hunger persisted, farm surpluses disappeared. After the war, efforts to revive food stamps were blocked by southerners who dominated the congressional agricultural committees. In 1961, President Kennedy initiated a pilot food stamp project; the purchase requirement was retained, both to stimulate consumption and to reduce stigma. The requirement was part of the Food Stamp Act of 1964, which still incorporated the two goals of reducing food surpluses and promoting nutrition (McDonald, 1977). However, as a concession to the South, the program was made optional; counties could choose either stamps or a commodities-distribution program (Finegold, 1988).

Significant reforms took place during the Nixon administration, in part as a reaction to the defeat of the Family Assistance Plan (see Chapter 4). Now, the program began to take on more welfare characteristics. More categories of poor people would receive free stamps, and benefit levels were raised. In 1974, the program became mandatory nationwide. In 1977, the purchase requirement was eliminated and enrollments rose significantly. While there is criticism as to how the benefits are calculated—the USDA's Thrifty Food Plan, which assumes that a household spends 30% of its income on food—they are indexed to the cost of living. Even though participation has increased, especially since the Nixon reforms, still only about half of all eligibles are enrolled, with lower rates for the elderly, singles, and the rural poor. Less than 60% of the poor are enrolled (eligibility is 130% of poverty) (Finegold, 1988; Lipsky & Thibodeau, 1990).

Significantly, as the food stamps program has taken on more welfare characteristics, notably the elimination of the purchase requirement, its structure has changed. The 1981 Omnibus Budget Reconciliation Act, which made significant cuts in all welfare programs, changed food stamps eligibility calculations by using gross income instead of allowing various deductions, and reduced outreach; approximately 1 million nonelderly were cut from the rolls, and benefits were reduced for millions, contributing to the increase in hunger in the 1980s (Lipsky & Thibodeau, 1990). Administrative barriers and hassles are increasing and now reflect a program more interested in preventing welfare cheating than in reducing hunger. Registration and reregistration requirements have become increasingly complex, raising barriers against the elderly and others who have difficulty in negotiating bureaucracies. As with AFDC, the federal government has instituted tough quality-control measures designed to reduce leniency errors. The USDA has adopted practices that, like AFDC and general relief, result in "churning"—the temporary denial of benefits for technical violations. Significantly, as of 1985, food stamp participants were required to participate in employment and training programs, again reducing the rolls (Lipsky & Thibodeau, 1990). In Los Angeles County, the food stamp program is administered by the same people who administer general relief. They apply the same work test and use the same work-relief projects and the same sanctions, which are very tough. Despite the fact that food stamps are legally available to otherwise eligible persons without regard to their eligibility for other assistance, including general relief, and a violation of general relief requirements is not a reason for termination of food stamp benefits, almost invariably persons who are terminated from general relief are also terminated erroneously from food stamps.[16]

What is significant about food stamps is how the program is changing. When the program was more centrally concerned with the distribution of agricultural surpluses, it was able to avoid most of the negative implications of the undeserving poor by either the purchase requirement or commodity distribution. The purchase requirement excluded the very poor and was thought to lessen stigma. Commodity distribution, which was an option with counties, is itself stigmatizing and enabled the South to maintain its racial subordination policies. The purchase requirement began to be eliminated for certain poverty groups; eventually it was eliminated altogether, and the program was made nationwide. It became a welfare program that included, of course, large numbers of undeserving poor. And now the food stamps program is beginning to resemble AFDC—there is concern about "waste, fraud, and abuse"; there are strict quality controls; there are significant administrative barriers; and there is a work test. In short, the program is becoming more interested in the social regulation of the undeserving poor than in nutrition.

General Relief

What has happened to those not covered by the major programs—the vast majority of the unemployed who either fail to qualify for insurance or have exhausted their benefits; families who are excluded from AFDC; those who do not fit into a category, such as childless couples and singles; half the potential eligibles who for whatever reason fail to enroll to receive food stamps? The general mass of poverty, the undifferentiated poor, have been supported, if at all, under state and local general relief. General relief, the historic program for the undeserving poor, remains to this day at the local level. It is the program for those who have been left behind, those who, for moral reasons, have never been considered worthy of societal support. Historically, and today, it is the first-line defense against all of the known and supposed evils of the indiscriminate outdoor relief of poverty—long-term dependency, indolence, vagrancy, begging, crime, and delinquency. The stereotypical general relief applicant of the past was the bum, the male malingerer, the tramp (First & Toomey, 1989, pp. 113–114); today, it is the African-

American male. It is to the general relief program that we owe the poorhouses, the stone piles, and other forms of harsh work-relief. The myth of general relief is that it is the bottom-line safety net; the ceremony is the moral degradation of those who are forced to apply. Although, historically, those who actually received general relief were usually totally unemployable—children, the severely disabled, the mentally ill, and the aged—the conditions of relief are made sufficiently onerous as to deter the able-bodied from applying (Katz, 1986, pp. 283–284).

General relief today is extremely varied. There is no federal participation at all, and in many states there is not even state-level participation and supervision. Thus a great many programs are at the county and/or municipal level. In many parts of the country there are no such programs at all, while in major cities programs are usually extensive. Benefits are rock bottom, for a short term, highly discretionary, and, if the applicant is considered employable, there is a stiff work requirement. In fact, most able-bodied are simply denied aid, except perhaps some temporary emergency assistance for a night or two.[17]

At present, AFDC is not general relief, but it is closer to general relief than to social security or Supplemental Security Income in its most important characteristics. While there is a significant federal role in AFDC, it is still predominantly a state and local program. Compared with the deserving poor programs, the attitude of AFDC toward its applicants and recipients is generally hostile and suspicious. Bureaucratic disentitlement is a major administrative characteristic. But the most important distinguishing feature is the central role of work requirements, which will be discussed in the next two chapters.

CONCLUSION

In more than a century of welfare change, existing ideologies were challenged by the maturing industrial state, immigration, race relations, the rise of the single-mother family, urban disorders, industrial accidents, the Depression, and, in the post-World War II period, the mass migrations and economic dislocations of African-Americans, the political activism of the 1960s and 1970s, and, as we shall see in the next chapter, the influx of women into the paid labor force. But what these events mean is not preordained; rather, social construction is always contested. In the late nineteenth century, there were sharp conflicts as to the nature and causes of pauperism and whether outdoor relief was the cure or the curse; whether children in poor and disorganized homes should be separated from those homes or supported in them. In this century, questions have included whether compensation for injured workers would undermine the work ethic, whether the elderly were in or out of the work force, and whether it was more important to meet the needs of the unemployed or to shore up capitalism.

We have traced three major ideological resolutions that arose in the New Deal and post-New Deal periods with which we live today. The first had to do with the central importance of the work ethic. The protagonists in this struggle were the masses of unemployed (mostly) males in the Depression. The basic decision that evolved was that the "problem" and the "solution" was capitalism, and that meeting need had to be subordinate to the goals of capitalism. The treatment of the unemployed and the working poor in this country illustrates the paramount importance of the work ethic, with its central component of individual moral responsibility.

The story of the aged is important for several reasons. It shows, first, that social constructions are malleable and contested. Here, there was a significant change in the construction of the problem and the solution. Prior to the Depression, the aged were considered part of the paid labor force, or at least they were not unambiguously excluded; accordingly, relief conflicted with the work ethic and, as we have pointed out, programs reflected this ambiguity. Social constructions for the dependent aged changed with the Depression—now, substantial groups wanted them out of the labor force; they were to be the deserving poor. But this conception was not determined by the Depression. One can imagine a society where work and dignity would be reserved for the elderly, and, indeed, contemporary attitudes have changed—witness the age-discrimination laws in existence today. But even then, this construction was sharply challenged by the Roosevelt administration and the Social Security Administration; they felt that the dependent aged were still the undeserving poor and that their stigma would threaten the retirement program, which was built on a different set of symbols.

The second conclusion about the story of the aged concerns the outcome of this contest. Eventually, the reconception of the dependent aged as deserving poor won out, and it resulted in the transformation of the social security system. Needs were translated into rights, thus preserving the social security myths of contract and entitlement, but now, ceremony gave way to real, substantive benefits. The great changes affecting the elderly—the Depression, changing family structure, their growing numbers and political influence—were mediated by the reconstruction of the moral basis of their dependency and eventually the combination resulted in a real change for most of the dependent aged.

This kind of moral conceptual transformation has not happened with single mothers and their children. Through patriarchy and race, this group of the poor was primarily excluded from welfare. They had to work in the lowest jobs and raise their children under slum conditions. Yet, they were condemned for working and for neglecting their children. Through their moral degradation, they defined the proper role of wife and homemaker. One would have thought that the social construction of this group might have changed in the 1960s and 1970s. This was the era of civil rights, welfare rights, and legal rights for a whole range of other dependent groups—women, the sick, the mentally ill, children, the disabled. Welfare mothers organized, demonstrated, and demanded dignity. There was strong support for civil rights. African-American electoral politics changed, and in many cities there was new leadership. And the welfare program did open. But society's attitudes toward the welfare mother have not changed. This group is still condemned by race and gender. Welfare for them is moral degradation. They are forced by the larger social and economic system to seek relief, but the relief system is harsh and meager and does nothing to improve their condition. In the next two chapters, we will see how the welfare system tries to set these mothers to work, historically the most important social control feature of welfare.

In three major programs—social security retirement (and SSI), AFDC, and food stamps—we see the power of social construction. All three programs were transformed by the moral conceptions of their clientele. Social security reflects the deserving poor status of the elderly. AFDC and food stamps are becoming increasingly regulatory.

NOTES

1. Initially, FERA was only for those who were able to work; the "unemployables" were to be handled by traditional relief at the state and local levels. However, the unemployables were included on the FERA rolls because of lack of public and private funds at the local level (Rose, 1989, p. 67).

2. The arts projects became the best known from this period.

3. For example, in 1879, soldiers who "discovered" war-related disabilities received a lump-sum benefit covering all of the payments that they would have received if they had applied when the program was enacted. In 1890, the combat-related injury requirement was repealed; any veteran of 90 days who could no longer perform manual labor could receive a pension. In practice, old age became the disability, and this was codified (age 62) in 1906. It was estimated that about half of the white males over 65 in the North were on the rolls (Orloff & Skocpol, 1984).

4. The tax-offset plan that was enacted was a 3% tax levied by the federal government on businesses with eight or more employees. If the state passed an acceptable plan, businesses would be credited with 90% of the federal tax; otherwise, the state would forfeit all of the taxes to the federal government. The offset plan provided a strong incentive for the remaining states to pass the appropriate legislation (Amenta & Carruthers, 1986, p. 143, n. 19).

5. The maximum federal ADC payment was $18 per month for the first child and $12 for the second, with a federal reimbursement rate of 30%. There was no aid to the caretaker. OAA allowed a monthly grant of up to $30; the reimbursement rate was 50% (Abramovitz, 1988, p. 316).

6. A matching grant for the mother was added in 1950 (Abramovitz, 1988, p. 316).

7. For a somewhat different interpretation, see Patterson (1981, p. 70).

8. There is a famous quote of a southern public assistance field supervisor: "The number of Negro cases is few due to the unanimous feeling on the part of the staff and board that there are more work opportunities for Negro women and to their intense desire not to interfere with local labor conditions. The attitude that they have always gotten along, and that 'all they'll do is have more children' is definite. . . . There is hesitancy on the part of lay boards to advance too rapidly over the thinking of their own communities, which see no reason why the employable Negro mother should not continue her usually sketchy seasonal labor or indefinite domestic service rather than receive a public assistance grant" (Bell, 1965, p. 35).

9. Aid to the blind was also continued at the state level. This program was noncontroversial, quite small, and, apparently, never became politically visible.

10. A full discussion of the Family Assistance Act can be found in Chapter 4.

11. SSI still has a means test, but it is simplified and nonintrusive. Not all income-maintenance problems of the elderly poor have been solved, as will be discussed shortly. SSI includes disability, which is extremely controversial (Stone, 1984). But, of course, disabled applicants are potentially still part of the labor force.

12. Martha Derthick (1979), commenting on the OAA pressure, states: "There is no telling how the congressional leadership would have reacted to a plan for universal flat payments if one had come to it carefully worked out, from a responsible and credible source. . . . Altmeyer later judged that flat pensions would have been ap-

proved had it not been for the 1939 amendments, which got old age insurance off the ground in a hurry" (p. 221).

13. The Family Support Act of 1988 mandates AFDC-UP in all the states by 1990, but states may limit benefits to 6 months out of 12. See Chapter 6.

14. Because of the strict emphasis on overpayments, workers will deny benefits or close cases when recipients fail to comply with procedural rules. Procedural rejections of applications increased almost 50% between 1972 and 1984; procedural terminations rose from 14% of all closings in 1972 to 41% in 1984. While these increases are dramatic, and many are reversed on appeal, it is not known how many procedurally denied families are substantively entitled to benefits (Brodkin & Lipsky, 1983; Chassman, 1987; Lipsky, 1984). The practice of denying or terminating benefits because of recipients' noncompliance with specified procedures is widespread in general relief, and is known as "churning" (Dehavenon, 1987–1988).

15. The states pay a portion of the administrative costs.

16. Practice varies. In some jurisdictions, all three programs—food stamps, general relief, and AFDC—are administered by the same offices. In others, general relief is separate. Lucie White (personal communication, October 11, 1989) reports that in North Carolina whole families will be cut from food stamps under the general relief 60-day penalty if one of the parents violates the work test. In this sense, the food stamps program is now much more severe than AFDC.

17. For a description of general relief in Los Angeles County, see Handler (1987–1988); for New York, see Dehavenon (1987–1988); and for Chicago, see Sosin, Colson, and Grossman (1988).

4

Welfare and Work:
The Institutionalization
of Moral Ambiguity

THE STICK AND THE CARROT

The contemporary approach to setting welfare recipients to work has been through a combination of regulatory and incentive strategies. The regulatory strategy makes the receipt of welfare contingent on participation in a work program. It sets up an administrative system through which welfare recipients are classified and typed as able-bodied or not. Two approaches are taken with the able-bodied. The most common approach—the historic approach—is simply to deny aid; these applicants are forced back into the market. Even today, there are no income-maintenance programs of any substance for most of the poor in the United States who are childless and nonelderly. If the able-bodied are accepted into a program, they are then required to participate in a work program, with sanctions imposed on those who fail to comply. If there is sufficient liberal objection that such programs are either punitive or will force welfare recipients into the low-wage labor market, services such as education and training may be provided. Symbolically, a regulatory strategy separates the welfare poor from the working poor by conferring the deviant status of "pauper labor," thereby reaffirming the work ethic. Behaviorally, the regulatory strategy controls the poor either by discouraging them from applying or by forcing others off the welfare rolls for failure to comply.

In contrast, the incentive strategy attempts to encourage welfare recipients to work by reducing the effective marginal tax rate on their earnings. Recipients are encouraged to combine wage work with welfare. In theory, the reduction of the welfare grant (the "marginal tax rate") is adjusted so that the recipient is always financially better off by working. The incentive strategy is based on the primacy of the capitalist market system in regulating human behavior. The incentive system is also administratively easier to operate than regulation. Symbolically, the incentive strategy blurs the distinction between welfare recipients and the working poor; therefore, it is strongly resisted by those who believe that labor discipline must be enforced through the segregation and stigmatization of the poor. As we shall note later, there is also a third strategy—a guaranteed minimal income—but it has generally been rejected in the United States.

As we have seen, the regulatory strategy has been used throughout most of welfare history. Starting in the 1960s, however, various combinations of incentives and regulation have been tried. The results of both strategies have been mixed, and the programs more often than not offered symbolic rather than real solutions to getting the able-bodied poor to work (Rein, 1982). The ebb and flow of these programs can be understood against a background of several social trends, including the changing number and characteristics of the poor, the increasing entry of women into the labor force and the changing labor market, and shifts in the domestic code.

As discussed in Chapter 3, AFDC recipients were always subject to state regulatory work programs. Characteristics of these programs varied. Generally, there was strict enforcement in the South and other areas where low-wage seasonal agricultural labor was in demand. There was no federal work requirement until the 1960s, when welfare became a "crisis" claiming national attention.

The first response of the federal government to the welfare crisis was rehabilitation through social services. In 1956, when the rise in welfare began to become evident, and again in 1962, the Social Security Act was amended to add a social service component to

AFDC. The real push for social services came in the Kennedy administration. The view was that welfare rolls would decrease as families became self-supporting through social services programs. Aid to Dependent Children was changed to Aid to Families of Dependent Children, and the states were authorized to provide "rehabilitation and other services" to "help maintain and strengthen family life," and to help families "to attain or retain capability for the maximum self-support and personal independence." In addition, the 1962 amendments adopted an incentive strategy. For the first time, AFDC recipients would be allowed to retain a portion of earned income (42 USC s.601, as amended, 1962; Handler & Hollingsworth, 1971, pp. 103–104).[1]

By 1967, the social services strategy was abandoned. The rolls and costs mounted steadily; the industrial states were claiming that poverty-stricken families were migrating to high-benefit states; it was charged that administration was lax, that the program encouraged immorality, and that people were discouraged from working (Handler & Hollingsworth, 1971, p. 135). Congress, in an angry mood, shifted strategies; it turned its attention to setting AFDC recipients to work. In that year, the first federal work program (WIN) was enacted.

Congress, of course, was responding to widespread demands to do something about welfare. Several factors contributed to the renewed interest in putting recipients to work. As has been the case throughout the history of welfare, the rapid rise in the number of recipients and especially the costs of caring for them created a backlash, triggering efforts to reduce the welfare rolls. States, for example, can freeze cost-of-living adjustments in welfare benefits, a key strategy used during the 1970s, or engage in bureaucratic disentitlement by imposing cumbersome administrative requirements. Now, however, as the result of the civil rights and legal rights movements, state and local officials were constrained by federal law and by threats of lawsuits. As a result of changes in attitudes and law, these officials lost control over the gates; the historic method of setting the poor to work by barring entry was no longer available, and the previously excluded streamed into the programs. Alternatively and concomitantly, imposing a work test is a time-honored strategy for reducing welfare costs.

States and local communities are especially sensitive to the rise in the number of recipients, and the expenditures that incurs, because of their relatively small tax bases—welfare and related social service expenditures consume a large share of their revenues. Local businesses and residents, especially white middle- and working-class residents, become increasingly resentful of welfare recipients because they increase taxes, reduce the availability of a cheap labor force, and raise low wages. Moreover, the changing characteristics of welfare recipients—single mothers with out-of-wedlock children, and disproportionately from ethnic minorities—add to the moral outrage of the white middle and working classes. Public opinion inevitably turns against welfare recipients and contributes to the pressures on politicians to curb expenditures. Moynihan (1973) quotes from an editorial in the *New York Times* in early 1971, a newspaper generally known for its liberal position on social policy:

> Welfare can be called an outrage because: it offers the equivalent of a tax-free income estimated as high as $5,624 to a family of four which may or may not actually have been deserted by its father; it holds out a bonus for additional illegitimate children; any recipient can double a monthly payment by claiming to have lost a check; it has even included, in extreme cases, fringe benefits beyond those in any union contract, such as a weekend at the Waldorf-Astoria or a ski trip to Vermont. (p. 44) (Copyright © 1971 by The New York Times Company. Reprinted by permission.)

The emphasis on a work requirement was undoubtedly also legitimated by the increased participation of women, mostly white women, in the labor force. From 1950 to 1980, the participation rate of white women 16 years and older in the labor force increased from 32.6% to 51.2%, compared with an increase of 46.9% to 53.2% for nonwhite women. Among married women with spouses present, the rate of participation in the labor force increased dramatically, from 28.5% in 1955 to 40.5% in 1970 and to 56.7% in 1988. For the widowed, divorced, and separated, who had a much higher rate of participation to begin with, the change over time was much smaller, from 40.7% in 1955 to 40.3% in 1970 and then to 46.2% in 1988 (U.S. Department of Labor, 1989, Table 6).

More remarkable, however, has been the shift in the "traditional" role of married women with young children. From 1950 to 1980 the labor force participation of married women with spouses present who have children under 6 years old increased from approximately

Table 4.1
Labor Force Participation Rate by Married, Separated, and Divorced
Women and by Age of Children: 1960–1987

Year	Children 6–17 Only			Children Under 6		
	Married	Separated	Divorced	Married	Separated	Divorced
1960	39.0	—	—	18.6	—	—
1970	49.2	60.6	82.4	30.3	45.4	63.3
1980	61.7	66.3	82.3	45.1	52.2	68.3
1985	67.8	70.9	83.4	53.4	53.2	67.5
1988	72.5	69.3	83.9	57.1	53.0	70.1

SOURCE: U.S. Bureau of the Census (1989, p. 386).

10% to 45%, and for those with children over 6 from under 30% to
over 60% (Garfinkel & McLanahan, 1986, p. 65). The labor force
participation rates of married women now approximately equal
those of single mothers (see Table 4.1).

Many factors may have contributed to this dramatic change in
labor force participation. No doubt an important cause was the
decline in family income, especially for blue-collar workers, and the
shift to service occupations.[2] The increased participation of women
in the labor force was also caused by an increased demand for
women workers as the labor market changed through the rapid
expansion of the service economy. As noted by Tienda, Smith, and
Ortiz (1987), "Since 1960 service employment has expanded continuously, while jobs in the manufacturing and agricultural sectors
have decreased so that by 1980 two out of every three jobs in the
U.S. economy were in service industries" (p. 195). While such
demand has had a positive effect in terms of higher wages, the
gender segregation of the labor market diminished only marginally,
and has not reduced appreciably the wage gap between men and
women. Indeed, as Tienda et al. point out, female-type jobs became
even more gender-segregated during the 1970s. Moreover, employment in a female-type job has a negative effect on earnings. Because
women workers tend to be concentrated in low-wage service occupations, the expansion of the service sector, while providing
employment opportunities in professional and managerial positions, also increased the demand for low-wage women workers.
Thus the service economy, especially in the low-wage occupations,

has increasingly become dependent on the supply of low-wage women workers. This in turn has generated pressure on welfare policy to regulate the flow of low-income women into these jobs. It does so not so much by insisting that welfare recipients seek employment as by using the work requirements to discourage poor women from leaving the labor force.

Needless to say, the dramatic shift in female labor-force participation coincided with a profound change in the domestic code. It not only became acceptable for married women with young children to work, it was indeed expected of them. The respectability of working married mothers only heightened the perceived deviance and moral depravity of single mothers, especially those with children born out of wedlock, who are on welfare rather than working. Paradoxically, the changing domestic code resulted in greater convergence between conservatives and liberals. Historically, conservatives justified punitive welfare policies that forced poor women to work on the basis of their failure to uphold the code of the "virtuous" woman who is married and stays home to take care of her husband and children. Now they could readily justify these policies on the basis of the new code. Liberals, who historically opposed punitive welfare policies by arguing that poor women should have the same right as other women to stay home and care for their children, have lost the legitimacy of their position. In accepting and advocating for the new code, they now acknowledge that single mothers on welfare should work (Garfinkel & McLanahan, 1986). In contrast to the conservatives, however, they argue that government has a major responsibility in helping these women to find employment by providing training, employment opportunities, and child care.

It is against such a background that current work policies and programs have been formulated. They are distinguished by their combination of inducements and sanctions, which reflect the tension between the expansion of the entitlement to welfare and the fear of its negative impact on the normative order. The tension, rooted in the moral ambiguity of poverty, is expressed in the prevalence of two competing ideologies about able-bodied poor. The first views the primary problem of able-bodied poor as deficiencies in human capital (i.e., lack of education, training, and skills), but also acknowledges unfavorable labor market conditions as a secondary factor. Thus, to assist the poor in gaining employment, investments should be made in training and skills acquisition, including the creation of employment opportunities. The second view attributes the unemployment of the able-bodied poor to lack of motivation, self-discipline, or knowledge of how to seek employment. As Mead (1986) puts it, "This 'pathological instability' in holding jobs, rather than lack of jobs, is the main reason for the work difficulties of the disadvantaged" (p. 73). Accordingly, the poor should be "weaned" from welfare that reduces motivation and should be encouraged, and even obligated, to seek employment.

It should be emphasized that the two ideologies nonetheless have a great deal in common. They arise and derive their legitimacy from the same dominant rule that views poverty as a personal rather than a social deficit. Specifically, they are rooted in an economic and social order based on a liberal capitalist market economy. They tend to accept an economic model of the person, namely, that a person's behavior is a function of a rational economic calculus of costs and benefits. Therefore, both ideologies are equally concerned about the trade-off between welfare and work, and seek to devise a system of economic incentives and disincentives that will induce people to work rather than remain on welfare. Both accept the proposition that welfare generosity reduces the incentive to work. They differ, of course, on what they consider an acceptable level of welfare generosity and on the emphasis on inducements versus sanctions to induce welfare recipients to work. It is this dialectic between the two contesting ideologies that has created the stick-and-carrot approach.

WORK PROGRAMS (WIN)

WIN has been the mainstay program in setting AFDC recipients to work since it was launched in 1967.[3] Although WIN combined both the incentive and regulatory strategies, regulation predominated. WIN, at its core, was coercive; it made the receipt of welfare by the able-bodied poor contingent on participation in the program and, subsequently, by imposing sanctions for nonparticipation. Although WIN was rationalized as a program providing employment services, it nonetheless distinguished between able-bodied poor and other poor by mandating the former to participate in the labor market.

From its inception and throughout its convoluted history, the rhetorics justifying WIN bore little relationship to its actual impact. All the available evidence indicates that the program has had dismal results. Analysis of the policies guiding the program, its implementation, and its accomplishments demonstrate once again the core difficulties of all work programs, emanating from the problematic linkages among institutional norms, policies, and programs. Specifically, we will show (a) that the translation of ambiguous institutional rules into policies generated myths and ceremonies, periodic revisions, reduced fiscal commitments, and organizational discretion at the local level; and (b) that the political economy of local WIN agencies generated organizational dilemmas that substantially hampered organizational performance.

The WIN legislation was driven by both social regulation and moral needs. The continuing rise in AFDC recipients and expenditures, coming on the heels of racial insurgency in numerous cities, pushed policymakers to find ways to curb this trend. The specter of single mothers with out-of-wedlock children being supported by public funds created a moral outrage because it threatened the domestic code, especially the patriarchal family ethic (Abramovitz, 1988). At the institutional level, the state needed to reassert the dominant moral order. Both themes were echoed by Representative Mills when he introduced the legislation:

> We want the states to see to it that those who are drawing as unemployed fathers, or drawing as mothers, unless there is good cause for them not to be required to take it, that they take training and then work. . . . What in the world is wrong with requiring these people to submit themselves, if they are to draw public funds, to a test of their ability to learn a job?

He went on to ask rhetorically, "Are you satisfied with the fact that illegitimacy in this country is rising and rising?" (U.S. Congress, 1967, p. 23053).

Much of the debate around the legislation centered on the definition of the able-bodied welfare recipient who would be required to participate in the work program (Malone, 1986). The Ways and Means Committee expected all adults and children over the age of 16 to participate, including mothers if appropriate child care could be provided for their children. To enforce participation, the committee stipulated a penalty of reduction in the welfare grant for non-compliance. The bill was opposed by various advocacy groups, including the AFL-CIO, the National Welfare Rights Organization, the American Public Welfare Association, the American Civil Liberties Union, and many others. They not only opposed the mandatory feature of the program, but also questioned the ability of the states to provide adequate child care. Mrs. Johnie Tillman, the chairwoman of the National Welfare Rights Organization, in objecting to the bill, graphically expressed the moral bind it would impose on welfare mothers when she stated:

> Forcing parents out of the home will only cause more delinquency. When we are out of the home working, our children are picked up by the police. The first think [sic] they are going to say is, "Where are your parents?" When they say "My mother is working," they are going to go before the judge and find out why these children are out in the street and why they were picked up. (quoted in Malone, 1986, p. 38)

The bill ultimately required mandatory participation by each appropriate child and relative who has attained age 16 and is receiving AFDC. While it did not specify criteria for "appropriateness," it did exempt persons who are disabled, a child attending school full-time, a person who cares for another member of the household who is incapacitated, and a person whose participation the state agency finds to be not in the best interest of the children. Priorities for referral were given first to persons with work skills needed in the local community, second to individuals needing training for jobs that are available in the area, and third to persons who cannot be employed in the regular economy but could participate in community work projects. The language of the bill was sufficiently ambiguous and broad to give the states considerable discretion in deciding who would be referred to WIN. Thus the legislation also planted the seeds of bureaucratic conflict between welfare departments and state employment services offices, which were expected to implement WIN.

In effect, WIN used a stick-and-carrot approach. The stick was applied mostly to fathers on AFDC-UP and children over the age of 16 who were neither in school or working. They were mandated to register for WIN and could be dropped from AFDC if they declined to participate without good cause. The decision of what constituted "good cause" was left to the discretion of the welfare officials. The carrot was in the form of work incentives (discussed below), promise of training and employment services, increased funding for day care, and encouragement of mothers with school-age children to volunteer for WIN and receive training and other support services.

In the first annual report to Congress, WIN was described as combining "social services, child care services, and manpower training services for potentially employable persons to equip them to get and hold a job, using a combination of on-the-job training, institutional training, work experience and counseling" (U.S. Department of Labor, 1970, p. 2). Much was made of WIN's service approach—employability development plan, team concept, and program flexibility. Nonetheless, this report already hinted at the problems that would plague WIN, including determination of who is truly an able-bodied recipient, attrition between referral and enrollment, large numbers of participants on "hold" waiting for services, labor market constraints, coordination difficulties among various services, and lack of child care.

Through fiscal year 1971, 2.7 million assessments were made, of which only 24% were deemed "appropriate for referral." From this pool only 118,000 were actually enrolled. Of those terminated, only 20% held a job for at least three months, and the median wage for employed WIN women was approximately $2.00 per hour (the minimum wage in 1971 was $1.60). Thus the WIN program was successful in obtaining jobs for only 2–3% of the eligible AFDC recipients (Goodwin, 1983; Rein, 1982). The budget for the program was $150 million in 1970. During that period there were more than 2.5 million families on AFDC, and the total expenditures were over $4 billion.

Rein (1982) attributes the failure of the program to its incompatible values of obligating recipients to register for work, thus reducing the welfare rolls, and helping them overcome barriers to gainful employment through training and other services. While this is a significant factor, it is necessary to view the policy in the context of having meager resources and limited scope, granting wide discretion to local welfare offices in referring "appropriate" clients, and bureaucratic unwillingness to enforce sanctions for noncompliance. This suggests that evaluating the program solely on the basis of its effects on the recipients and welfare rolls is to ignore its institutional purpose. The program served a mostly symbolic function, a form of myth and ceremony affirming cherished values that have been questioned by the reality of rising welfare rolls and expenditures. By upholding the institutional rule of work, WIN defused the normative threat of the rapid expansion of welfare. The main purpose of the program was to engage in the ceremony of requiring able-bodied recipients to register for training and employment in accordance with the institutional rule it was designed to uphold. The key feature of WIN was thus the certification of able-bodied recipients. The certification, however, was only loosely connected to the actual provision of employment services. Thus providing employment and training services and placing recipients in the labor market were of secondary importance to the survival of the program.

WORK INCENTIVES
AND DISINCENTIVES

Work incentives represent an alternative strategy to participation in a work program by encouraging welfare recipients to supplement their income through voluntary participation in the labor market. Such a strategy does not have regulatory or coercive features, and does not insist on the distinction between able-bodied and other welfare recipients.

One of the major issues in inducing AFDC recipients to work has been the potential decrease in assistance for every dollar of earned income. If every dollar of earned income reduces assistance by that amount, the recipient is, in effect, being levied a 100% tax. Recognizing this, the 1962 amendments to the Social Security Act required states to disregard any expenses reasonably attributable to the earning of wages in the calculation of the AFDC grant. The 1967 amendments to the Social Security Act further expanded the incentives by stipulating that the first $30 per month of earnings plus one-third of the remainder would be exempted. It is important to emphasize that the income disregard was computed on earnings before work-related expenses and child-care costs were subtracted. Thus it was estimated that the average "tax" rate dropped to 34.4% (Moffitt & Wolf, 1987).

However, when work incentives become embedded in a regulatory program such as WIN, it is likely that the distinction between the two strategies will become blurred, and it is doubtful that welfare recipients will respond differently to each strategy. In a review of studies on the impact of these incentives, Rein (1982, pp. 53–59) concludes that they had no discernible impact on the work efforts of AFDC recipients. During the 1970s the effective tax rate rose again as state welfare regulations became more restrictive about allowable work-related expenses, and by 1979 it reached the same level as prior to the 1967 Social Security Amendments (Fraker, Moffitt, & Wolf, 1985).

THE NEGATIVE
INCOME TAX EXPERIMENTS

A third strategy that has rarely been considered in the history of welfare reform in the United States is that of a guaranteed minimum income. Its marginal place in the national debate over welfare reform mirrors the dominant normative institutions of American society. An income strategy runs counter to the symbols of individual responsibility, primacy of the market, the deviance of the able-bodied poor, and the moral denigration of poor single mothers. It disturbs the economics of labor and gender, especially in low-wage industries, and reduces local regulatory discretion. Nonetheless, this option was seriously considered during President Johnson's War on Poverty. With the emergence of a wide variety of programs, including talk about income redistribution, a political climate was created that stimulated liberal economists both within and outside the Office of Economic Opportunity and the Department of Health, Education and Welfare (e.g., James Lyday, Worth Bateman, James Tobin, Robert Lampman) to propose a guaranteed minimal income scheme to eradicate poverty.

They were not alone. Milton Friedman (1962), a conservative economist, proposed a negative income tax (NIT) by which individuals whose income falls below the federal income tax exemption and deductions would receive a subsidy set at 50%. While Friedman preferred private charity as the way to alleviate poverty, he acknowledged that in contemporary society such a solution was not feasible. Thus he justified the negative income tax scheme as compatible with the tenets of classical liberalism and capitalism, namely, that it would not distort the market economy, and it would minimize the intervention of government and eliminate the vast welfare bureaucracy, thus protecting the freedom of all the poor as well as providing some measure of economic security.

There was still the question of whether guaranteed welfare benefits would increase dependency by eroding the work ethic. Accordingly, the liberal economists of the Johnson administration marshalled social science research to study the trade-off between welfare and work. They had hoped that the moral ambivalence of providing the poor with assistance while preserving the work ethic could be resolved by examining scientifically the consequences of different levels of benefits and tax rates on the incentive to work, thus providing an answer as to the optimal mix of the two. It was expected that increased benefits would result in some reduction in work effort. The magnitude of the reduction remained unknown, however, and any welfare reform hinged on this issue. This was the impetus for the NIT experiments initiated by the Office of Economic Opportunity (Levine, 1975). Several experiments were launched in the 1960s and early 1970s, the most prominent among them being the New Jersey Negative Tax Experiment and the Seattle-Denver Income Maintenance Experiment.

The Seattle-Denver study, the most comprehensive, enrolled 4,800 families, of which 39% were African-American, 43% were white, and 18% were Chicano. The sample also included families headed by single adults. The experimental design attempted to test several conditions. First, it included guaranteed benefits for 3, 5, and 20 years in order to determine long-term consequences. Second, it included three benefit levels, starting with $3,800 for a family of four (approximating the poverty level) and moving to $4,800 and $5,600. Third, it consisted of four different tax rates, including a constant and a declining rate. Finally, it had three alternative manpower treatments, consisting of different mixes of counseling and training subsidies, to see if they could counteract the work disincentives. In estimating the reduction in work effort (i.e., annual hours of work), Robins (1980) found that for those with income below the break-even point and not on a declining tax rate, on the average, husbands reduced their work hours by 5%, wives by 22%, and single female heads of households by 11%. In terms of employability, the probability of working for husbands declined by 5%, for wives by 8%, and for female heads by 11%. Robins and West (1980) also estimated the long-term effects of the experiment (i.e., five years). The proportion of reduction of hours of work for husbands was 9%, for wives 20%, and for female heads 25%. Clearly, women were far more likely to opt out of the labor force when they had a secure income. Moreover, the long-term effect on nonwhite males was twice as high as that for white males. Moffitt (1982) points out that for the males much of the reduction in work effort was due to a small number of men who opted to leave their jobs altogether rather than reduce their hours of work.

Interestingly, the results of the experimental condition on training subsidies have generally gone unnoticed. Hall (1980) reports that the subsidies clearly induced the recipients to take additional schooling, and this was true for husbands, wives, and single female heads of households. For the last group, the subsidies had a greater effect in inducing women to go back to school than it had on those already in school. The strongest effect was on young women.

One of the most controversial findings of the Seattle-Denver experiment was the impact of the negative income tax on marital stability (Groeneveld, Tuma, & Hannan, 1980). For the five-year sample the overall increase in marital dissolution for African-Americans was 61%, and for whites 58%. For Chicanos there was a 4% decline. The increases occurred at the lower levels of the income guarantee. These rates varied, however, according to number of children and other demographic characteristics. These findings were frequently cited by opponents of welfare reform based on an income strategy, and were critical in persuading key politicians that an income-guarantee plan was incompatible with supporting family stability among the poor (Steiner, 1981).[4]

The NIT experiments have been criticized on both substantive and methodological grounds (for a review, see Ferber & Hirsch, 1978). For our purpose, however, the issue is the extent to which the experiments served to guide social policy by helping diminish the moral ambiguity of welfare and work. From this perspective, the experiments only added to the moral debate. The congressional debates on welfare reform were heavily colored by the political fall-out of the experiments (Neubeck & Roach, 1981). Senator Moynihan, for example, expressed concern that the findings about work effort and marital dissolution would erode support for a negative income tax program. Contesting ideological interest groups seized upon the findings to support their own views. Martin Anderson (1978), advocating a reaffirmation of a needy-only philosophical approach to welfare and a clear work requirement, buttressed his argument by concluding from the experiments that a guaranteed income would cause substantial reduction (perhaps as much as 50%) in the work effort of low-income workers as well as massive marriage breakups. Charles Murray (1984), who advocated the elimination of public assistance to the able-bodied poor, used the results of the experiments to support his view that welfare has a morally corrupting impact on its recipients. Proponents of an income support program charged that such critics overlooked the fact that the experiments provided income support far more generous than had been contemplated by any welfare reform proposal, that the reduction of the work effort for heads of households was very moderate, and that the negative consequences of income support programs on family stability have been overstated (e.g., Danziger & Gottschalk, 1985; Garfinkel & McLanahan, 1986).

Assessing the impact of these experiments on policymakers, Neubeck and Roach (1981) conclude that "political elites are likely to see as significant and useful those research results that fit well with their already formed ideological predispositions, and ignore or challenge those that conflict with them" (p. 315). Much of this was evident in the debate over the major welfare reform initiative undertaken in the next administration.

THE FAMILY ASSISTANCE PLAN

The failure of WIN to stem the rising tide of welfare expenditures occurred in a context of increasing fiscal difficulties in the industrial states, the aftermath of racial insurrections in the major cities, and a newly elected Republican president who campaigned against the "welfare mess." While the NIT experiments were under way, another window of opportunity was created by several of President Nixon's domestic advisers, especially Moynihan, Finch, and Shultz, who proposed a radical change in welfare policy, based on a concept of the negative income tax, which came to be known as the Family Assistance Plan (FAP).

The essential features of FAP, as presented to Congress in October 1969, consisted of a low cash benefit packaged as negative income tax for families with children, regardless of whether the family head was employed or not, while excluding childless couples and single poor. It established an "income floor," which was set at $1,600 per year for a family of four (approximately 45% of the poverty level). Recipients would continue to be eligible for food stamps, Medicaid, public housing, and other social services.[5] It provided a work incentive by excluding the first $720 earned and a 50% tax on each additional dollar earned. When the yearly income of a family of four reached $3,920, it would no longer be eligible for cash benefits. By establishing a nationwide minimum income standard for all of the poor and a system of wage supplementation, FAP merged the welfare and the working poor. FAP required that states with higher AFDC benefits than stipulated by the bill would be required to maintain them and extend them to families with unemployed fathers. However, it also provided fiscal relief to the states. Every state would have to spend at least 50% of the amount it would have to spend under the present public assistance programs, but no state would have to spend more than 90% of its current expenditures.

That was the incentive strategy of FAP. The bill also had its regulatory component. FAP essentially adopted the WIN work requirements. A family member's failure to register with the local public employment office or to accept "suitable" employment without a showing of good cause would result in that person's not being counted in the family's eligibility for benefits. In addition, FAP provided funds for work training and child care. However, it was estimated that these funds could reach only 150,000 recipients out of 1.1 million eligible who would be required to register for work, and could provide child care to only 450,000 children (Marmor & Rein, 1973).

It was estimated that FAP would have added over $4 billion to welfare expenditures (an increase of 138%); added 10 million new recipients, mostly working poor; and eliminated AFDC in 16 to 18 states, mostly southern. Indeed, in 15 states more than 15% of the population would be eligible for FAP, including 35% of the population in Mississippi, 25% in Louisiana, 24% in Kentucky, and 22% in Georgia (Moynihan, 1973).

FAP (with some minor revisions) was approved by the House Ways and Means Committee and passed in the House in April 1970. It was, however, defeated in the Senate Finance Committee. A revised bill, H.R. 1, which attempted to respond to the various objections raised against FAP, was introduced by Congressmen Mills and Byrnes in January 1971 (Bowler, 1974; Burke & Burke, 1974). H.R. 1 established a minimum income guarantee for a family of four of $2,400, but eliminated eligibility for food stamps. There was no requirement that states continue any benefits above the federal floor, but it gave them an inducement to continue supplementation by guaranteeing that if the state expanded the supplementary benefits in the future it would not have to spend more than it did in 1971. Bowing to conservatives, H.R. 1 strengthened the regulatory features. It distinguished between families with an able-bodied adult and those without. Those with an able-bodied adult were required to participate in a program titled Opportunities for Families (OFF) and were given a wage supplementation. The work incentive was reduced from 50% to 33%. It also tightened the work requirements by requiring women with children over the age of 3 rather than 6 to register for employment, insisting that recipients employed full-time register for programs to upgrade their skills, and deleting the "suitable" clause as an excuse from the work requirement. The work training projects of FAP were replaced by a new public service employment program. A cap was set on federal funding for social services to welfare recipients. The application procedures for FAP and OFF were also tightened.

In addition, H.R. 1 proposed what is now known as Supplementary Security Income, which merged and federalized the grant-in-aid programs for the dependent aged, the blind, and the disabled.

H.R. 1 passed the House in June 1971, but again was rejected by the conservative Senate Finance Committee. The Finance Committee fashioned its own alternative, which replaced AFDC with a comprehensive work program. It sought to reaffirm the separation of the welfare poor from the working poor by denying welfare payments to families headed by an able-bodied father, and families headed by a mother whose youngest child was over the age of 5. Instead, it would guarantee them a job opportunity and a wage supplement, if the job paid less than the minimum wage. The moral justifications for this approach were the extensive participation of mothers in the labor force and the nation's need for public works. As the committee's report put it:

> Does it make sense to pay millions of persons not to work at a time when so many vital jobs go undone? Can this Nation treat mothers of school-age children on welfare as though they were unemployable and pay them to remain at home when more than half of mothers with school-age children in the general population are already working? (U.S. Congress, 1972)

This alternative also failed to pass in the House-Senate Conference.

Undoubtedly, FAP presented a radical welfare reform. What is especially illuminating about it is not merely its ultimate failure to become law, but the national debate it evoked. This debate illuminates, in sharp relief, the many countervailing forces that shape welfare policy. The heart of the debate was precisely the daring attempt of FAP to blur the distinctions between able-bodied and disabled poor, and between the welfare and the working poor. By softening these distinctions, especially through the inclusion of the working poor, FAP produced an irreconcilable tension between the provision of a guaranteed minimum income to all citizens and the preservation of the incentive to work, while trying to contain the fiscal burden of welfare. That is, FAP heightened the conflict between the relief of misery and the maintenance of the work ethic, in a context of a capitalist economy that abhors raising the overall costs of welfare. As Marmor and Rein (1973) put it:

> More intractable problems were inherent in a strategy to use low marginal tax rates to encourage work, relieve distress, and reduce the fiscal burdens of states and localities. . . . the more adequate the basic allowance at which economic insufficiency is met, the more demanding the task of encouraging self-sufficiency. Again, the more attractive the incentives (the proportion of benefits retained as earnings rise), the steeper the cost and the larger the program. (p. 17)

The conflict is between two contending moral principles battling for supremacy in the political arena through the manipulation of symbols. According to Burke and Burke (1974), "Nixon cloaked the family-income guarantee in conservative rhetoric," and presented FAP as a proposal to reinforce America's work ethic (p. 110). He told the nation: "What America needs is not more welfare but more workfare." The president added: "To put it bluntly and simply any system which makes it more profitable for a man not to work than to work, and which encourages a man to desert his family, is wrong and indefensible" (quoted in Burke & Burke, 1974, p. 111). But this was exactly what FAP was accused of doing.[6] The Chamber of Commerce denounced FAP as a federal relief subsidy for fully employable fathers that "could tend to 'lock' them in their present occupations. Such payments could prove to be a strong disincentive to improve their learning capacities" (quoted in Moynihan, 1973, p. 289).

The most powerful image of FAP as a threat to the work ethic was presented by Senator Williams of the Senate Finance Committee, who showed that FAP contained a serious "notch," namely, that at a certain level of benefits, any additional earning would result in a net loss of income. The notch was illustrated through the calculation of the benefits of a recipient in Chicago receiving FAP, state supplementation, food stamps, Medicaid, and public housing bonus. Williams directed his questions to Robert Patricelli, deputy assistant secretary of HEW:

Senator Williams: If they increase their earnings from $720 to $5,560 under this bill, they have a spendable income of $6,109, or $19 less than if they sit in a rocking chair earning only $720. Is that not correct?
Mr. Patricelli: That is correct. . . .
Senator Williams: They are penalized $19 because they go out and earn $5,500. Is that correct?
Mr. Patricelli: That is correct.
The Chairman . . . What possible logic is there to it?
Mr. Patricelli: There is none, Senator. (quoted in Moynihan, 1973, p. 481)

The facts that only a small proportion of the poor lived in public housing and that Medicaid could not be counted as "spendable income" were not considered.

Equally vehement attacks came from the liberals, on the grounds that FAP set its guaranteed income too low to afford the poor a decent living. Indeed, FAP was interpreted as a symbol of a noncaring society. Prosocial welfare groups such as the National Conference on Social Welfare and the National Association of Social Workers demanded a guaranteed annual income based on the Bureau of

Labor Statistics low-income budget ($5,500 for a family of four). They argued that the lot of welfare recipients in the industrial states would hardly improve under FAP. They echoed the position taken by the National Welfare Rights Organization, whose constituency included mostly AFDC recipients in the highly industrialized states with relatively generous AFDC benefits, for whom FAP did not present a significant improvement in income. NWRO adopted the slogan "$5,500 or Fight." Senator George McGovern, who advocated a children's allowance, stated, "If we rush to support that program as the push button answer to poverty, we are wrapping our hopes for those 10% of our citizens who are poor up in a neat little package, addressing the package to Strom Thurmond and hoping he will deliver it to the needy" (quoted in Moynihan, 1973, p. 443). FAP provided an opportunity for liberal Democrats to outbid the president with impunity and thus score a moral victory. Senator Eugene McCarthy, with the blessing of NWRO, introduced the Adequate Income Act of 1970, which included a minimum income guarantee of $5,500 and no work requirement. Senator Fred Harris introduced the National Basic Income Maintenance and Incentive Act, which started with a minimum income guarantee of $2,520 and rose over three years to poverty level. Yet, this attack on FAP resulted in a tragic irony of pitting the welfare of one group of poor against another. FAP clearly represented a major improvement to the most destitute of the poor in the country, especially those living in the South. Under H.R. 1, 3.6 million poor in 11 southern states and 3.4 million in other states barred from any cash assistance would have become eligible for assistance (Burke & Burke, 1974, p. 172). Yet it was the political power of the poor, and their allies, in the industrialized states that helped derail FAP at the expense of the poor in southern states.

Closely intertwined with this debate was the issue of work requirements, especially their effects on regulating the low-wage labor market and maintaining industrial discipline. FAP included the WIN work requirements, which, as noted earlier, proved to be mostly symbolic, given the resources allocated for such a purpose. Moreover, FAP adopted the same standards of employment "suitability" used for unemployment insurance (Moynihan, 1973, p. 406). Nonetheless, the liberals objected to the work requirements, viewing them as coercive and draconian. In contrast, conservatives feared that the workfare provision of FAP was an empty gesture, or, as Buckley phrased it, merely "boob-bait for conservatives" (quoted in Moynihan, 1973, p. 370). More ominous, however, was the perceived impact of FAP on regulating the supply of low-wage workers. The image of the Speenhamland system was evoked again, this time to demonstrate that employers would exploit the working poor because they would have no incentive to raise their wages. The labor unions opposed FAP for that reason; the United Auto Workers feared that FAP would subsidize sweatshop employers (Burke & Burke, 1974, p. 140). Moreover, opponents of the work requirements could visualize that FAP would force the poor to accept the most demeaning of jobs, such as sweeping city streets and parks. In the NWRO's publication, the *Welfare Fighter*, a cartoon was printed showing two poor and raggedly dressed charwomen. The African-American woman asked the white, "What's that FAP mean?" The white responded, "Fuck America's Poor!" (Burke & Burke, 1974, p. 138).

This fear was fueled, in part, by the response of southern politicians and businesses to FAP. "Many white Southerners feared that FAP's guaranteed income would shrink the supply of cheap labor, bankrupt marginal industry, boost the cost of locally produced goods and services, increase taxes, and put more blacks into political office" (Burke & Burke, 1974, p. 147). As Lester Maddox, the governor of Georgia, put it: "You're not going to be able to find anyone willing to work as maids or janitors or housekeepers if this bill gets through, that I promise you" (quoted in Moynihan, 1973, pp. 378–379). Because African-Americans were historically concentrated in low-wage jobs and were overrepresented in the welfare rolls, the debate quickly took on racial overtones. For African-Americans, the work requirements provoked the symbols of servitude and "slave work." In an article for *Fortune* on the impact of FAP on the South, Richard Armstrong quoted the Reverend Rims Barber, a civil rights worker with the Delta Ministry in Mississippi, who viewed the work requirement as "slave labor. That's just subsidizing lazy white women who shouldn't be allowed to have maids at that price" (quoted in Moynihan, 1973, p. 390). Whites simply could not appreciate how the history of exploitation of African-American men and women generated deep distrust of the work requirement provisions of FAP. This distrust was effectively used by NWRO to denounce FAP as racist. In a hearing conducted by

Senator McCarthy on FAP's work requirements. Beulah Sanders, NWRO's vice chair, testified:

> You can't force me to work! You'd better give me something better than I'm getting on welfare. I ain't taking it. . . . I heard that Senator Long said as long as he can't get his laundry done he's going to put welfare recipients to work. . . . Those days are gone forever! . . . We ain't gonna clean it! (quoted in Burke & Burke, 1974, p. 162)

Racism was blatantly manifest when NWRO was described, presumably by Senator Long, as the "Black Brood Mares, Inc." (Moynihan, 1973, p. 336).

As is always the case in discussions of welfare reform, issues of racism, the domestic code, and deviant behavior became intermingled in the debate over FAP. There were concerns that FAP would do little to stem the tide of illegitimacy, that it would erode the patriarchal domestic code, and foster dependency. This attitude was best epitomized by Senator Talmadge when he questioned the under secretary of HEW on the cash penalty for a man refusing to accept work:

> *Senator Talmadge:* So he could do a little casual labor on somebody's yard from time-to-time and maybe sell a little heroin or do a little burglary and he would be in pretty good shape, wouldn't he?
> *Mr. Veneman:* He would be in about the same shape as under the present program. (quoted in Moynihan, 1973, p. 473)

Similarly, Senator Long (1971) argued that H.R. 1 would promote family illegitimacy and immorality. He calculated that in his own state of Louisiana the bill could give a family a bonus of $2,650 for the father and mother not to marry if the father was earning $5,000. He termed it an incentive to immorality, and stated:

> If the mother admits that she knows the whereabouts and identity of the father, the family income is reduced. Therefore, she does not admit it. . . . Mother tells the children, "That man over there is your father, but do not tell anybody. Keep it a secret because if the government finds out about it, we will lose our welfare money." (p. 4)

Long's solution to the "welfare mess" was to make child desertion a federal crime and to have a tougher paternity identification law.

As we shall see, a solution in a similar spirit was incorporated in the Family Support Act of 1988.

Once again, women on AFDC were caught in the cross fire of the debate around the domestic code. Those upholding the patriarchal code viewed these women as deviant because of the failure of their men to support their children. In an attempt at social control, they were required to register for work, but when they went to work, they were accused of neglecting their domestic duties. On the other hand, those who expected mothers to participate in the labor market tried to deny women on AFDC the opportunity to stay home and care for their children, but if the recipients did just that, they were accused of being lazy.

Finally, FAP also touched on such sensitive issues as state discretion and the role of the welfare bureaucracy. While states wanted fiscal relief, they were reluctant to give up their discretion in the administration of welfare. They wanted to be able to continue to administer welfare to fit their own political economies and moral values. Similarly, welfare bureaucrats did not want to lose their own autonomy, especially in determining the conditions of their work. Indeed, the American Federation of State, County and Municipal Employees, representing more than 30,000 welfare workers, opposed FAP.

WIN II

The ever-present moral and political conflicts over welfare doomed radical welfare reforms such as FAP. Moreover, the national debate sharpened hostility and frustration toward AFDC. It came to symbolize government waste and uncontrollable costs; it was seen as morally corrupting, in terms of both sexual behavior and work incentives; and it reinforced racial and gender prejudices. These symbols were expressed in the amendment to the Social Security Act introduced by Senator Talmadge in 1971. WIN II, as it came to be known, expanded the definition of able-bodied poor to include mothers with children 6 years of age or older, required their mandatory registration in the program, changed the focus of the program from educational and institutional training to employment services and subsidized employment, and provided tax incentives to prospective employers. Further policy oscillations concerning emphasis on direct job placement versus training occurred in 1975, when a balance between the two was attempted, and in 1980, when job placement was reemphasized and sanctions against AFDC recipients refusing participation were strengthened. As a result, job-search activities, in the form of job clubs and supervised job searches, became the primary focus of the program. They required minimal expenditure of resources, were relatively simple to implement and administer, and put much of the onus of responsibility on the welfare recipient to find a job.

Law (1983) sees WIN II as a "backlash" against legal rights women had earned during the 1960s, including entitlement to welfare, control of their reproductive capacity, and access to male-dominated occupations. These gains had challenged male dominance and traditional conceptions about family structure. In contrast, she argues, welfare policy, in general, and the work requirement policies, in particular, are intended, in effect, to "enforce the patriarchal requirement of female dependence upon men" (p. 1249). Since the work requirements move a very small proportion of the women on AFDC into the labor market, their function is more symbolic, casting a moral shadow over single mothers with young children. Moreover, those who do enter the labor market are typically in traditional female jobs.

Much of Law's argument rests on the analysis of the WIN program to be discussed below, which indeed gave preference in job placement to male recipients and exempted their wives from the work requirement. Yet, the majority of WIN registrants and job entrants were women (U.S. Department of Labor, 1980). Furthermore, males on welfare did not fare well at all. Prior to the Family Support Act of 1988, only about half the states permitted unemployed fathers to receive AFDC, and when they did they were more likely to be forced into the labor market and into low-wage jobs without improving their financial situation. The unemployed parent provision of AFDC forced male heads off the rolls once they worked more than 100 hours per month, regardless of their level of earnings. Law, however, is correct in pointing to the moral and symbolic meaning of the work requirements for women on welfare. They do, as the poor laws have always done, reaffirm patriarchy and stigmatize and discriminate against the poor, male and female, although in different ways.

In fact, WIN II has had marginal impact on both the employability of AFDC recipients and the reduction of the welfare rolls. Although the budget grew to more than $300 million in 1974 and stayed so until 1981, when it began to decline, it was wholly inadequate to handle the number of new registrants as required by WIN II, which jumped to more than 1 million recipients. At its peak, the average funding per registrant was $250 (Nightingale & Burbridge, 1987). Although the job placement record improved by 30%, it still represented a very small fraction of those enrolled. Furthermore, the achievements of the program, as will be noted below, were affected by a process called "creaming," that is, selecting the most employable recipients for participation in program components.

A persistent characteristic of the program, from a policy perspective, was its minimal impact on AFDC recipients and expenditures. A report by the U.S. General Accounting Office (1982) notes that only 40% of AFDC recipients were required to register. This was essentially a "paper registration" that accompanied application for AFDC. Of those registered, only half were selected to take part in any program component, and these were generally selected because of their potential employability. The rest were placed in a "hold" category for lack of resources or jobs. Of those who participated in WIN, 25% became employed; of those employed, 70% claimed that they found the jobs on their own. Table 4.2 shows the "funneling" effect of WIN and its marginal impact on both its registrants and the AFDC population.

Furthermore, of those who had obtained employment, 40% left the welfare rolls altogether, 48% experienced some grant reduction, and 11% continued to receive the full grant. Thus under the best scenario WIN was able to remove less than 2% of the AFDC recipients from the rolls and reduced the grants by an additional 2%. Finally, of those attaining employment, 33% were paid less than the minimum wage. In a follow-up study of WIN participants, Schiller (1978) found a modest gain in earnings but very little in welfare grant savings. The most effective component of the program was subsidized employment, either private on-the-job training (OJT) or public service employment. Although less than 1% of the WIN participants were in OJT, 6.3% of the successful job entrants came from OJT (J. E. Gordon, 1978).

WIN II failed for roughly the same reasons as prior work programs. The political economy of the local WIN programs can be

Table 4.2
The Funneling Effect of WIN in 1980

		Percentage of AFDC Recipients	Percentage of WIN Registrants
Total AFDC recipients	4,100,000		
WIN registrants	1,600,000	39	
WIN participants	769,000	19	48
Enrolled in training	83,000	2	5
Obtained employment	204,474	5	13
found job on their own	143,132	3	9
found job through WIN	61,342	1	4

SOURCE: U.S. General Accounting Office (1982).

best described as volatile and unstable and riddled with contradictions, resulting in administrative solutions that greatly impeded their effectiveness. The funding allocation formula created incentives to cream because job retention rate, entry wage rate, and number of job entries together made up approximately 80% of the weight in the formula, compared with a 20% weight on reduction in welfare grants (Mitchell, Chadwin, & Nightingale, 1979, p. 23). Consequently, it was more advantageous to the local programs to focus on employable recipients. As in previous work programs, local WIN offices were plagued by the triple problem of uncontrollable local labor market conditions, multiple employment barriers facing AFDC recipients, and a demand for services that far outstripped resources. A comprehensive organizational study by Mitchell et al. (1979) found that one-third to one-half of the variance in the performance of local WIN programs was accounted for by socioeconomic factors in their external environment. More important, these factors had opposite effects on different organizational performance measures.[7]

Creaming, paper registration, and other decoupling devices were reinforced by the environments of the local offices. These offices were caught in the classical dilemma of "street-level bureaucracies" (Lipsky, 1980) of demand outstripping resources, thus requiring some sort of a rationing system. The rationing system was dictated

by the nationally set evaluation criteria that determined the allocation of resources to the local programs. These criteria revolved
around job placement and job retention, which, as noted, encouraged the local offices to focus their resources on the most employable recipients even though those who could have benefited most
from the program were the long-term recipients. Lack of resources
and the desire to score well on these evaluation criteria also reduced the incentive to sanction noncooperating clients. Indeed, paper registration to WIN during the welfare intake, whereby recipients were merely placed in an administrative hold category, was a
tactic used to comply with the policy of ensuring complete certification of all "able-bodied" recipients, but had little effect on the
actual delivery of services.

Within these economic and political constraints, the evolving
service delivery system was a function of the local administrative
leadership and choice of the service technology. As one would expect, the more attention given to the needs of the clients, the more
effective the program. This included providing clients with training
in systematic job-search activities, individualized assistance in job
placement, and supportive services beyond child care and including counseling, emergency transportation, family planning, and
household management. Providing these services required close coordination between the employment services and the social service
agencies. In short, to develop an effective service delivery system
required both economic and political incentives that were not typically found in WIN.

Organizationally, the WIN programs became only loosely coupled with the very policies that brought them into existence. As
long as the programs were able to develop structures that complied
with the institutional rules enunciated in the policies, they could
further decouple their actual operations—services to the recipients—from these structures.

EARNED INCOME TAX CREDIT

WIN II, by attempting to distinguish between able-bodied and
other poor, provided a symbolic reaffirmation of the moral inferior-
ity of unemployed poor married men and single mothers, and the

primacy of the work ethic; but it could not address the moral dilemma presented by the working poor. The persistence of poverty among working men and women challenges the basic ethical foundations of the capitalist market economy. It is difficult to blame them for their poverty status, or to take the position that they are undeserving. Yet, the working poor were among the main casualties of the defeat of FAP. This did not go unnoticed, even among conservative legislators. Senator Long proposed, as an alternative to FAP, a "work bonus" to low-wage workers, consisting of 10% of wages (up to $400 annually, with a phase-out starting at an income of $4,000 and a cutoff at $5,600). It was also rationalized as an offset to the social security payroll taxes paid by the working poor. While the Senate passed the work bonus legislation, it was not until 1975 that the earned income tax credit (EITC) became law as part of the Revenue Adjustment Act of 1975. Limited only to families with dependent children, EITC provided a refundable 10% tax credit up to $400 on earned income of $4,000 or less. The credit was phased out on higher earnings and eliminated when earned income reached $8,000. A family could qualify only if more than half of its income was earned.

Subsequent legislation made EITC permanent (1978) and indexed to the consumer price index (1986). In 1989, the tax credit was 14% for earned income up to $6,500, the maximum credit was $910, and the credit was phased out at a 10% rate for income exceeding $10,240. It was estimated that among those families eligible for EITC, about 35% had incomes below the poverty line. Yet, less than half of the poor families with children are eligible, mostly because either they lack any earned income or it does not constitute over half of their total income. Thus families that rely mostly on AFDC for their income are not eligible for EITC.[8] It is further estimated that EITC can lift about 5% of all poor families with dependent children above the poverty line (Gabe, 1989). For 1989, the total number of families receiving credit was projected to be more than 10 million, and the amount of credit was over $5 billion (U.S. Congress, 1989).

EITC thus represents one of the few income strategies to combat poverty, mirroring in concept the negative income tax scheme, but with one crucial difference—EITC preserves the historic distinction between the working poor and the welfare poor. AFDC recipients are excluded—to participate, one must have *earned* income. EITC is for those who work but do not earn enough. And the more one works, the higher the benefit. Consensus around EITC was achieved because institutionally it avoids much of the moral ambivalence about poverty, and behaviorally it has marginal impact on the labor market, especially on the supply of low-wage workers. Institutionally, it embraces highly acceptable symbols—that is, the deserving working poor who care for their dependent children. To receive the tax credit one must file a federal tax return, a symbol of an earned economic citizenship. Because the EITC does not apply to most welfare mothers—those who do not earn, those who are most stigmatized—it escapes much of the debate over the domestic code, and it is generally devoid of the gender and racial undertones that have beset much of the controversy on AFDC. Behaviorally, EITC has been viewed as providing incentives to work, especially at low earning levels and for part-time workers. Finally, it is relatively simple to administer.

Critics of EITC point to some obvious shortcomings. The benefit increases with earned income; it disregards family size; a married working couple might gain by dividing the household into separate units; and it adds an implicit tax rate of 14% to the tax rates from federal and state income taxes. When combined with other welfare benefits, the marginal tax rate may create a disincentive to work (Campbell & Pierce, 1980). Nonetheless, the symbolic attractiveness of EITC has generally shielded it from the ideological debate about welfare, and has led to its consideration as a strategy for welfare reform, both by President Carter and in recent congressional initiatives (see Chapter 6).

WELFARE REFORM THROUGH WORK INCENTIVES: CARTER'S BETTER JOBS AND INCOME

While Nixon tried to reform welfare through a guaranteed minimal income strategy, Carter adopted a work incentives strategy. His Program for Better Jobs and Income (PBJI), announced in the summer of 1977, was based on a complex combination of work incentives and regulations coupled with a public jobs program. The long shadow of the failure of FAP moved the framers of PBJI to redraw sharply the distinction between able-bodied and disabled poor, adopting an income assistance approach for the latter and a jobs program for the former (Storey, Harris, Levy, Fechter, & Michel, 1978). To accomplish both aims, PBJI had to resort to a complex mix of inducements and deterrents that proved, again, to be elusive and self-contradictory. Several constraints, some working in opposite directions, shaped the evolution of PBJI. First, there was considerable congressional opposition to any form of guaranteed annual income. Second, the leadership of the Senate Finance Committee, especially Senator Long, remained committed to the idea that welfare mothers should work. Third, Carter insisted on a zero-cost plan. Finally, within the Carter administration there were interdepartmental rivalries, especially between the Department of Health, Education and Welfare, which advocated an income policy, and the Department of Labor, which insisted on a jobs program (Lynn & Whitman, 1981).

PBJI developed a two-tier system differentiating between the poor who were not expected to work—such as the elderly, blind, disabled, and single parents with preschool children—and all other poor households in which one adult was expected to work. This distinction was reinforced by differential levels of benefits and taxation of additional income. As shown in Figure 4.1, a family of four not expected to work was to receive a basic benefit of $4,200. Any income beyond that level would be subject to a 50% tax until the total income reached $8,400, at which point the tax rate reached 100%. A family of four that was expected to work was to receive a basic benefit of only $2,300. It was entitled to keep all its earned income until its total income reached $3,800. Thereafter, additional earned income was subject to a 50% tax until total income reached $8,400. In this scheme, refusal to accept a job without good cause would prompt a sizable reduction in the level of benefits (i.e., $1,900).

To make sure that able-bodied recipients worked, the proposal included a program of job-search and subsidized public employment and training opportunities, and an expanded earned income tax credit. If recipients could not find jobs in the private sector, the public service employment and training program was to provide up to 1.4 million job and training slots. Only if private and public jobs were not available after an eight-week search was the family able to move to the higher benefit schedule.

PBJI was debated in the 95th Congress, but neither the House nor the Senate approved any of it. The Carter administration returned

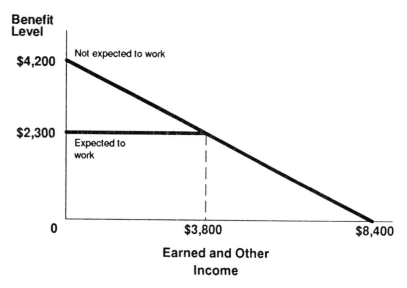

Figure 4.1. PBJI Benefit Schedule for a Family of Four

to the 96th Congress with a much more modest proposal, but it too failed to pass.

Like its predecessors, PBJI was caught in a tangle of moral, political, and economic countervailing forces that prevented its enactment. The framers of PBJI took the high ground by claiming that the program was profamily and prowork. In a symbolic sense, this was indeed the case. PBJI reinforced the domestic code of a two-parent family in which the husband was expected to work (Lynn & Whitman, 1981). The male breadwinner would have been the main beneficiary of the public jobs and training program, since only single parents with children over the age of 14 were required to participate in the jobs program, while single parents with children ages 7–13 were expected to work part-time during school hours. Thus PBJI echoed the differential status of men and women in the labor market. The domestic code and the work ethic were further reaffirmed through the differential work incentives. The cumulative marginal tax rates for single-parent families not expected to work remained high for all income classes, ranging between 66% and 72%. In contrast, for four-person families with a member expected to work, the tax rate would have been nonexistent up to $3,800 and then reached a high of about 53% (Hoagland & Korbel, 1978).

The boundaries set between able-bodied poor and disabled poor proved too ambiguous and permeable. Although there was general consensus that the aged, blind, and disabled should be assigned to the higher tier and male heads of poor households to the lower, no consensus existed about the place of female heads of poor households (Friedman & Hausman, 1977). The debate on whether poor women should be expected to work or to stay home was resolved by establishing three categories of women—those with children over the age of 14, who were expected to work full-time; those with school-age children, who were expected to work part-time; and those with children under the age of 7, who were expected to stay home. In defining these categories, the Carter administration acknowledged the changing role of women in the economy, but nonetheless maintained the patriarchal domestic code and confirmed women's inferior position in the labor market.

The distinctions made between able-bodied and disabled poor and between male and female heads of poor households only highlighted the program's moral ambiguity. Those who viewed welfare as morally corrupting saw the income assistance as a threat to the work ethic, while those who viewed welfare as a right viewed the jobs program as coercive and exploitative. Senator Long, for example, commented at a hearing on PBJI, "It just seems to me . . . that we have no business paying any citizen to sit there and do nothing, just to sit there and vegetate" (U.S. Congress, 1978, p. 170). In contrast, Congressman Hawkins was concerned that the required jobs program would be used to keep low-paying, dead-end, meaningless jobs in the private economy for both men and women. Moreover, the complex incentive system directed at maintaining these distinctions could not escape the notch problem, thus encouraging a two-parent family to split because each adult would be better off alone and not working (Friedman & Hausman, 1977, pp. 63–64). In addition, it was argued that lowering the benefit level for those expected to work might result in individuals not committed to work actually attempting to reclassify themselves as disabled in order to obtain the higher benefit level. In this context, the success of PBJI depended heavily on the effective administration of a work test. Yet, as we have seen, much of the history of welfare reform is marked by failure to administer such a test.

As in other welfare reform proposals based on work, PBJI was caught in the contradiction between providing jobs for the poor and preserving the low-wage private economy. Conservatives objected to substantial government intrusion into the labor market through the creation of public jobs, fearing that it would drive out small businesses depending on low-wage workers. Liberals felt that the government had a responsibility to guarantee employment and that the Carter administration greatly underestimated the demand for public jobs. In addition, the labor unions objected to the income supplementation of low-wage work, fearing that it would serve as a subsidy to low-wage industries. Both camps acknowledged that, with the exception of the Depression, the government had little experience in mounting a massive public jobs and training program.

Regional differences in labor market conditions and welfare generosity and the issue of state autonomy also surfaced to affect support for PBJI. Southern states clearly saw in PBJI a threat to their racist economic and social institutions, including their low-wage industries. As was the case with FAP, 36% of all nonwhite families would have gained from the program, compared with only 14% of all white families. In addition, 35% of all families removed from poverty by PBJI would have resided in the South (Hoagland & Korbel, 1978). On the other hand, northern states, burdened with high welfare expenditures, were disappointed by the low level of relief offered to them by PBJI. The states were generally lukewarm about the federalization of welfare because the expected benefits did not make it worthwhile for them to give up their autonomy in controlling their own poor.

Finally, although the Carter administration projected a small increase in the costs of the welfare reform, the Congressional Budget Office estimated that PBJI would add 3.5 million families to the welfare rolls and would increase the costs of welfare by $14 billion (Hoagland & Korbel, 1978).

CONCLUSION

Every president since Truman—Eisenhower, Kennedy, Johnson, Nixon, Ford, Carter, Reagan—has tried his hand at welfare reform.[9] What conclusions can be drawn from this steady stream of political activity? One consistent theme, true to our basic liberal, capitalist orientation, is that poverty is an individual responsibility. Thus, from the brief experiment with rehabilitation through social services (Eisenhower and Kennedy) to the concentration on the various work strategies, the focus has been on reforming the individual rather than on addressing the structural conditions of poverty.

After the quick rejection of social services as a strategy, the country returned to basics—how to get the welfare poor to work. Three strategies have been noted—regulation, incentives, and the attempt to enact a guaranteed income. In some ways, the failed attempt to enact the Family Assistance Plan is the most illuminating. Those debates and subsequent policy changes reaffirmed the traditional symbolic and regulatory approaches to welfare. The Family Assistance Plan was a radical initiative in that it sought to remove the distinction between the working poor and the welfare poor, a distinction that has been steadfastly maintained ever since the organized relief of the poor began. The very purpose of the poorhouses was to segregate and stigmatize the welfare poor; the means test, pauper labor, the very structure and administration of welfare all serve the same purpose. Through symbols as well as regulation, labor discipline is maintained by segregation, by creating the "other" as deviant. FAP would have changed all that; vast numbers of the poor would have received both welfare benefits and earnings.

A similar objection could be made more generally to the incentives strategy, whereby the system encourages welfare recipients to work by allowing them to retain a portion of their earned income. Prior to 1967, this was not allowed; there was a clear separation between work and welfare. But this approach—in effect, a 100% tax rate—created strong disincentives to leave welfare. As is true of so much of welfare policy, a compromise was reached; welfare recipients could retain some earned income. As we shall see in the next chapter, a conservative Reagan administration cut back the incentive strategy on the traditional grounds of separating work and welfare.

The difference between FAP and the welfare incentive strategy was that FAP was sold differently. Welfare incentives were embedded in major regulatory changes (WIN I, II) that emphasized both the welfare poor and stiff work tests. FAP emphasized major support for the working poor as well. Its political rhetoric and symbols were different, which aroused strong opposition among conservatives; they were not about to see millions of working people merged with the welfare poor under the guise of "welfare reform."

The importance of the separation is illustrated by two subsequent policy initiatives. The earned income tax credit, which has been growing steadily (and is about to be expanded significantly) does two things: It provides wage supplementation to the working poor, but it specifically excludes the welfare poor. In terms of utilitarian economics, this makes no sense. Why should an AFDC mother who is working part-time not also be supplemented and encouraged to increase her work effort? The answer is that, symbolically, the welfare poor must be segregated from the working poor and stigmatized. EITC draws its political strength, in part, because it is not associated with welfare.

The other interesting initiative was Carter's ill-fated Program for Better Jobs and Income, whereby the able-bodied welfare poor were to be separated from the disabled poor and the former were to be given only half the welfare benefit. This was a partial return to the work requirements that were used before the 1960s. Recall that under traditional welfare, there are two types of work requirements. For the able-bodied applicant, the denial of assistance forces the applicant back into the labor market. By closing the door, welfare imposes the market work requirement. For those admitted to the program, welfare will also impose a regulatory or administrative work requirement. PBJI split the difference—by declaring certain categories of the welfare population "able-bodied," the plan would have forced them into the labor market by giving them only half of the benefits. Since AFDC benefits, on average, are considerably below the poverty line, Carter's grants for the able-bodied would have been below subsistence. This was the reason a liberal administration had to have a program of public jobs as a last resort; otherwise, families would have starved.

Carter's plan failed, but we will demonstrate in the next two chapters that the basic idea of legislatively declaring certain categories of the welfare poor to be able-bodied is taking hold, in the form of lowering the age of children at which their mothers are declared to be in the work force. Moreover, liberals are joining conservatives in this approach.

In any event, the main story through the period from Eisenhower to Reagan is the increasing stringency of the regulatory work test. For the reasons spelled out—the rising rolls and costs, the changing composition of the rolls, race, gender, and sexual morality—the work test evolved from a somewhat benign early WIN program to the harsh WIN II. WIN II not only imposed sanctions on women, but, significantly, cut down services and training. The able-bodied welfare poor were to be forced into low-status work. In fact, of course, not much happened. But welfare is largely myth and ceremony, and the harsh symbols of segregation and stigma reemerged. Nixon even tried to sell FAP on the basis that it would stiffen the work requirements.

Throughout this period, race, as always, figured prominently in the policy debates. There is little doubt that a major part of the "crisis" of welfare was due to the changing racial composition of the recipients. As pointed out, the debates in Congress frequently and openly were cast in racist overtones. As we shall show in the next two chapters, with rising racial tensions in the country, race continues to play an important role in welfare policy.

Gender issues for the welfare poor both changed and remained the same. The big change occurred in the domestic code. With the dramatic entry of women, including mothers of small children, into the paid labor force, women were now expected to earn income. Poor women, of course, always had to work, and there were always work tests for mothers on welfare. But now, the rhetorical *justification* for requiring welfare mothers to work had changed. Even the liberals joined the chorus. After all, if nonwelfare mothers were working (in the paid labor force), why should welfare mothers be treated differently? The problem, however, is that welfare mothers have an even more difficult time making a satisfactory transition to the paid labor force than women in general. In addition to the problems of gender discrimination, they are poorer, have fewer skills, are disproportionately minority, have more disabilities, and so forth. The symbols of the work programs now demand that these mothers enter the paid labor force, but the programs are designed so that only a few will do so. The great bulk of welfare mothers will remain on welfare; they will be considered failures and deviants, affirming the value of those who succeed. The symbols of the mothers' pensions have been turned on their heads. In that day, poor mothers who had to work affirmed the values of the patriarchal domestic code. Now, the poor mother on welfare who cannot work will be considered the "other."

As welfare continued its journey in "crisis," labor discipline and race and gender discrimination were affirmed and hardened through the segregation and stigmatization of the welfare poor in the next, most conservative administration.

NOTES

1. The 1962 amendments did not add that much substantively to the 1956 amendments. More was done about training and financial incentives to the states (Steiner, 1966, chap. 2).

2. The average weekly earnings in constant dollars for production workers in manufacturing declined from $187 in 1970 to $171 in 1986; for construction workers they declined from $304 to $262; for retail trade workers, from $128 to $99; and for service workers they changed slightly, from $151 to $149 (U.S. Bureau of the Census, 1989, p. 392).

3. There were several precursors to WIN. In 1961, Congress approved extension of AFDC to two-parent families, authorizing federal matching grants to families in which the fathers were either out of work or employed for fewer than 100 hours per month. States had to provide for work registration and periodic reregistration of the unemployed parents and for maximum utilization of job placement services. In fact, states were required to deny aid to a child if the unemployed parent refused to accept employment without good cause. Fear of rising AFDC-UP cases and of condoning relief to able-bodied fathers brought about an amendment to the Social Security Act in 1962 that permitted expenditures for AFDC-UP to be made up in the form of payments for work. The Community Work and Training (CWT) programs, however, were mostly symbolic. Funds allocated to the program were very meager and their use was quite restricted. Only 13 states opted for such programs. CWT was folded into Title V of the Economic Opportunity Act of 1964—the Work Experience and Training Program. Being locally administered, the program quickly turned into low-wage jobs in the public sector. Thus most of the costs per enrollee went for relief. The jobs, as expected, were for unskilled labor, and few meaningful training or educational opportunities were provided. Attrition rates were high, with 75% leaving without completing their assignments, and with half of the trainees who left the program continuing on public assistance. Thus the program seemed to contribute little to economic self-sufficiency (Levitan & Mangum, 1969).

4. Recent reanalysis of the data by Cain and Wissoker (1990), using somewhat different assumptions, including excluding childless couples, raises serious questions about the validity of the original findings. These authors found that for the sample as a whole, when adjusting for attrition, pure NIT increased marital breakups by only 7%, which was not statistically significant. For African-Americans, however, the rate increased by 21% (still not statistically significant), while for Hispanics it declined by 25%. It was only the *combination* of NIT with a program offering training, education, and job counseling that had a sizable destabilizing effect on marital stability. For the sample as a whole, the rate of marital breakup increased by 38%, for blacks by 77%, and for Hispanics by 8%.

5. Adding the value of food stamps, the family's income would reach $2,460.

6. Martin Anderson, aide to Arthur Burns, who was counselor to the president, attacked FAP by evoking the image of the Speenhamland system of 1795. Under that system the justices of Berkshire devised a scale to subsidize the wages of the poor if family income was below the price of a loaf of bread (i.e., a guaranteed minimal income, such as proposed by FAP). Anderson quoted the historian Polanyi, who argued that despite its best intentions, the system eroded incentive to work, thus further pauperizing the poor. Polanyi concluded that "neither the rulers nor the ruled ever forgot the lessons of that fool's paradise" (quoted in Burke & Burke, 1974, p. 71).

7. For example, the job entry wage is positively correlated with population density, unemployment rate, proportion employed in low-wage industries, and proportion of WIN registrants who were male. Some of the same variables are negatively correlated with welfare grant reduction.

8. Under the Omnibus Budget Reconciliation Act of 1981, EITC, whether actually received or not, was counted as income in calculating AFDC benefits. This was repealed in 1984.

9. EITC was enacted during the Ford administration.

5

Welfare-Work Programs:
The New Poorhouse?

THE OMNIBUS BUDGET
RECONCILIATION ACT OF 1981

The election of Ronald Reagan as president and the passage of the 1981 Omnibus Budget Reconciliation Act (OBRA) signaled a further shift in public policy toward welfare and work. Ideologically, this shift was driven by several principles: (a) Welfare should be granted only to the "truly needy," (b) a strict work-test requirement should be enforced, and (c) responsibility for welfare should be shifted from the federal government to state and local governments and private institutions (Anderson, 1978).

Instituting a strict work requirement was expected to weed out those who were capable of taking care of themselves, and shifting the responsibility to the local governments was aimed at reducing the fiscal obligation of the federal government. In addition, the delegation of federal responsibility for work programs to the states was intended to accomplish several objectives. First, the moral controversies over work and welfare, and the potential political liabilities—always a danger in welfare—would be shifted from the national spotlight to the local level. Second, by decentralizing the moral debate to the local level, the federal government encouraged much greater ideological pluralism regarding welfare and work, and, in so doing, made it much more difficult to sustain any national coalition on behalf of the poor. Such a coalition had been viewed as a major force in promoting large expenditures for welfare (Butler, 1985). In a decentralized system, the protection of the rights of the poor becomes immensely difficult if for no other reason than the variety of state laws and the uneven distribution and resources of liberal advocacy groups (Houseman, 1990). Third, with some of the burden shifted to the local community, the reduced tax base would make it harder to provide generous programs for the poor (Peterson, 1984). Thus local communities would have a greater incentive to mandate recipients to work for their relief as a way of deterring applications and reducing costs.

In introducing the Reagan administration's proposed changes to AFDC, Secretary of Health and Human Services Richard Schweiker argued:

> The American public is not willing to bear the burden of supporting people who can work. We believe that everyone receiving assistance who is capable of working should be involved in the work program. . . . To this end . . . we would require States to establish community work experience programs. . . . This work would be performed in return for AFDC benefits. (U.S. Congress, 1981, p. 7)

As usual, the proposed work requirement was also justified by the other set of symbols, namely, that it would be for the benefit of the poor. It would increase employability through actual work experience and training, encourage identification with the labor market, provide work history, and develop the discipline necessary for accepting employment.[1]

While Congress rejected the proposed work requirements, it permitted states to adopt several options. These included (a) establishing a single agency to operate the WIN program (WIN Demonstration), (b) requiring AFDC recipients to participate in a community work experience program (CWEP) as a condition of their eligibility, (c) requiring recipients to participate in job-search activities, and (d) establishing grant diversion programs under which a portion of the AFDC grant could be used to subsidize on-the-job training (Nightingale & Burbridge, 1987). The federal government continued to provide 90% of WIN funding up to a fixed amount for each state. The other options received AFDC administrative funds for which the federal share was 50%, with the total amount unlimited.

To some extent the federal strategy succeeded. WIN funding declined by 70% from 1981 to 1987 (U.S. General Accounting Office, 1987), forcing many states to replace lost federal funding with state funding and to develop the new program options. The attraction of these options, on the one hand, was the lack of a cap on the AFDC administrative funds, but they required, on the other hand, greater commitment of state matching funds. States did take advantage of the new options available to them: 26 states opted for the WIN Demo, 27 states had CWEP programs, 17 states had some type of AFDC grant diversion program, and 22 states had job-search programs (Nightingale & Burbridge, 1987, p. 49). For fiscal year 1985, the budget outlay for WIN was $278.8 million, of which $162.4 million was used for WIN Demonstration and CWEP. As noted in Table 5.1, AFDC administrative funds and other special federal funds added approximately $33 million to the new initiative, and the states themselves contributed $67.2 million, or approximately 25% of all funds. If one adds the remaining regular WIN funds (approximately $116 million), the total approximates the level of funding of WIN in 1981. That is, the combination of increased state funding and use of AFDC administrative funds has restored most of the WIN budgetary cuts to their 1981 level.

By shifting the responsibility to the states, the federal government succeeded in making AFDC work programs a local political issue (Nightingale & Burbridge, 1987, p. 28). States had to scramble to cope with the reduction in federal funding while trying to take advantage of the new options. More important, the devolution of federal responsibility shifted the moral debate to the states, because it created both a fiscal constraint (i.e., reduced funding) and a programmatic opportunity (i.e., increased autonomy). In doing so it attracted and mobilized interest groups, including politicians, both liberals and conservatives, who saw an opportunity to advance their welfare ideologies; business enterprises, who saw an opportunity to obtain a better-trained low-wage work force; and labor unions concerned about competition from work programs.

As anticipated by the federal government, a significant number of states did implement CWEP programs requiring AFDC recipients to work for their assistance. Clearly, economic and political considerations at the state level influenced the emphases and choices. There is evidence to indicate that states experiencing economic growth and low unemployment (mostly northeastern states) tended to develop more extensive programs emphasizing job placement, training, and supportive services while deemphasizing work-for-relief. Several such state initiatives received national attention for their programmatic innovation, such as Employment and Training Choices (ET) in Massachusetts and Greater Avenues for Independence (GAIN) in California. In contrast, some economically depressed and rural states tended to emphasize the work-for-relief option (Nightingale & Burbridge, 1987). Yet, despite the considerable increase in state initiatives, funding, and program reorganizations, the cumulative results point, with few exceptions, to modest changes and accomplishments. As was the experience with previous work initiatives, the gap between intentions and reality remained wide and, once again, the role of myths and ceremonies dominated.

The scope and impact of the AFDC work programs initiated by the Reagan administration generally built upon the WIN program. According to a study by the U.S. General Accounting Office (1987), approximately 22% (714,448) of all AFDC recipients participate in these programs nationwide, with great variations by states (ranging from 2.8% to 62%). Of the participants, 89% were enrolled in WIN Demo, 4% in CWEP, 7% in job search, and less than 1% in grant diversion. Participation, however, does not mean receiving services. Rough estimates would suggest that 70% of the participants received some services. Of those receiving services in WIN Demo, 72% participated in either individual or group job-search counseling. Only 12.5% received some form of training, and 11.7% direct placement assistance. The emphasis on job search is probably due to the its lower costs. Indeed, the median expenditure per participant in WIN Demo was $309. In contrast, on-the-job training costs more than $2,700 per participant. Determining the impact of these programs is very difficult for lack of any systematic data. Based on several experiments conducted by the Manpower Demonstration Research Corporation, discussed in the next section, it seems that such programs increase the employability of the participants by 5% to 7% over the control groups. The U.S. General Accounting Office (1987) survey indicates that most of the jobs were in entry-level low-wage occupations with a median wage of $4.14, and that over 48% of the participants who obtained jobs remained on welfare (pp. 104–105).

Overall, then, these findings do not vary appreciably from the record of WIN, although a few individual states might have achieved better results. This is not surprising in light of the fact that at the policy level the changes, although symbolically significant, were actually accompanied by a severe reduction in fiscal resources. As noted above, the initiatives by the states were aimed primarily at restoring the budget cuts in WIN. It is unclear to what extent the states will be able to continue to do so in the face of continued decline in federal allocations and the uncertain economic picture in many states. Most states have not been able to maintain pre-1981 staffing levels for work programs. It is still apparent that the states rely heavily on federal funds, and especially WIN. Furthermore, 94% of all funding is allocated to WIN Demo, which, at best, represented a modest programmatic innovation. At the local level, only in isolated instances did the political economy of AFDC work programs change in any significant way. Only six states— Delaware, Maine, Massachusetts, New York, Virginia, and California—maintained or improved the allocation of resources to the program (Nightingale & Burbridge, 1987). In most communities the demand for services continued to outstrip the supply of resources dramatically. Local economic conditions, especially labor market characteristics, continued to have a major impact on the nature and outcome of the program. To quote the U.S. General Accounting Office (1987) study:

> Strong economies such as those in Massachusetts and San Diego offer very different opportunities to work program participants than do those of Pontiac, Michigan, where the decline of the auto industry has forced men and women who had well paying jobs onto welfare, and Beaufort County, South Carolina, where seasonal resort jobs that are geographically inaccessible to many welfare recipients are among the few sources of employment. (p. 111)

Administratively, states experimented with different organizational structures to improve the coordination of services between the welfare agency and the employment services, especially the agencies administering Job Training Partnership Act (JTPA) programs.[2] Burbridge and Nightingale (1989) found various models of coordination, but they caution that improved coordination was attained only when the local economy was strong. In some states, greater attention was paid to participants' needs for other services, such as child care and transportation assistance. However, these organizational arrangements do not necessarily offer a solution to the unavailability of services. JTPA programs, for example, served only about 10% of all welfare recipients over the age of 13, and most of the work programs depended on external funding sources such as Title XX to pay for child care.[3] Finally, the service modalities of most of these work programs did not change; job search has remained the most prevalent mode of activity.

OBRA also presented a significant reduction in the work incentives for welfare recipients. Returning to the first principle, the notion that AFDC recipients could receive welfare and work was anathema to the Reagan administration, which sought to distinguish sharply between able-bodied and disabled poor and to reduce the welfare rolls. The act set a lower income ceiling (150% of the state's standard of need) above which eligibility was lost and eliminated the "$30 and one-third" income disregard in lieu of work expense after 4 months of earning (changed to 12 months in 1984). It also eliminated the latitude the states had in determining work expenses by permitting deduction of the first $75 of a full-time worker's earnings and up to $160 per month for child care. In contrast to the work programs, these strategies appeared to meet the administration's goals. It is estimated that while 5% of the total AFDC caseload lost eligibility, 35% of those who worked lost eligibility, and the tax on earnings for those working over 4 months was effectively raised to 78% (Moffitt & Wolf, 1987).

A study by the U.S. General Accounting Office (1985) in five localities found a substantial loss in income among those terminated and those whose AFDC grants were reduced. However, contrary to the liberals' predictions, the reduction in work expenses did not result in a return to welfare. The rate of return of closed cases to AFDC after one year ranged from 7% to 18%, well below pre-OBRA, in three out of the five sites. Those terminated from the rolls coped with the loss of AFDC through increased earnings—not by changing jobs or increasing hours of work, but rather by receiving a higher hourly wage. The reasons are unclear and may range from poor recall by the respondents to employers compensating for the loss of AFDC. This pattern, however, occurred only in high-benefit sites, where the job picture was brighter. Local conditions such as the generosity of the assistance, the behavior of local officials, and the labor market characteristics seem to mediate the impact of the harsher regulations. For those on AFDC and working, the reduction in the work incentives apparently did not reduce their work effort. Most of those who lost their assistance simply managed somehow to live with a substantially reduced income, and yet have not changed their work behavior in either direction.[4] In any event, OBRA did achieve a reduction of approximately 9% in AFDC expenditures. In 1984 Congress liberalized the treatment of earned income by AFDC recipients by raising the income ceiling to 180% of the state's standard of need, by extending the $30 income disregard for an additional eight months, and by allowing the $75 work expenses deduction to part-time workers as well.

Despite the various changes in the work incentives, Burtless (1989) concludes that there is no evidence that they appreciably affected the work behavior of single mothers. Welfare recipients, caught in their struggle for daily survival, are much less likely to understand or appreciate the intent of such policies, and they simply cope as best they can with administrative decisions imposed on them, without significantly altering their normal behavior. This should come as no surprise. Goodwin (1972; 1983) has shown convincingly that welfare recipients identify as strongly with the work ethic as nonrecipients; however, they have less self-confidence in finding jobs because of failure in the world of work, and thus find welfare more acceptable. Hence those who do work will generally continue to do so, and those who can find ways to get off welfare will do so irrespective of the work incentives. The only obvious way to push welfare recipients into the labor market is to reduce their basic grants.

DEMONSTRATIONS OF
ALTERNATIVE WORK PROGRAMS

The emerging ideological consensus on the role of women in the paid labor force focused attention on the social effectiveness and efficiency of various work programs. Liberals and conservatives alike searched for a design of work programs that could be justified and legitimated on social utilitarian grounds. In a capitalist society, symbols gain legitimacy when they can be justified on the basis of a social utilitarian calculus. Such a calculus defines the success or failure of a work program on the basis of a benefit-cost analysis from the perspective of the participants, the taxpayers, and society at large. *Benefits* are defined as outputs produced by the participants in the program and postprogram earnings, reduced dependence on welfare programs, and reduced use of alternative training and employment services. *Costs* are defined as program operating costs, administrative costs, participant labor costs (i.e., in-program earnings, forgone earnings), and increased work-related costs (Kemper, Long, & Thornton, 1981).

It is important to emphasize that benefits and costs that cannot readily be assigned a monetary value are not included. As a result, there are many important social and psychological consequences of such programs that are ignored. From a political economy perspective they omit, for example, the impact of these programs on displacing other low-wage workers, their consequences on the wage structure in low-wage industries, and their effect on maintaining gender-segregated industries and occupations (since most of the participants are women). They also fail to consider the extent to which such programs serve as a deterrent (i.e., as a work test) to applying for welfare as well as the intangible benefits and costs for those who have to administer such programs. From a social psychological perspective, the cost-benefit analysis ignores the impact of such programs on the social and psychological well-being of the participants and their families, including, for example, positive or negative self-image in working in low-wage jobs, coping with job insecurity associated with low-wage jobs, impact on physical and mental health, and the trade-off between working and caring for one's dependents.

The point is not to enumerate all of the possible benefits and costs that are left out, but rather to sharpen and highlight the normative context of such an analysis. The issue is not merely technical, but rather ideological and political, because the dominant explanation of the "welfare mess" frames and constrains the discussion and debate on work programs to a narrow social utilitarian perspective. Such a choice is consistent with the need to affirm the legitimacy of "successful" programs by showing their adherence to and reinforcement of the dominant institutional norms about welfare and work, namely, that they sustain the economic order.

Even from a social utilitarian perspective, the policy implications from the different work program experiments and demonstrations are invariably ambiguous for two reasons. First, because the results are sensitive to contextual variations, generalizations become exceedingly difficult. These variables include changing national and local economic conditions, the composition of the populations participating in the programs, changes in national and local welfare policies, the scope of each program, and the administrative capacity of the welfare agency. Second, the program that may be the most cost-effective for participants may not be so for taxpayers, and vice versa, while one that is cost-effective for both may produce only marginal benefits.

Under the Reagan administration, there were two sets of work programs—WIN and the OBRA experiments. In a review of a series of evaluation studies of various work programs, Grossman and Mirsky (1985) conclude that "they have increased the employment and earnings of AFDC recipients, but that they have had little effect on hourly wages, and quite modest effects on welfare receipt" (p. 17). They note that welfare recipients who have had little or no work experience benefited substantially more from the programs than those with some recent work experience. Moreover, for welfare recipients with no work experience, public service employment, CETA, and on-the-job training provided the greatest improvement in earnings, ranging from $1,201 to $2,793, compared with $495 in job placement. Nonetheless, despite these generally positive results, the Reagan administration essentially eliminated or reduced substantially the funding for these programs, mostly because public employment for welfare recipients is not generally compatible with the symbols of a capitalist market economy. Furthermore, as we shall note below, many of these programs did not provide significant savings in welfare expenditures in the short run, making it difficult for policymakers to justify their continuation. Thus even social utilitarianism has its limits within the current structure of our economic and political institutions.

The 1981 Omnibus Budget Reconciliation Act also provided the opportunity to design a rigorous set of experiments in several types of work programs for AFDC recipients in eight states. The evaluation of these programs, using experimental and control groups, has been conducted by Manpower Demonstration Research Corporation. The programs range from a mandatory community work experience program in West Virginia to a voluntary on-the-job training program in New Jersey. The results of the evaluation of these programs in seven areas are summarized in Table 5.1. Gueron (1990) notes that the programs did lead to consistent and measurable increases in employment and earnings, and also led to some welfare savings. Women who were first-time applicants and with recent work history did not gain from the programs, while women with no work experience showed significant gains. Yet, long-term welfare recipients with no recent employment did not show consistent gains.

It is instructive to examine the variations in some of the programs in greater detail. West Virginia, having one of the highest unemployment rates in the nation, established a straight work-for-relief program whereby recipients of AFDC-UP and AFDC WIN were required to work in unpaid jobs (CWEP) as long as they were on the rolls. The results indicate that participation by the AFDC recipients assigned to the experiment who worked in CWEP reached 33%, compared with 70% of all AFDC-UP registrants. The CWEP assignments were often lengthy, but participation was neither full-time nor continuous, mostly because of adjustments to child-care needs. CWEP had no short-term impact (and was not expected to) on the employability or earnings of the AFDC women and men, and only a small reduction in welfare receipt was evident at the end of the 21-month follow-up period. Few participants acquired new skills. CWEP cost the government more than it saved, unless one included the value of the services provided by participants while in CWEP. When the value of the services is included, the net benefit to the government was $734 per recipient. Most participants felt that the work-for-relief was fair, but that the work-site sponsor had the better end of the bargain. Thus the experiment pointed out, once again, that it is possible to set the poor to work, particularly poor men, under certain conditions. These include (a) an economic and political climate, such as that existing in West Virginia, characterized by high unemployment and a very depressed economy, a demand for subsidized labor, an acquiescent target population, availability of special demonstration funding, and a welfare agency with an administrative capacity to manage such a program (Friedlander, Erickson, Hamilton, & Knox, 1986, p.

Table 5.1.

Summary of the Impacts on AFDC Eligibles of Welfare Employment Programs in Seven Areas

Location, Outcome, and Follow-up Period	Experimental Group Mean	Control Group Mean	Difference	Percentage Change
Arkansas				
average earnings($)				
year 1	674	507	167[d]	33
year 2	1,180	957	223	23
year 3	1,422	1,085	337[d]	31
employed at end of(%)				
year 1	20.4	16.7	3.7[c]	22
year 2	23.9	20.3	3.6	18
year 3	24.5	18.3	6.2[e]	34
average AFDC payments($)				
year 1	998	1,143	−145[e]	−13
year 2	793	982	−190[e]	−19
year 3	742	910	−168[e]	−18
on welfare at end of(%)				
year 1	51.0	59.1	−8.1[e]	−14
year 2	38.1	46.0	−7.9[e]	−17
year 3	32.8	40.1	−7.3[e]	−18
Baltimore				
average earnings($)				
year 1	1,612	1,472	140	10
year 2	2,787	2,386	401[e]	17
year 3	3,499	2,989	511[e]	17
employed at end of(%)				
year 1	34.7	31.2	3.5[d]	11
year 2	39.5	37.1	2.4	6
year 3	40.7	40.3	0.4	1
average AFDC payments($)				
year 1	2,520	2,517	2	0
year 2	2,058	2,092	−34	−2
year 3	1,783	1,815	−31	−2
on welfare at end of(%)				
year 1	72.0	73.3	−1.4	−2
year 2	58.7	59.0	−0.3	−1
year 3	48.2	48.4	−0.2	0
Cook County				
average earnings($)				
year 1	1,227	1,217	10	1
employed at end of(%)				
year 1	22.6	21.3	1.3	6
average AFDC payments($)				
year 1	3,105	3,145	−40	−1

Table 5.1. (cont'd)

Location, Outcome, and Follow-up Period	Experimental Group Mean	Control Group Mean	Difference	Percentage Change
Cook County (cont'd)				
on welfare at end of(%)				
year 1	78.9	80.8	−1.9[d]	−2
San Diego I				
average earnings($)				
year 1	2,379	1,937	443[e]	23
employed at end of(%)				
year 1	42.4	36.9	5.5[e]	15
average AFDC payments($)				
year 1	2,524	2,750	−226[e]	−8
on welfare at end of(%)				
year 1	45.8	47.9	−2.0	−4
San Diego Saturation				
average earnings($)				
year 1	2,029	1,677	352[e]	21
year 2	2,902	2,246	658[e]	29
employed at end of(%)				
year 1	34.7	26.9	7.7[e]	29
year 2	34.7	29.3	5.4[e]	29
average AFDC payments($)				
year 1	4,424	4,830	−407[e]	−8
year 2	3,408	3,961	−553[e]	−14
on welfare at end of(%)				
year 1	66.0	72.4	−6.4[e]	−9
year 2	51.3	58.7	−7.4[e]	−13
Virginia				
average earnings($)				
year 1	1,352	1,282	−69	5
year 2	2,268	1,988	280[d]	14
year 3[a]	2,624	2,356	268[c]	11
employed at end of(%)				
year 1	34.7	31.0	3.8[d]	12
year 2	39.3	33.3	6.0[e]	18
year 3[b]	38.7	34.1	4.6[e]	13
average AFDC payments($)				
year 1	1,961	2,029	−69	−3
year 2	1,480	1,516	−36	−2
year 3[a]	1,184	1,295	−111[d]	−9
on welfare at end of(%)				
year 1	59.8	59.4	0.4	1
year 2	44.0	44.9	−0.9	−2
year 3[b]	36.6	39.3	−2.6	−7

Table 5.1. (cont'd)

Location, Outcome, and Follow-up Period	Experimental Group Mean	Control Group Mean	Difference	Percentage Change
West Virginia				
average earnings($)				
year 1	451	435	16	4
employed at end of(%)				
year 1	12.0	13.1	−1.0	−8
average AFDC payments($)				
year 1	1,692	1,692	0	0
on welfare at end of(%)				
year 1	70.9	72.5	−1.5	−2

NOTE: These data include zero values for sample members not employed and for sample members not receiving welfare. Estimates are regression adjusted using ordinary least squares, controlling for preenrollment characteristics of sample members. There may be some discrepancies in experimental-control differences because of rounding. In all programs except the San Diego Saturation program, year 1 begins with the quarter of random assignment. As a result, "average earnings" in year 1 may include up to two months of earnings prior to random assignment. In the San Diego Saturation program, year 1 begins with the quarter following the quarter of random assignment. "Employed" or "on welfare" at the end of the year is defined as receiving earnings or welfare payments at some point during the last quarter of the year. Earnings and AFDC payments are not adjusted for inflation.
a. Annualized earnings and welfare payments are caluated from six and nine months of data, respectively.
b. Percentage employed and on welfare at the end of 2½ and 2¾ years, respectively.
c. Denotes statistical significance at the 10% level.
d. Denotes statistical significance at the 5% level.
e. Denotes statistical significance at the 1% level.
SOURCE: Gueron (1990). Reprinted by permission.

xxiii); and (b) a willingness by policymakers to suppress moral ambiguity by abandoning the hope of reducing the welfare rolls, achieving significant savings in welfare expenditures, or claiming to improve the employability of the poor.

The San Diego experiment is of special significance because its has influenced the formulation of the AFDC work legislation in California known as Greater Avenues for Independence, or GAIN, considered to be a model for the Family Support Act. San Diego experimented with two program approaches: (a) job search and (b) job search followed by work experience (Goldman, Friedlander, Gueron, & Long, 1985). The first approach included one-day job placement followed by a three-week job-search workshop and two weeks of self-directed job search in a group setting. In the second program, following the job-search workshop those unable to find a job were required to work in an unpaid job in a public or private nonprofit agency (Experimental Work Experience Program, or EWEP), with monthly work hours determined by the family's AFDC grant divided by the minimum wage.

Certain contextual factors existed in San Diego that might have had special impact on the character of the program and its outcomes. First, San Diego experienced a period of rapid economic growth. Second, the local political leadership and the public in general identified strongly with an ideology that views welfare as morally corrupting and eroding the work ethic. Third, the work history and level of education of the participants in the experiments surpassed those of the national welfare population.

Participation levels were generally high, but the threat of sanctions for noncompliance were ever present. Almost three-quarters of the sample in the EWEP were identified as noncompliant, and 10% of them were actually sanctioned. Nonetheless, most EWEP participants expressed satisfaction with the work assignments and felt that the program was fair.

For AFDC recipients in both of the San Diego programs, the employment rates of the experimental group were between 5% and 10% higher than those of the control group, and their quarterly earnings gains averaged between $96 and $213. There were very modest welfare savings, mostly in the EWEP ($206 over a year). The results for the AFDC-UP showed no consistent increase in employment or earnings; however, there were significant reductions in welfare payments, mostly because of higher reduction rates in the AFDC-UP grants as a result of earnings and the application of sanctions.

A cost-benefit analysis shows that AFDC participants gained between $313 and $367 in both types of programs, but the taxpayers lost $87 on EWEP and $215 on job search per participant. In contrast, for the AFDC-UP, the recipients lost $91 in job search and $400 in EWEP while the taxpayer gained $24 and $557, respectively.

The results of this study are even more revealing when we note the differences in outcome between AFDC and AFDC-UP. They demonstrate how policies and regulations governing the provision of welfare grants play a major role in affecting the costs and benefits of various AFDC work programs, especially the trade-off between benefits and costs to the recipients versus benefits and costs to the taxpayer.

San Diego subsequently also experimented with a saturated work initiative model, known as SWIM (Hamilton & Friedlander, 1989). The experiment tested the feasibility and effectiveness of including a high proportion of mandatory WIN eligibles in an ongoing job-search, work experience, and education and training program. Although the targeted monthly participation rates were 75%, the actual monthly rates averaged 22% for program-arranged activities and increased to 33% if education and training initiated by the participants were added. The researchers conclude that the participation rate was probably the best that could be expected for a program of this type. This is an important finding, since there is a public misperception that all welfare recipients of working age not only should but could participate in a work program.

For participants on AFDC, the SWIM program achieved significant gains in employment (12% over the control group), and earnings—$354 increase per participant in the first year and $658 increase in the second year. There was also reduction in welfare payments—$407 per participant in the first year, and $553 in the second year. Most notably, earning gains and welfare savings were especially higher for the recipients compared with the applicants. Similar gains and savings were achieved for participants on AFDC-UP. From a cost-benefit analysis, over a five-year period SWIM produced a saving to government of more than $1,500 per participant, which is quite impressive. However, the economic well-being of the participants hardly improved. Indeed, AFDC applicants experienced a net loss ranging from $878 to $883, while recipients showed a net gain of $613 to $818. For AFDC-UP, applicants gained and recipients lost. Thus the program succeeded in moving recipients from welfare to work, thereby reducing welfare costs to government, but at the potential expense of the recipients, whose poverty status did not improve.

The relationship between welfare generosity and program effectiveness can also be seen in comparisons between states. In Arkansas, where in 1984 the average AFDC monthly payment per family was $151, compared with $489 in California, the experimental work program (job search and work experience) created a net benefit to the taxpayer of an estimated $1,177 and a net loss to the participant of $535 (Friedlander, Hoerz, Quint, & Riccio, 1985). In San Diego, for the job search and EWEP, it will be recalled, the taxpayer experienced a net loss of $87 and the participant gained $367. In a low-benefit state such as Arkansas, it is much easier to place participants in minimum-wage jobs, where earnings will make them ineligible for continued support from AFDC, resulting also in the loss of other benefits, such as Medicaid. In San Diego, in contrast, because of the relative generosity of the welfare grant, it is more difficult to place participants in minimum-wage jobs that provide sufficient earnings to *remove* them from the welfare rolls.[5]

Finally, we review the results of the Options Program in Baltimore, Maryland, because of the program's emphasis on improving the long-term employability of AFDC recipients (Friedlander et al., 1985). This program emphasized work experience, basic literacy and general equivalency diploma preparation, and skill training. The program was able to provide a substantial proportion of the participants with various services, in contrast to the regular WIN program. Evaluating the impact of the program, researchers found an increase of 7% in employment, and a slight gain in earnings compared with the control group. There were not, however, immediate reductions in welfare receipt or grant expenditures. The impact of the program was more manifest among those who lacked recent work experience. From a benefit-cost analysis standpoint, the participants gained $547. When the value of the community work is included, the benefits and costs to the taxpayer are even. It can be concluded, therefore, that with a significant commitment of resources such a program can provide improvement in the employability of AFDC recipients. However, it must be emphasized that these recipients must continue to depend heavily on welfare grants for their income.

These and other experiments provide general support for the notion that some welfare recipients can be assisted in obtaining employment, resulting in modest savings in welfare expenditures. Moreover, they show that social utility is maximized if such programs target recipients with little work experience, although long-term recipients with no recent employment have not shown consistent improvement in earnings (Gueron, 1990).

More important, however, is that work programs such as SWIM in San Diego or CWEP in West Virginia demonstrate that with strict enforcement and use of sanctions, adequate fiscal investment, and a requirement that the poor work for their welfare benefits if they cannot find jobs, it is possible to substitute work for welfare, especially if the concern to improve the economic well-being of the poor is abandoned. For conservatives such a program is proof that the poor can be put to work at significant savings to government, but this does not lift them out of poverty. Undoubtedly, the experiments have strengthened the claims made by proponents of setting the poor to work, who can point to the gains in employability while minimizing the continued dependency of the majority of the poor on welfare for their sustenance. Another important policy contribution of these experiments to the Family Support Act of 1988 has been the targeting of long-term recipients with no work experience for the work programs. Indeed, as we indicate in the next chapter, these recipients have become the "new" able-bodied poor.

However, the experiments did not fully resolve the political and economic dilemmas of implementing such programs. Local political and economic conditions are key factors in determining the choice of programs, whether work-for-relief or voluntary training programs, and their cost-effectiveness. In the short run, most of these programs are costly to the taxpayer, and their benefits may not exceed costs for several years. It is therefore uncertain how well policymakers can mobilize sufficient political support to invest heavily in large-scale implementation of such programs. They have to contend with other interest groups competing for the same resources to promote education, health, child care, highways, the protection of the environment, and the business climate. It is not surprising, as we noted earlier, that only a few states with prospering economies are willing to make such commitments. Finally, although the experiments have demonstrated an organizational capacity to implement such a program, they do not address the organizational issues arising from large-scale implementation encompassing a significant proportion of the poor. The historical evidence indicates that attempts to implement such programs on a large scale and with a broad scope typically falter and become overwhelmed by organizational difficulties, mostly emanating from the external environment, over which the programs have little control.

INNOVATIVE WORK PROGRAMS?
ET VERSUS GAIN

Despite the dismal results of most work programs, there has been no surcease in the search for an AFDC work program as a centerpiece in any overall welfare policy. The attachment to work clearly exceeds its potential impact as indicated by the available research. And despite very modest (at best) results, the various experiments and demonstrations have given renewed impetus to the institutionalization of new forms of work programs, as the San Diego experiment had on the work program legislation in California. Policymakers have selectively used research findings that programs "work" while ignoring negative results to buttress new legislative initiatives. Yet, as has been the case historically, ideological considerations and the need to affirm dominant cultural norms have dominated much of the policy-making process. Consequently, the innovations, two of which are discussed here, do not and cannot represent radical departures from the past, because the basic cultural and normative ambivalences about poverty have not changed, and the programs must still cope with many of the same local economic and political exigencies that have existed in the past.

Under OBRA, states were encouraged to innovate and revamp their own work policies and programs. Studies have shown that size, wealth, industrialization, environmental changes, and level of activity by interest groups determine the degree of innovation by states (Downs, 1976; Walker, 1969). Not surprisingly, the two leading states in innovating work programs have been Massachusetts, with its Employment and Training Program, and California, with Greater Avenues for Independence. Interestingly, each represents a distinctively different solution to the moral ambiguity of welfare and work. ET has attempted to reduce the moral ambiguity by making the program practically voluntary. GAIN, on the other hand, has heightened the moral ambiguity by simultaneously pursuing a carrot-and-stick policy. Both models were products of negotiations and compromises between contending interest groups trying to resolve the moral ambiguity of welfare and work within political and economic constraints and opportunities at the state level.[6]

It is important to note the economic and political environments in which these two programs emerged. In Massachusetts and California the per capita income for 1983 was more than $6,000, among the highest in the nation. However, the unemployment rate in 1985 was 3.9% in Massachusetts, the lowest in the nation, and 7.2% in California. The proportion of welfare recipients in the total population in 1985 was 5.9% in Massachusetts, compared with 8.7% in

California. Between 1980 and 1983, before ET became operational, Massachusetts experienced a substantial decline of approximately 29% in the AFDC rolls, compared with an increase of 7.6% in California.[7] In Massachusetts, the decline continued into 1985 and reached 32% in comparison to 1980, while in California the increase reached 9%. Most of the increase in California was due to the influx of refugees (Albert & Wiseman, 1986). The average monthly payment per family in 1984 was $389 in Massachusetts and $489 in California. Politically, in 1982 Massachusetts elected a liberal Democratic governor, while California reelected a conservative Republican but the Democrats maintained control of the legislature.

Shortly after the passage of OBRA in 1981, Governor King of Massachusetts proposed a comprehensive work and training program that was mandatory for all recipients with children over the age of 3 and consisted of a job search for 5 weeks and a required community work experience for 26 weeks for those unable to find a job. This cycle was to be repeated. Heavy sanctions for failure to cooperate, including total loss of the grant, were attached to the proposed program. A very effective coalition was organized to oppose the proposal that included trade unions, the Catholic church, major human service organizations, and legal advocacy groups. The coalition's main objective was to advocate for a voluntary program, and, with the election of Governor Dukakis, it achieved its aim. Undoubtedly the rapid decline in the AFDC rolls also had a significant impact on the success of the coalition (Savner, Williams, & Halas, 1986).

ET virtually eliminated mandatory participation within the limits of the federal law. Although nonexempt recipients were still required to register for WIN, there was no effective enforcement to participate, and those refusing to participate were put on a "future participation list," which meant that they continued to receive information about the program periodically. The list was merely a device to circumvent federal regulations and to avoid the imposition of sanctions for nonparticipation. By these administrative maneuvers, ET managed to minimize, but not eliminate, some of the policy contradictions that typically accompany work programs. It did not attempt to serve as a deterrent or to control the behavior of the recipients by imposing a work requirement, and it did not penalize the able-bodied poor for not working.[8] Instead, it attempted to induce the able-bodied poor to enter the labor market by offering an array of services, including extensive education and training.

ET represented a symbolic departure from WIN by viewing welfare recipients as potential customers to be attracted to the program. Indeed, ET engaged in a very active marketing campaign through publicity in newspapers and television and presentation of videos on ET in the larger welfare offices (O'Neill, 1990). Moreover, while WIN promised support services, such as child care, but lacked funding to provide them, Massachusetts actually committed the necessary resources. Even prior to the Family Support Act, ET provided transitional services up to one year for child care and health care. In 1980, expenditures on WIN were approximately $20 million, of which the state contributed 10%. In 1985 the expenditures jumped to $30 million, of which the state contributed close to 60%. In 1988, the state appropriation reached $68 million. ET is relatively expensive, with expenditures per participant approximating $2,000.

ET also departed from WIN in its scope and impact. Preliminary findings by Nightingale et al. (1989) indicate that for fiscal year 1987 about 67% of all adults on AFDC participated in the program.[9] About 50% were active in a program component beyond the initial assessment and orientation. Of those who participated in some substantive component, 44% obtained jobs, with a mean starting wage of $5.70 per hour. Of those who found jobs, about 49% stayed off welfare. Few WIN programs achieved such a high rate of participation and job placement.

Critics of ET have argued that the dual emphasis on voluntary participation and use of performance-based contracting may result in creaming—that is, selection of the most motivated and job-ready recipients (O'Neill, 1990). Nightingale et al. (1989) also report that the starting wages were higher for participants in areas with lower unemployment rates and for participants with any of the following characteristics: male, previous work experience, short welfare spells, and participation in vocational training. Thus there are indications that female and minority participants were not immune from the racial and gender biases in the labor market. Job retention seemed to be related to the provision of health care and child care, participation in GED or college and supported work experience, short welfare spells, and placement in administrative and professional jobs.

Undoubtedly, the characteristics of ET and its potential success were a function of the unique labor market conditions that existed in Massachusetts when the program was launched. It provided, at relatively high public cost, motivated and trained low-skilled workers to an economy, dominated by finance, service, trade, communication, and construction industries, that operated in an exceptionally tight labor market. A study by the Massachusetts Taxpayers Foundation (1987) found that the increases in jobs in the service, finance, and trade industries played a major role, together with ET, in reducing the AFDC caseload. However, a recent study by O'Neill (1990) argues that ET has had no discernible independent effect on reducing the AFDC caseload; rather, local economic conditions were responsible for the change.

It is clear that ET benefited from an unusual combination of favorable economic and political conditions that converged to make the program possible. One can speculate that the business community was willing to support such a program as long as it served its interests, and that political support for the program would be sustained only as long as the economy remained robust, the AFDC rolls continued to decline, and the state's revenues could provide sufficient public funding to maintain the program without facing competition from other programs and interest groups. Put differently, the success of ET hinged on considerable expenditure of resources, which is acceptable only under very favorable political and economic circumstances. But these economic and political conditions are changing and are likely to affect the character of ET. As the state struggles with an increasing budget deficit, a rise in the welfare rolls, and a political climate that is becoming less tolerant of welfare recipients, pressures will mount to reduce funding and to insist on mandatory participation in community work experiences.

ET opted to downplay certain symbolic elements of the dominant cultural norms about welfare and work, especially by not mandating the able-bodied poor to work and by emphasizing incentives over regulations. Thus the program is vulnerable to moral and political attacks, and could become a victim of the very symbols it represents.

California's GAIN program, in contrast, embodies and epitomizes the moral ambivalence of poverty. Indeed, many of its ideological underpinnings can be found in the Job Opportunities and

Basic Skills (JOBS) component of the Family Support Act of 1988. It is a patchwork of compromises among contending ideological perspectives, resulting in immensely complex yet ambitious legislation. As recounted by Kirp (1986), California's governor wanted to revive the CWEP (i.e., work-for-relief) on a statewide basis, but his efforts were blocked by the Democrat-controlled legislature. Yet, the continuing increase in the AFDC rolls, coupled with public support for tax limitations (i.e., Proposition 13), provided the impetus for negotiations. The liberals accepted the idea of a mandated work program, while the conservatives agreed to the provision of services—education, training, and child care—to help recipients become employable. Thus the symbols on both ends of the moral spectrum were affirmed. Underlying the GAIN legislation were diverse ideological declarations ranging from the belief that recipients do want to work and will do so if provided the opportunity to the statement that able-bodied recipients are expected to work.

The objective of GAIN has been to reduce welfare costs by increasing earnings of participants in unsubsidized employment. Emphasis is given to the importance of providing adequate services to attain this objective, but the added costs had to be justified on the basis of long-term personal and community payoff.

GAIN requires all eligible recipients to participate in the program until they become employed or are off AFDC. Following JOBS regulations, mandatory registration is required of all AFDC-UP recipients and AFDC recipients whose youngest children are 3 years old or older. Other recipients can volunteer to participate if resources are available. All registrants must undergo an initial orientation and appraisal to determine if they might be exempted or deferred from the program. Those not exempted or deferred undergo a basic appraisal for literacy skills and participate in remedial education if necessary. Registrants who had employment experience within two years prior to registration are referred to job search and job clubs. Those without work experience and those unable to find jobs are then reassessed and an employment plan is developed that could include training, education, and job services, as well as supportive services such as child care. The plan may also call for short-term work-for-relief (Preemployment Preparation Program, or PREP). Those who complete the plan but fail to find a job within 90 days are assigned to long-term PREP (up to a year). Those who fail to obtain unsubsidized employment following PREP are reassessed again, and they repeat the process as long as they are on AFDC.

The inherent policy contradictions in the program are quite apparent. The program is expected to serve as a deterrent for able-bodied recipients, yet if it provided all the resources it claims, it could actually attract new recipients. Based on the results of the San Diego experiment, the program places priority on long-term recipients, yet the contract requirements with the various educational, training, and placement vendors encourage creaming by insisting on payments based on performance (e.g., placement in unsubsidized employment). The program emphasizes job search and placement, but concedes the need for services to those failing to find a job. While the ultimate aim of the program is job placement, there are numerous safeguards enabling participants to refuse jobs, including net earnings (after mandatory deductions such as taxes, social security, union dues, and costs of health insurance if not covered by the employer) that are less than the monthly AFDC grant. This would mean that a mother with two children would have good cause to refuse a job paying $1,100 per month.[10] The program has emphasized the need for an individualized plan fitting the unique needs of each participant. However, it is very prescriptive in the phases each participant must follow. The program emphasizes rehabilitation, via its educational, training, and job placement services, but it simultaneously pursues a mandatory work-for-relief provision for those who fail to obtain employment. In this instance, interestingly, the policymakers did not heed the negative results of the San Diego experiment.

The program is expected to provide extensive services, but has a built-in disclaimer in case of lack of resources—temporary deferral. While the program is mandatory, and requires the application of sanctions for noncompliance, it provides many loopholes for "deferring" compliance, including emotional and mental problems, substance abuse, and severe family crisis. The program requires participants to sign a contract for each phase of the service provision process obligating the participant and the agency to certain activities. Inability of the agency to meet its contractual obligations provides the participant with good cause to discontinue participation. Violation of the contract by the participant could trigger sanctions for noncompliance. Yet, the program has specified a very complex and cumbersome hearing system that renders sanctioning difficult. Finally, although the program is mandated by the state, which assumes all additional administrative costs, it leaves much of its implementation to local county initiative. Moreover, although it emphasizes the need for a full array of services, it also puts a premium on using existing local services before commitment of additional state resources.

The political economy of implementing GAIN, at both state and county levels, has pointed to onerous issues not much different from those experienced in WIN. Recognizing the complexity of the program enacted in 1985, the legislation allowed the counties up to five years to plan and phase in the program. By 1988 the phase-in period had already been extended by one year. The budgeting of GAIN also points to its fundamental precariousness. First, the original projected costs of the program when fully operational were $266.3 million. By 1988–1989, the appropriations exceeded $368 million, partly due to the underestimated demand for basic education. Second, approximately a third or more of the funding comes from redirection of existing resources appropriated to state agencies that are mandated to serve welfare recipients, such as adult schools, community colleges, and JTPA programs. This is termed the "maintenance of effort" principle. The rest of the budget consists of approximately 50% new federal funds and 50% new state general funds. In fiscal year 1988–1989, more than $90 million represented maintenance of effort, and new state general funds amounted to $213.7 million. The maintenance of effort principle creates an annual tug-of-war between the state department of finance and other state agencies (adult schools, community colleges, and so on) that fight for their own agendas.

Third, because the state faces serious fiscal difficulties in balancing its budget, GAIN has already fallen prey to budget reductions. For fiscal year 1989–1990, the total budget was $374.5 million, but the allocation of general funds declined to $150 million. Most of the difference was made up by increases in federal funding under JOBS and increases in maintenance of effort. Thus new federal funding is used to substitute for state funding rather than to increase the scope of the program. For fiscal year 1990–1991, the governor proposed an actual reduction in total appropriation to $364.3 million, reducing the allocation in general funding even further, to $120 million. The budget reductions anticipated serving fewer participants. Yet, the projected budget needed for a full implementation of the program was $528.8 million. Already, local counties and agencies are voicing concerns and fears about lack of adequate funding. Because the largest urban counties, such as Los Angeles and Alameda, delayed the implementation of GAIN, they are more likely to be underfunded in relation to their eligible GAIN populations. Thus, unless the program can produce early favorable results, difficult under the best of circumstances, the political support for GAIN, vulnerable to begin with, may be short-lived, particularly if the state continues to experience further fiscal difficulties. As was the case with WIN, in the competition for limited resources, work programs for the poor come in last when it comes to actual public dollars.

Experience from the early implementation of GAIN points to several significant trends. First, participation rates are not unlike those experienced by previous work programs. Approximately 70% of those registered for the program attended the orientation. Only 34% of the registrants actually attended an initial program component (i.e., basic education, job search, or self-initiated training) (Riccio, Goldman, Hamilton, Martinson, & Orenstein, 1989). Thus almost two-thirds of the registrants were either deregistered or deferred from the program. The high rates of deregistration and deferral point to an inherent difficulty in a complex work program such as GAIN. The program assumes a systematic progression from basic education to job search, and, for those failing to obtain employment, to further assessment, vocational training, and possibly work experience. However, the dynamics of the welfare caseload impede such a progression. Even long-term welfare recipients experience welfare in a series of interrupted welfare spells, making their participation in GAIN discontinuous as well.

Second, there are some initial indications that a much larger than expected proportion of the registrants have literacy deficiencies (Wallace & Long, 1987). Indeed, almost 60% of the registrants who attended orientation were determined to need basic education (Riccio et al., 1989), which has now become the major service component of GAIN. Thus, de facto, GAIN has become a massive compensatory educational program rather than a jobs program. The need for basic education is likely to prolong the length of stay of participants in the program and increase its costs. Already, there are pressures in some counties to move the registrants to job search rather than to remedial education.

Third, as expected, there are wide variations among the counties in the operation of the program. Because GAIN requires the formation of an extensive interorganizational network of services, counties vary in their ability to develop such networks, depending on the richness and accessibility of the services available. In general, there has been a tendency to rely on existing public services, some of which—such as JTPA programs and the state employment services agency—have not in the past demonstrated a commitment to the needs of welfare recipients. Counties rich in educational resources such as community colleges have better capabilities to respond to the educational needs of their participants. Counties also vary in their orientation to the GAIN participants and the organization of the program (Riccio et al., 1989). Some counties are more client oriented, as reflected in their attitudes toward participants during intake and orientation. Caseload sizes vary greatly, from a low of 64 to a high of 225. There are some preliminary indications that counties with unfavorable labor market conditions are more likely to emphasize the work-for-relief aspect of the program.

Los Angeles County, which encompasses over a third of the AFDC caseload in the state, has experienced severe difficulties in implementing the program. Developing a network of services through contracts with various service providers proved to be difficult, and involved protracted negotiations. On the one hand, the county insisted that the services be tailored to the needs of the participants as seen by the county planners. On the other hand, many of the service providers, mostly public agencies, having a monopoly over the services, resisted and wanted the contracts to reflect their own conceptions and interests. Ultimately, the county had to capitulate. The county also decided to contract out to a private, for-profit agency the case management function, partly because it did not want to expand the number of county employees, and partly because it did not expect that funding for the program would last more than a few years. The contract, resisted by labor unions and Democratic legislators, produced serious political fallout in the form of a legislative cap on the funding available to case management. As a result, the county has not been able to serve more than approximately 11,000 active cases in any given month, which is less than 10% of the projected eligible GAIN participants in the county.[11] Moreover, because of a late start, the county is receiving a much smaller share of the GAIN funding than its projected eligible population indicates it should have. For 1989–1990, the county was allocated $33.3 million, which was less than 9% of the total state GAIN budget. Even without the dispute over the contract of the case management, the county faces the prospect of hardly any significant raises in its GAIN budget, which means that it will be unable to reach any significant proportion of GAIN eligibles. This will further strain the county's relations with its service providers, who have expected and budgeted for a much larger pool of participants.

What is the likelihood that GAIN will achieve its intended objectives? If history is any guide, the prognosis is not very favorable. Governor Deukmejian (1990) recently stated that "GAIN should be transformed into a true 'workfare' program, where immediate priority is to remove people from the welfare rolls and put them on payrolls as quickly as possible." The governor especially objected to the extensive emphasis of GAIN on education, since more than 60% of GAIN registrants are found to be needing basic education. To delegitimate this emphasis he used the time-honored strategy of pointing to sensational but rare misuses of the program by suggesting that welfare recipients abuse the system, using taxpayer money to pursue graduate education. Instead, the governor would require all participants to look for jobs before being diverted into any education or training program. As he put it, "Let the job marketplace, not caseworkers, determine who is employable."

A program that is beset by such conflicting policies is likely to become decoupled from the policies and to engage in activities that reaffirm the conflicting symbols but provide limited, if any, substantive outputs. Thus the ultimate virtue of GAIN might not be in the number of recipients who become economically self-sufficient or in its ability to reduce the welfare rolls, but rather in giving a symbolic expression, by its very existence, to contesting ideologies about the poor.

CONCLUSION

Work policies and programs have persisted in various forms, despite the overwhelming historical evidence that they have generally failed to reduce the welfare rolls in any appreciable way or to improve the economic self-sufficiency of the poor. The reasons for their survival cannot, therefore, reside in their salutary effects on the poor and welfare, but rather in their apparent utility to the nonpoor. It has been proposed that work programs serve a social control function by deterring potential applicants, by sanctioning noncomplying recipients, and by forcing the poor into low-wage jobs (Katz, 1986; Piven & Cloward, 1971). Undoubtedly, the history of work programs is replete with such attempts. Nonetheless, even as an instrument of social control, work programs have not been very effective or efficient. There are clearly more efficient ways to control the lives of welfare recipients—through policies governing the provision of cash relief and through administrative procedures (Brodkin & Lipsky, 1983), for instance—than through cumbersome and costly administrative programs. Local policymakers and program administrators know this; at the local level, where the administrative and fiscal pressures are most acute, they have repeatedly preferred the manipulation of the gates and the amount of direct cash relief rather than setting the poor to work.

Yet, the idea of setting the able-bodied poor to work has remained ingrained throughout the ideological spectrum on poverty and welfare. Both the advocates of the view of poverty as a personal and moral deficiency (the "moralists") and the proponents of the view of poverty as a consequence of debilitating circumstances (the "structuralists") have embraced the idea of work programs, albeit with different emphases. The former present it as a key solution to the problem of poverty, while the latter accept it as an important supplementary solution. They do so because poverty among able-bodied persons presents to both groups a moral ambiguity for which work programs are an attempted solution. For the moralists, the persistence of poverty brings into doubt the legitimacy of the moral order by questioning the righteousness of the work ethic and self-sufficiency. Work programs are viewed as the affirmation of these norms because they insist that the able-bodied poor should work and be removed from the welfare rolls. For the structuralists, the persistence of poverty among the able-bodied challenges the political order by questioning its ability to provide equal opportunities to all citizens. Work programs confirm the role of government in protecting social rights, including the right to work, by insisting that the able-bodied poor can work and escape poverty. Moreover, in both instances, the institution of work programs reaffirms the capitalist market economy, which both views uphold and accept as the foundation for common institutional rules about work and welfare.

The fact that the resulting work policies and programs point to an overwhelming disjuncture between ideology and organizational reality is a strong indication that work policies and programs serve a primarily symbolic purpose. In many respects both the moralists and the structuralists use work programs as an institutional safety valve for the continued reliance on cash relief for the able-bodied poor. Decoupling the symbols from the programs ensures that failures at the programmatic level do not undermine the legitimacy of the symbols. These failures are addressed by periodic and almost ritualistic modifications of the policies and the programs. These oscillate, for example, between providing training and employment services versus job search; mandatory versus voluntary participation; and enforcement of work requirement versus inducements to work. Yet, the critical functions of these programs are to certify who is able-bodied, to mandate registration for work, and to be able to present sufficient testimonials of setting some of them to work.

Nonetheless, even in carrying out these functions, work programs cannot escape the moral ambiguity of the symbols they attempt to uphold. It is the political economy of coping with the moral ambiguity that gives work programs several distinct organizational characteristics. First, these programs are beset by contradictory goals, such as providing recipients with services while forcing them to work or inducing them to work while insisting on mandatory participation. Second, the programs are generally starved of sufficient resources to meet their mandate. Third, they serve a very small fraction of the eligible poor. Fourth, they are highly sensitive to local labor market conditions, which are the key determinant of their success in getting the poor to work. Fifth, while most eligible recipients are registered and certified, only a few actually receive employment services or are placed in jobs. Finally, these programs are caught in bureaucratic dilemmas regarding the enforcement of sanctions for noncompliance in the face of limited resources and problem-ridden recipients.

Although the institution of work programs primarily serves the needs of the nonpoor in confirming their cultural norms, the poor, especially poor women, do not escape without cost. Periodically they encounter a mixture of fear of losing their welfare benefits and hope of escaping poverty. They face the fear that work requirements will force them to work under exploitative conditions or force them off welfare while keeping them in poverty. For some, indeed, the fear becomes reality; for the majority, however, the fear dissipates into a bureaucratic nuisance to be borne as a cost of being on welfare. Their hopes are raised that the program will indeed help them obtain employment and escape poverty. For some the hoped-for changes materialize, but for the vast majority the organizational reality of lack of resources destroys the hope. In both instances, the poor become entrapped in what surely must be perceived by them as bureaucratic capriciousness in which official edicts and declarations have double and contradictory meanings.

It is clear that requiring welfare recipients, women and men, to work for their relief does little to improve their economic well-being. It is also abundantly clear that for the majority of women on AFDC, even when they work, periodic dependency on welfare benefits is unavoidable. Thus the dominant cultural norm of viewing welfare as antithesis to work contradicts the social reality, in which work and welfare must complement each other. Because the institution of work programs is based on these cultural norms, it finds itself in conflict with this reality. As long as the moral ambiguity of poverty is not resolved at the institutional level, work programs will continue to serve their symbolic function while being mostly marginal to the social reality of poverty and welfare.

Forgotten in the institution of work programs are the children of the poor. They are the silent partners whose voices are seldom heard and whose needs are seldom considered in the moral debate about welfare and work. At best, they are viewed as an impediment to setting the poor to work that could be remedied through the provision of child-care subsidies. At worst, they are viewed as the result of the moral depravity of the poor. The impact of welfare in general and work programs in particular on the well-being of children is generally ignored. In the studies of the costs and benefits of work programs, mention of children is generally nonexistent, and benefits and costs to them are not calculated. It might be argued that there is a conspiracy of silence among the framers of welfare and work policies, because having to address directly the needs of the children of the poor requires solutions that may run counter to dominant institutional norms. The legacy of work programs is to have the children bear the costs of whatever failings and misfortunes their parents have accrued.

NOTES

1. The proposed community work experience program was based on a three-year demonstration project conducted in California in 1972–1975, when Ronald Reagan was governor. The evaluation of the program, although flawed, pointed to dismal results, including very low participation rates (2.6%) and resistance by counties to implementing the program (State of California Employment Development Department, 1976).

2. The Job Training Partnership Act of 1982 also exemplified the Reagan administration's welfare ideology. It replaced the Comprehensive Employment and Training Act (CETA) by greatly reducing overall funding, eliminating public service employment, reducing the scope of employment services, and giving states considerable discretion in managing the program.

3. The ET program in Massachusetts was the exception, spending 32% of its budget on child care through a voucher system.

4. Although the results were replicated by several other studies, they suffered from serious methodological problems that cast doubt on their validity (Moffitt, 1985). Moffitt (1986) suggests that OBRA had a lagged negative effect on the incentive to work.

5. In the second experimental work program, SWIM, most of the savings were in *case closure*. Some portion of the welfare savings may have stemmed from the imposition of sanctions, and the fact that a number of the experiment's participants who became employed but later lost their jobs remained off welfare (Hamilton & Friedlander, 1989, p. 56).

6. Since their inception, both programs have had to undergo some changes as a result of the passage of the JOBS program under the Family Support Act of 1988. The legislation could make it more difficult for Massachusetts to maintain the voluntary character of ET, although it does give priority to recipients who volunteer. It will require only minor changes in GAIN.

7. O'Neill (1990) suggests that most of the decline in AFDC caseload in Massachusetts can be attributed to the changes in AFDC eligibility as a result of OBRA, since a large percentage of the recipients in that state were working.

8. Mandatory participation was still required for recipients of AFDC-UP and mothers with adolescent children.

9. However, this proportion also includes 17% who participated in the prior year. A U.S. General Accounting Office (1987) study reports a rate of participation of 28% for 1986.

10. Assuming the recipient is employed 40 hours per week, the equivalent hourly wage will be just under $7.00.

11. The cap was lifted in FY 1990.

6

The Contemporary Reform "Consensus": Symbolic and Structural Ambiguity Redux

THE REFORM CONSENSUS

Today, we are embarking on what has been called a major reform of welfare policy. We have just enacted the Family Support Act of 1988, which, in our customary political rhetoric, is hailed as a major change in welfare policy. Whether or not *reform* is an appropriate term, there appears to be an emerging consensus on what changes ought to be made in AFDC (Kosterlitz, 1987). According to Robert Reischauer (1989), the consensus, embraced by both liberals and conservatives, centers on five broad themes: responsibility, work, family, education, and state discretion.

Responsibility involves reciprocal obligations. In contrast to the ideology of entitlement, which characterized the 1960s and early 1970s, it should now be made clear to welfare recipients that in return for support, they, too, have obligations to try to become self-sufficient. The new term is *workfare*. Workfare means that all able-bodied recipients will be required to prepare themselves for employment, look for jobs, and accept jobs if offered.[1] If this fails, the recipient will be required to accept a public job in return for the welfare grant (work-relief). The work obligation is cast in rehabilitative terms, as "an opportunity to join the nation's mainstream" (Reischauer, 1989).

Historically, as we have seen, required work has been one of the most bitterly contested issues between liberals and conservatives. Why the consensus now? Reischauer (1989) offers several reasons. There is the traditional value placed on work in liberal capitalist society; it is the measure of one's worth, self-respect, and identity. The value of work has now been extended to mothers. There has been a fundamental change in our attitudes toward working mothers; most Americans believe that it is not only appropriate for mothers to work outside the home, but also desirable. These views reflect reality: The majority of mothers are in the paid labor force; this is especially true of divorced women.[2] And since most mothers of young children are now in the paid labor force, it is only reasonable to expect welfare mothers to do the same (Garfinkel & McLanahan, 1986). In addition, a bargain has been struck: As part of the workfare package, there is to be a full range of education, training, and job placement activities as well as adequate day care; health insurance will be extended for low-income workers.

The family issues relate to the dramatic changes in the composition of the American family—that is, the increases in divorce, in the numbers of those who never marry, in the numbers of children born out of wedlock, and in the numbers of children living in single-parent households—and the increase in poverty among this group of women and children. While there is debate as to how much poverty and welfare dependency is the direct result of changes in family composition compared with the decline in wage rates and working conditions in general (Bane, 1986), female-headed households are often welfare-dependent for considerable periods of time. It is assumed that the effects of being on welfare are harmful for both mothers and children. The rise of female-headed households, the incidence of poverty and welfare among this group, and beliefs about the apparent harmful effects of this condition on both parents and children in these households have led to a growing concern about the creation and perpetuation of a more or less permanent "underclass" (Katz, 1989; Wilson, 1987). There is, of course, little agreement on how to reduce out-of-wedlock births, but there is now strong consensus on strengthening child-support mechanisms.

There is also consensus that educational failure leads to welfare dependency. Young women who do poorly in school are more likely to become single mothers. Many poorly educated female household heads cannot even qualify for entry-level jobs, and a minimum-wage job provides only three-quarters of the amount that a mother and two children need to get out of poverty. There has been a significant increase in child poverty (now about one-fifth of all children), which, it is felt, could have serious implications for the nation's economy. Poverty affects the future prospects of children, and the poor children of today will not only have to compete with Asian and German workers but will also have to support our retirement programs. Accordingly, there are recommendations to improve the quality of our public schools and to require teenage welfare mothers to graduate high school.

The final area of consensus, according to Reischauer (1989), concerns state discretion. Conservatives have always favored state control over welfare policy; liberals have distrusted the states, especially in matters of race. Liberals now are more amenable to state discretion. State experimentation has appeal, given the prevailing consensus as to the general inadequacies of the present system. Several states have adopted innovative programs. There is great variety within and among states as to the range of people on welfare, labor market conditions, educational systems, and bureaucratic capacities; and there is growing agreement that education, training, and employment programs ought to be sensitive to local labor market conditions.

Those familiar with welfare history will be puzzled, amused, or cynical about Reischauer's five areas of consensus. Each decade, it seems that we are rediscovering the wheel. As we have seen (Chapter 2), from the initial enactment of the aid to dependent children programs in the second decade of this century, there have been obligations of responsibility on welfare mothers; they had to be "fit and proper" and had to have a "suitable home," and there always was a work requirement. Throughout various "reform" periods, contracts have been tried, as well as various work tests (Schorr, 1987). Some 25 years ago, an ambitious program of job training and work incentives was enacted (Chapter 4). State discretion is also curious. Aid to dependent children started as a state and local program; AFDC is still primarily a state program. True, there are federal requirements, but they are not nearly as substantively important as the state provisions.

What seems to precipitate this new round of welfare reform? As a nation we have become alarmed with the rise of the underclass (Katz, 1989). There is a growing perception that large segments of our population, especially African-Americans and Hispanics, are trapped in poverty-stricken, crime- and drug-ridden ghettos, and that young people and children growing up in these circumstances have at best only minimal chances of leading decent, productive lives.[3] The underclass has grown and become visible especially in the urban centers of the Northeast and the Midwest, particularly in cities such as New York and Chicago (Massey & Eggers, 1990). While "during the 1970s, black poverty became more persistent and geographically concentrated in American cities" (Massey, 1990, pp. 350–351), the nature, extent, and reasons are contested (Kasarda, 1989; Mead, 1986; Testa, Atone, Krogh, & Neckerman, 1989; Wilson, 1987). Massey shows that racial segregation interacting with a rising rate of African-American poverty was mostly responsible for the social transformation of the black community and the concentration of poverty during the 1970s. He argues that

> because segregation concentrates disadvantage, shifts in black poverty rates comparable to those observed during the 1970s have the power to transform the socioeconomic character of poor black neighborhoods very rapidly and dramatically, changing a low-income black community from a place where welfare-dependent, female-headed families are a minority to one where they are the norm, producing high rates of crime, property abandonment, mortality, and educational failure.

The contemporary consensus on welfare reform is our current attempt to try to do something about this deep and frustratingly complex problem. Yet, as has been the case throughout welfare history, the victims of poverty are again blamed, and little attention is given to the structural issues, especially racial segregation, that have created the so-called underclass. Rather, it is easier to formulate the problem as the failure of entitlement, that welfare is to be had for the asking, and that easy welfare encourages dependency in mothers that is transmitted to children. There is the feeling that somehow AFDC families have lost the sense that there are mutual obligations, that citizens of society ought to contribute as well as receive, and, in today's terms, *contributing* means productive, paid labor.[4] It is true that there always have been work tests and other requirements, but they have been weakly enforced and have produced minimal results.

Conservatives believe that it should be clearly communicated to welfare recipients that they are expected to get into mainstream paid labor, develop discipline and motivation, and become self-sufficient. Required participation, even for mothers with very young children, and even though part-time, is necessary to make the message clear and to develop the proper attitudes among welfare children. While conservatives favor supports such as day care, they are more inclined to favor activities that lead to quick placement and actual experience, including required workfare jobs for those who cannot find private sector jobs. Since many Americans work in low-wage jobs with poor working conditions and no fringe benefits, conservatives are less inclined to worry about the kinds of jobs that welfare recipients should be required to take. They believe that if an individual keeps working, he or she will be able to get better jobs (Mead, 1989; Reischauer, 1989). For the most part, work requirements have been opposed by liberals, who have charged that these requirements are administered harshly and arbitrarily. The consensus on education, job training and preparation, and day care are the incentives that have brought the liberals on board.

In sum, the reform consensus is tough, but it is deeply infused with rehabilitative overtones—responsibility, education, training, the moral values of work and independence, honestly recognizing and trying to do something about changing the culture of poverty. Great emphasis is placed on supportive, rehabilitative programs, and on the seemingly generous day-care provisions.

Have we really turned a corner in AFDC? Are we really going to enact a change that is both responsible and constructive, a program that is aimed at meeting the needs of women and children in poverty rather than the needs of the majority? There is strong reason to doubt that we have changed our ways. We will argue that the current consensus represents yet another attempt at a reconciliation of the historical contradictions and moral ambiguities in welfare policy. To some extent, the consensus is trying to respond to real structural needs in the political economy; to a large extent, the consensus is reproducing traditional symbols in new forms to take account of the large changes that have occurred in American society.

Welfare reform policy is a symbolic reflection of two major changes in the political economy: the increased demand for low-wage service work and the massive entry of women and mothers into the paid labor force. The education components and the work and training programs of welfare reform are justified by the need to increase the supply of workers. The dramatic shift in the ideology of AFDC from *excusing* mothers of young children from work to now *expecting* them to work reflects the changing labor force participation and societal attitudes of nonwelfare mothers.

We argue that the reform consensus represents yet another act of symbolism, reflecting persistent themes in welfare history, including racism and deep hostility to the female-headed household in poverty. This hostility has always been present in American social welfare history, and the changes in AFDC over the past decades and especially today reflect that hostility. The tip-off is the myth of workfare, the centerpiece of the reform consensus. As we have shown, the issue of work has always been at the heart of welfare policy. Welfare is about the status of poor mothers—the real and imagined social problems of working women, working mothers in degraded jobs, threatening the moral concept of the family, and spawning a permanent dependent criminal class. From its earliest days, AFDC has been more concerned with maintaining the work ethic, patriarchy, and racial subordination than with relieving the plight of poor mothers and their children. With the dramatic changes in AFDC in the 1960s, this exclusionary policy was breached and the question was raised: Should the formerly "degraded to begin with"—African-Americans, unwed mothers, those at the bottom of the socioeconomic ladder—now be morally excused from work? The answer was no. Starting in this period, federal work requirements began to be imposed on the new AFDC recipients. They were required to work; they were still not considered to be "proper" wives and mothers.

Liberals, who previously had opposed work requirements for welfare mothers primarily on the grounds that mothers (nonwelfare) should stay at home, now support the welfare work requirements on the grounds that since most nonwelfare mothers are in the paid labor force, it is reasonable to expect welfare mothers to work as well (Garfinkel & McLanahan, 1986). If this reconceptualization is accurate, it means that the welfare population has now been *incorporated* into the dominant class; welfare mothers now have the same moral characteristics and expectations as nonpoor mothers. In other words, we are no longer affirming dominant ideologies by constructing deviant behavior.

We argue that this is not the case, that we are still engaged in constructing enemies. Work requirements say that dependent mothers are expected to work, but are designed to ensure that most welfare recipients will not be able to escape welfare through employment. As with the early mothers' pension programs, a few will be anointed into majoritarian society—in that day, it was the "worthy widow"; today, it will be the model welfare mother who progresses through training, gets a decent job, and is no longer dependent. Those success stories will validate majoritarian ideologies; the great majority of welfare mothers will remain deviant by failing the work expectations. Once again, women of color will be victimized by both the economy and the welfare system. They will be less able to work because of race and gender, and now welfare reform will penalize them for failing to secure mainstream employment.

We have created a new category of able-bodied poor who are the target of welfare policy. These are women at high risk of long-term welfare dependency. Ellwood (1988), using longitudinal survey data, found that 25% of recipients have 10 or more years of welfare dependence and account for almost 60% of those who are on welfare at any given time, thus presumably consuming at least 60% of the program's resources. He further found that education, marital status, number of children, work experience, and disability status are the key predictors of welfare spells, and the group at greatest risk of becoming long-term recipients is that of young never-married women who enter the program when their children are less than 3 years old.

Long-term welfare recipients, including young unmarried mothers with very young children, are now the "new" able-bodied poor. They are the target of the renewed emphasis on workfare. But how successful is this targeting likely to be? Grossman, Maynard, and Roberts's (1985) evaluation of the various work programs indicates the following: (a) White recipients tend to benefit more from the employment and training programs than do minority recipients; (b) welfare recipients with little or no work experience benefit substantially more; and (c) the longer and more costly employment and training programs seem to have significant impact on earnings. These researchers also found that different programs optimally benefit different subgroups. For example, the employment and training programs they examined seem to be of most benefit to women with no recent work experience, women with previous job training, women over 40, and women with four or more children. When these findings are juxtaposed with Ellwood's (1988) analysis of welfare dependency, the best that one can conclude is that welfare-work programs are more cost-effective for women without recent work experience. However, as Ellwood notes, marital status, not employment, is the main route to economic self-sufficiency. In addition, even among the highest-risk group more than half of the women do not have long-term welfare spells. Finally, targeting long-term recipients will not accrue sizable welfare savings in the short run.

What the social scientists and top-level policymakers are trying to do is replace traditional moral and political conceptions of the able-bodied poor with technical, social utilitarian considerations. But surely work and training programs cannot exclude minority recipients because these programs are less successful with them. Similarly, it is unlikely that men will be excluded, even though the programs do little to improve their employability. And it is by no means settled that it is socially desirable to have young never-married women with children under the age of 3 work outside their homes, especially considering current child-care costs and lack of availability of quality day care. Finally, in an era of declining federal and state economies and increasing unemployment and welfare rolls, it may be politically and bureaucratically impossible to avoid creaming when the accrued benefits of the target group will be realized only in the long run. In sum, targeting may be good social science, but in this case there will be significant moral and political disagreement over its practical meaning; the programs will be difficult to administer, especially since multiple agencies will have to be coordinated (e.g., training, schools, child care, employers), as well as costly in the short run; and, most important, a weakening economy will mean fewer unsubsidized jobs.

Hence we may be setting up a targeted group of welfare recipients for failure. The status of welfare recipients who "fail" will be even more degraded because of the myths and ceremonies of opportunity accompanying the reform consensus. True to its mission, welfare policy affirms the values of middle-class mothers; in a prior age, these concerned the home, but now they involve the paid labor force. Those who cannot conform will still be outcasts. These are the old themes in welfare policy; they are alive and well in the current welfare reform.

THE FAMILY SUPPORT ACT
OF 1988

The latest manifestation of the welfare reform consensus is the newly enacted Family Support Act of 1988 (FSA). This law requires that every state establish a Job Opportunities and Basic Skills program by October 1990, and that such programs be fully operational by October 1992. Rather than providing detailed guidance, however, the Family Support Act is, in fact, only a broad outline. It has so many qualifications, and so many of the crucial decisions have been left to the states to fashion their own programs, that the new legislation amounts to little more than a codification of the existing waiver policy, or a block grant—but without much money in the grant.

Generally speaking, all mothers whose youngest children are 3 years old or older ("nonexempt") are required to participate in JOBS. States can decide to include mothers with children as young as 1 year old. Those who are "exempt" from JOBS include children under 16 attending school full-time (unless the child was nonexempt and assigned to school) and individuals who are ill (verified), who are 60 years or older, who live too far from a JOBS program, who are needed at home to care for an ill or incapacitated member of the household, who work 30 hours per week, who are three or more months pregnant, who provide child care to a young child, and/or who are full-time VISTA volunteers. Also, the second parent of an AFDC-UP family is considered exempt if he or she meets the child-care exemption requirements (Greenberg, 1990, p. 18).

The law requires that all states adopt an AFDC Unemployed Parent program. However, in those states that do not have such a program (about half), the state may elect to terminate benefits after the first six months. With an AFDC-UP family, the state can decide whether the second parent is exempt from the work requirements, but the parent who is exempt must satisfy the child-care provider exemption.[5]

It is up to the states to decide which categories of recipients will participate. However, to get the maximum federal money, the state has to commit 55% of its JOBS resources to the following targeted groups: recipients or applicants who have received aid for at least 36 of the preceding 60 months; parents under 24 years old who have either not completed or are not enrolled in high school or have had little or no work experience in the preceding year; and members of a family in which the youngest child is within two years of being ineligible of AFDC because of age. The idea is to ensure that at least the majority of state resources are focused on recipients who are most likely to be long-term dependents. However, the requirements can be waived on the grounds of infeasibility.[6]

Of course, not all nonexempt recipients will participate. Because of limited resources, states will have to formulate some sort of priority system; a state may choose to select volunteers within categories as a first priority or, conversely, may decide that certain persons should be "deferred" for particular reasons—for example, homelessness. While the federal government does not recognize a "deferral" category, a state can define particular characteristics as "good cause" for not participating (Greenberg, 1990, p. 19).

The secretary has to define what constitutes "participation," and, as we have seen under WIN, this is an important issue. States have claimed high participation rates even though large numbers of recipients are in varying stages of administrative "hold." The law says that registration alone will not constitute participation, but even under a strict definition, the participation rate has to be only 7% in fiscal years 1990 and 1991, and there are no penalties for a state's failure to meet this goal prior to fiscal year 1991.

A state may rely to a large extent on voluntary participation by recipients within categories. Federal law requires that states give "first consideration" to volunteers, but does not necessarily require that volunteers, in fact, be enrolled before others; regulations allow states to consider a variety of other factors in addition to individual preferences (Greenberg, 1990, p. 24). If a state chooses to concentrate on volunteers, it will probably save on administrative and compliance costs. However, it should be recognized that a program that selects volunteers first is not the same as a volunteers-only program (like Massachusetts). Under a volunteers-first program, if participants fail to comply without good cause, they are subject to sanctions because they still have nonexempt status (Savner et al., 1986). Federal law requires custodial parents under 20 years old who have not completed high school or its equivalent to participate in educational activities. However, the requirement is applicable only if a program exists in a particular political subdivision and there are available state resources to cover the costs. Moreover, work or training, rather than education, can be required if the recipient already has basic literacy skills or a long-term employment plan that does not require a high school diploma or its equivalent; in these circumstances, education is considered "inappropriate." States have discretion to let persons attending post-high school education continue working and count it as JOBS participation, and pay child-care and transportation costs with JOBS funds.

The states' JOBS programs must provide the following four services: (a) education below postsecondary level, which can include high school or its equivalent, basic and remedial English or English proficiency programs; (b) job skills training; (c) job readiness activities; and (d) job development and placement. In addition, every program must also include at least two of four optional services: group and individual job search, on-the-job training, work supplementation (i.e., using AFDC grants to subsidize wages), and community work experience or an alternative work experience approved by the Department of Health and Human Services. The emphasis on education is new, and, if implemented, could result in significant changes at the state level.

It should be emphasized that these requirements and options are bare-bones descriptions only; it is up to the individual states to decide not only the precise character and scope of the various components but also, with some exceptions,[7] the allocation of participants to the various components (Greenberg, 1990). It is up to the states to decide how many people will participate in each activity; again, a state might concentrate on education and training for relatively few participants, or job search and work-relief for larger numbers. There are restrictions on community work experience (CWEP, work-relief). Generally, the maximum hours of obligation are tied to the federal or applicable state minimum wage.[8] Other than the hours, the work-relief restrictions are very general. CWEP projects must be limited to some sort of public service (e.g., health, social service, environmental protection, education, development, public facilities or safety, day care) and, "to the extent possible, the prior training, experience, and skills of a recipient shall be used in making appropriate work experience assignments." A participant is not required to accept a job if that job would result in a net loss of income. However, states have discretion to supplement a low-wage job if that person would otherwise lose AFDC.

In addition to transportation and other work-related expenses, states must guarantee child care if it is necessary for a participant's education, training, or employment, although, again, it is very unclear just what a guarantee of child care means. In an important change, federal law requires that states must provide child care for up to a year for persons who go off of AFDC as a result of increased hours of employment, wages, or loss of AFDC earnings disregards as long as the state determines that the extended child care is necessary for employment.[9]

The state can provide child care directly, through purchase of service or vouchers, reimbursement to the family, or any other arrangement the state deems appropriate. The state can choose to pay the local market rate for child care, which has been defined as 75% of the cost of slots in the community, or as little as $200 per month for full-time care for a child under 2, and $175 for a child age 2 or over. But the state rate cannot exceed the local market rate. If the state chooses to pay below the market rate, then this virtually ensures reliance on informal and unlicensed care (Greenberg, 1990, p. 7). But to be federally reimbursable, the child care must meet applicable standards of state and local law.

In another important provision, the states must extend Medicaid for up to one year for recipients who lose AFDC due to employment.[10] Moreover, even if a state chooses to limit an AFDC-UP family to six months per year, the Medicaid coverage continues for the entire year, thus lessening some of the welfare discrimination against poor children in intact families. There are many details and state options under this provision. Costs and methods of payment vary. Generally, for the first six months coverage is free to the recipient, with the state paying the family's costs for the employer-provided health insurance. After six months, states must provide an additional six months of coverage for families with incomes below 185% of the poverty line, but can impose a premium on families exceeding 100% of poverty (Greenberg, 1990, p. 35).

Generally speaking, the participation process in JOBS follows procedures similar to those in GAIN and other state programs. There is an assessment, followed by an employability plan. There are notice, information, and timing requirements on the part of the state, including the availability of assistance in obtaining appropriate child care. Again, as with most matters, there is state flexibility in deciding how to conduct the assessments, in defining what "entering the program" means, and in developing an employment plan. The state is told to take various factors into account, including participant preferences, but is not told how to assign weights. After the assessment and development of the employability plan, the state may require the participant to enter into an agreement. Among other things, the agreement is to spell out the participant's obligations, the terms and conditions of participation, and what services (including child care) and other assistance the state is to provide. It is up to the state to decide whether the agreement is to be considered a contract under state law (Greenberg, 1990, p. 44).

Nonexempt recipients are subject to sanction if, without good cause, they fail to participate in JOBS, refuse to accept or quit employment, or otherwise reduce their earnings.[11] "Failure to participate" means failure to meet the requirements for all of the stages in the process—orientation, assessment, developing the employment plan, and so forth. If an individual disagrees with her assignment, it is unclear whether she has a right to a hearing at that point or must first refuse and be sanctioned (Greenberg, 1990, p. 43). If an individual is sanctioned, then that person's needs are excluded from the grant. If that person is a parent or caretaker, then the grant is paid to a protective payee. In AFDC-UP families, if only one parent is participating, then both parents' grants are subject to sanction even if the second parent is exempt. If both parents are participating, then only the grant of the sanctioned parent is affected. The sanctioned participant also loses Medicaid, unless there is some other basis for Medicaid eligibility. For the first violation, the sanction lasts until there is compliance; for the second violation, for three months or until compliance, whichever is longer; for the third and subsequent violations, the sanction lasts for six months or until compliance, again, whichever is longer. "Good cause" is defined by the states, except it must include the absence of needed child care, a job that would require the mother of a child under 6 to work more than 20 hours per week, or a job that would reduce the family's net income.[12] States are required to establish conciliation procedures to resolve disputes and to provide hearings for unresolved disputes. There are no federal requirements concerning the conciliation process. States may use the welfare fair-hearing process or create a separate one for JOBS. Under federal law, states cannot terminate welfare benefits prior to the hearing, but, according to HHS regulations, they can terminate child care and supportive services (Greenberg, 1990, pp. 55–56).

JOBS reflects the states' recent experiences with work programs under the Reagan administration's waiver policies. In that sense, the new law reflects traditional patterns of reform. Many domestic federal programs trace their origins to state experimentation and development. But in two other respects, JOBS is new. It was part of the Reagan administration's philosophy of reducing the role of the federal government; JOBS represents a major shift of responsibility for the design and implementation of welfare work programs from the federal government to the states (Kamerman & Kahn, 1989).

Yet, as we shall point out, it is quite likely that the rhetoric of JOBS will not be matched by its operational reality. The probable emphasis on myths and ceremonies is already apparent in the disjuncture between the promises of JOBS and the actual allocation of federal funds. Federal funding is limited and capped, rising from $600 million in fiscal year 1989 to $1 billion in fiscal year 1996 and subsequent years. Adjusted for inflation, the funding for 1989 essentially restores the WIN funding for 1981, but the pool of mandatory participants has been greatly expanded by the lowering of the age of the children for nonexempted recipients from 6 to 3.[13] It has been estimated that JOBS would permit 15,000 more AFDC recipients to participate in the program in 1989, and an additional 100,000 in each subsequent year. This is, at best, a modest increment. Furthermore, the states have to come up with their share of the matching funds, and they are unlikely to reach the federal cap. Since many states are now running budget deficits, available state funding for JOBS will be tight and the states will have to decide how many recipients will actually participate.[14] It is also likely that states will use the federal funding to reduce the commitment of their own resources to save money, as has happened already in California. Since the federal participation requirements are low, it is up to each state to decide how extensive a program it will have. Serious education and training programs are expensive, implying a small number of participants; unsupervised job search and work-relief without training would allow broad participation.

We argue that the main purpose of the Family Support Act is to provide an affirmation of the moral values expressed in the consensus on welfare reform: responsibility, work, family, education, and state discretion. The FSA deals directly with each area. It provides for contracts spelling out mutual obligations between the state and the welfare recipients (responsibility); its centerpiece is work and employment preparation; it strengthens and expands child support (family); states are authorized to use "learnfare" for teenage recipients (education); and the structure of the legislation, to a large extent, amounts to a codification of the delegation of responsibility to the states. Accordingly, we now turn to the broader consensus on welfare reform. How much is going to change?

Mutual Contractual Obligations (Responsibility)

Under JOBS, states have discretion as to whether to require recipients to enter into participation contracts. The contract is ideologically important. It is a central element of the conservative approach. As Reischauer (1989) points out, in contrast to the ideology of the 1960s and 1970s, it will now be made clear to recipients that in return for cash assistance and services, they, too, have an obligation to themselves and their families to try to become self-sufficient (see also Mead, 1989). Liberals are also in favor of contracts; they view the contract as a form of empowerment that will allow recipients to play a meaningful role in their future.

Not surprisingly, contracts in social welfare are not a new idea. They exist in a wide variety of settings, and experience with them has varied. Some say that contracts help in focusing both clients and staff on what is expected; some claim that contracts even aid in monitoring staff performance. On the other hand, it is claimed that, at best, contracts are useless paperwork; that they are easily manipulated by staff to suit their own purposes and increase their control over clients (Nelkin, 1987).

How are these contracts likely to work out in the current welfare reform? The county promises cash assistance, child care, and employment preparation in return for conscientious participation. This seems reasonable and just. But what are the mutual obligations and responsibilities, and how will they be enforced? The county has a variety of ways of enforcing its end of the bargain. If the participant does not perform as specified, the county can reduce and take control of the family grant. What can the participant do? Suppose that a participant needs English and math classes to upgrade her skills but there is nowhere available for her to take them, and instead she is offered either training for a low-skilled job or a workfare slot? Suppose the day care that is available is not suitable? Basically, the participant has three options: She can accept what is offered, she can leave welfare, or she can invoke the formal grievance procedure.[15] For well-established reasons, the grievance procedure is not an effective remedy for the vast majority of recipients (Handler, 1986). This means that in reality the participant has only two options—accept the conditions or leave welfare. What she cannot do is hold the county to its part of the bargain. She cannot get, in fact, the services or day care that she needs.[16]

The lack of sufficient day care well illustrates the problem of mutual responsibilities. As part of the consensus compromise, the liberals extracted significant promises for improvements in child-care funding. GAIN recognized the importance of child care to training and employment; passage of the California legislation was linked to other legislation designed to increase the supply of school-age child-care programs throughout the state. And, unlike many other programs, GAIN promised to pay market rates for child care (Strassburger, 1987). At the time of enactment, it was estimated that when GAIN was fully implemented, $118 million per year would be spent on child care. However, this was based on a rate of $1.50 per hour to provide care for 50,000 to 90,000 school-age children of the mandatory participants. In addition, there would be a one-time appropriation of $22.5 million for capital costs—for example, for portable buildings that could be set up on school grounds.

The emphasis of the GAIN program is for recipients to use relatives and other care that is exempt from state licensing laws. The administration refused to use the well-regarded child-care programs currently administered by the State Department of Education (SDE) (with a current budget of more than $300 million). SDE mostly contracts with agencies and school districts to operate child-care programs for low-income families. Instead of SDE, the State Department of Social Services would administer the child-care funds. Governor Deukmejian's Child Care Task Force rejected using the SDE programs on the grounds that GAIN could provide cheaper "basic" child care rather than quality care.[17]

Counties are required to pay for care for children under 12. They can set up their own programs or contract with agencies already providing services for the Education Department. Many counties are using their own systems to minimize costs. Most are choosing a vendor/voucher system. Aside from relatively minor restrictions on costs, parents are free to choose their child-care programs, but they have only two choices before risking sanctions.

GAIN requires counties to "encourage" care by relatives. This benefits the counties. Informal caregivers usually will accept less pay and can be paid only for the hours they work. Licensed care, in addition to being more expensive, must be paid for in part- or full-day slots, and erratic hours for mothers (training, classes, interviews, and so forth) cause problems. Most counties will pay only for the exact hours that the parents are occupied, which effectively precludes parents from choosing licensed providers. Informal care may be satisfactory for the relatively short periods of job search, education, and training, but is probably a less viable solution once a parent has long-term, permanent employment (Strassburger, 1987).

The real issue of day care will be the supply. At present in California, no area has sufficient day care to meet the needs of GAIN participants once the program is fully implemented. Licensed facilities are at 100% of capacity, and family day-care homes are at 83%. The current funding for latchkey child care will provide for 8,000 children; GAIN will add between 50,000 and 90,000 children, but the state report behind the bill estimated that between 620,000 and 815,000 children were in need of this service (Strassburger, 1987).

The Job Opportunities and Basic Skills program is not going to improve the California situation. JOBS and accompanying regulations require the states to guarantee necessary child care for JOBS participants, but there is substantial discretion as to how much the states have to pay for care. The range of the guarantee is from a low of $175 for full-time care for a child 2 or over, or $200 for a child under 2, to the market rate (defined as the rate that will cover 75% of the providers) (Greenberg, 1990, p. 122). According to the Children's Defense Fund (1988), the average cost per month per child for child care is $250. There are many unresolved issues as to just what this guarantee means—whether a state can limit its obligations because of lack of resources, whether it can deny or limit child care in non-JOBS areas or for non-JOBS participants, whether only certain components of JOBS carry the guarantee, whether only AFDC children in the family are entitled to the guarantee, and so forth (Greenberg, 1990, pp. 123–124). The regulations provide for restrictions on child care—for example, if an individual is not making satisfactory progress in education or training, or pending a hearing. The guarantee applies only to "necessary" child care, again a matter to be determined by the states. Individuals may choose informal care, but, according to the regulations, are not required to do so.

Thus the major issues of day care are not legal guarantees or whether the failure to supply day care results in a good-cause refusal to participate, but rather whether poor families will be able to get quality day care. After all, there will be substantial numbers of welfare families who will want to participate, who want to take advantage of education and training opportunities. The federal matching funds are open-ended for child care that meets federal requirements (Greenberg, 1990, p. 128). However, if past policies are any guide, it does seem doubtful that substantial federal assistance will be made available for the welfare poor. Consistent with its overall philosophy of reducing direct government involvement, the Reagan administration shifted from subsidizing the supply of child care to the demand side. Financial assistance was increased significantly for those who use child care via the dependent care tax credit; at the same time, the child-care credit for AFDC recipients was reduced (Kamerman & Kahn, 1989).[18] These changes were also consistent with the Reagan administration's overall policy of reorienting federal policy away from the poor to middle- and upper-income families. Tax credits now amount to more than $4 billion in federal financial assistance for child care (Liebman, 1989). Kamerman and Kahn (1989) report that almost two-thirds of the families who have claimed the credit had incomes above the median; only 7% with incomes below $10,000 have claimed the credit. Only 13% of federal tax dollars go to families with incomes below $15,000 (Liebman, 1989). Some states have tried to help the poorest single working mothers, but the subsidies are very low, and preclude any sort of quality care. Overall, child-care funding in the majority of states has declined (Kamerman & Kahn, 1989).

The decline in subsidies to child-care providers also hurt the poor, since the most heavily subsidized centers tended to be in low-income areas. There has been an increase in the supply of for-profit centers (now about one-half of the total licensed facilities),[19] but these benefit the middle class—they shun poor neighborhoods, and they try to cream by avoiding children with problems. The result is that now fewer children from low-income families are being served in the organized system (Kamerman & Kahn, 1989).

Currently, Congress and the administration are in the process of trying to resolve their differences over new child-care legislation. The Democrats favor an expanded state and federal role in subsidizing and regulating the supply, with sliding-scale subsidies for families. The Republicans favor an expanded income tax credit.[20] Under the Republican plan, there would be no federal standards; families could use any kind of day care they wanted, or none at all. The only requirement would be that one of the parents is working. Curiously, the Republicans' plan is targeted more at the poor than the Democrats', which could benefit more than half the population (Liebman, 1989). In any event, the best guess is that in view of the present budget crisis, not much in the way of new funding (or child care) will be made available. In the meantime, the pressures increase; more families are using child care and paying more for the services. For families at or near the poverty line, child-care costs can amount to as much as one-fifth of family income ("Average Child Support," 1987).

The short supply of child care is only one part of the problem of funding welfare reform. In addition to day care, in this era of very tight budgets, how much education and training will be available? In California, a Manpower Demonstration Research Corporation (MDRC) study of a sample of GAIN registrants in eight counties indicated that approximately 60% were in need of basic education (Riccio et al., 1989). In the Los Angeles County Participant Needs Assessment, it was found that 40% of the mandatory participants do not speak English, and almost 80% had less than a high school education. Providing the necessary educational resources is likely to increase the length of stay of the participants in the program and to escalate the costs as well. Will these pressures result in creaming and the tracking of clients into less costly program activities such as job search? (See Chapter 5.)

Creaming and tracking are also reinforced by administrative constraints. Welfare departments, which are typically understaffed and deprofessionalized, will be under severe pressure to process participants—to make assessments, to get contracts signed, to move participants through the system. It is in this environment—an environment of scarce resources and severe administrative constraints—that the ideology of contract, contract as empowerment and contract as moral obligation, is supposed to take root. The reality, of course, is that recipients will be given a set of requirements as they have in the past—the only difference will be that at the top of the page there will appear the word *contract* and at the bottom there will be a place for a signature.

Work: Changing AFDC
From Cash Relief to Work-Relief

So far, current work requirements have been applied to only a few recipients. While many objections have been raised about all aspects of the work requirements, major questions concern the feasibility of a nationwide program. Judith Gueron (1990), in a recent review of the MDRC experiments, points to some uncertainties. States will have to find a balance between coverage and intensity, and there is no clear sense whether greater investment in education and training will generate sufficiently greater returns to justify the added costs. Even less is known about the implications of serving women with very young children.

How much better off would recipients be if they worked? As noted in Chapter 5, the average increase in earnings in the MDRC experiments ranges from 10% to 30%, representing a significant increase in participants' disposable income. In the Supported Work Demonstration, the average increase was $900, nearly 50% over the earnings of the control group. Thus, in general, work programs can be expected to decrease welfare dependence by reducing either the absolute number of recipients or the proportion of total income derived from welfare.[21]

Yet, as pointed out in Chapters 4 and 5, there are limits as to what these programs can achieve. Even though welfare costs may be reduced, most poor single mothers will not be able to escape poverty through work. While only a small minority probably cannot work at all, about three-quarters of all welfare recipients cannot get jobs that will pay enough even if they work full-time.[22] Thus to reduce poverty substantially among mother-only families it will be necessary to supplement the earnings of single mothers who head families through some form of government transfer.

Moreover, the scope of JOBS is such that it will affect a very small fraction of welfare recipients, and cannot possibly, even with adequate funding and services, reach more than a third of the eligible recipients. Finally, experience with work programs has shown that much of their success is dependent on the conditions of the labor market. A notable example is ET in Massachusetts. Yet, when unemployment rises and wages become depressed, there is little that recipients can gain from such programs, as the experience of West Virginia points out. Therefore, liberals such as Garfinkel and McLanahan, who support the work requirement, argue that the government must create or locate jobs.

Changing the basic direction of AFDC from cash relief to work-relief is the key element of the welfare reform. However, because it is assumed that the various parts of the reform consensus will work together in changing the lives of welfare recipients—for example, contracts, child-support, and education are supposed to change values and resources—we will return to the work requirements and Garfinkel and McLanahan's analysis and proposals after considering the other reform initiatives.

Strengthening the Family: Child Support

Child support is one area where there is strong consensus. As with so many other welfare reforms, increased efforts to collect child support are also intimately tied to reducing welfare costs and caseloads. The first federal involvement took place as far back as 1950, when Congress authorized state welfare agencies to notify law enforcement officials when an AFDC child was deserted or abandoned; they would have the option to prosecute for failure to provide child support. In the 1960s, various statutory changes were designed to strengthen state child-support efforts—for example, federal help in locating absent fathers, requiring states to enforce support and establish paternity, allowing states to request addresses from the Internal Revenue Service and HEW. In 1975, the first significant legislation was passed. Sponsored by Senator Russell Long and explicitly sold on the basis of reducing welfare costs and caseloads, the legislation required the federal government to pay 75% of the cost of establishing paternity, locating absent fathers, and collecting child support, and authorized the use of Internal Revenue Service data to aid in collecting support for AFDC recipients; in 1980, the IRS provision was extended to nonwelfare families (Garfinkel & McLanahan, 1986, pp. 118–119).

The trends of federal assistance in the enforcement of child-support obligations accelerated during the Reagan administration. The 1984 Child Support Amendments broke new ground in that they go beyond the goal of reducing welfare costs; they apply to all parents. The two most important provisions require the states to adopt income-assignment laws that require employers to withhold child-support obligations from wages if the noncustodial parent is delinquent for one month, and to appoint a state commission to establish statewide standards for child support. According to Garfinkel and McLanahan (1986), the reason for the inclusion of nonwelfare parents is the emerging consensus in the country that the current child-support system condones parental irresponsibility (p. 136). In 1985, of the 8.8 million women with at least one child under 21 and an absent husband, 39% were never awarded child support. Of the 4.4 million women who were supposed to receive money from child-support awards, less than half received the full amount owed; of the rest, about half got less and half got nothing (Kosterlitz, 1987).

The FSA would strengthen the 1984 amendments in a number of ways. States would be required to meet new federal paternity establishment standards, which include establishing paternity in a certain percentage of cases of children receiving AFDC or child-support services.[23] There would be 90% federal matching funds for the paternity establishment program. The new law also requires the withholding of wages for all new child-support orders entered on or after January 1, 1994, unless the court finds good cause not to or both parties agree in writing to an alternative arrangement. Courts and other officials are encouraged to establish child-support guidelines for setting awards with periodic review. The guidelines will be rebuttable presumptions; awards that vary from the guidelines must be based on a finding that the guidelines would be unjust or inappropriate. By 1993, states must implement periodic review to measure the adequacy of child-support awards against the guidelines. States must, at the request of either parent, determine whether an award should be reviewed. By October 1, 1995, states are to have in place automated tracking and monitoring systems to increase child- or spousal-support collections. The Federal Parent Locator Service is to be given access to wage and unemployment compensation claims information and Department of Labor and state employment service data. States must require each parent to furnish his or her social security number upon the birth of the child, unless there is good cause not to do so, and that number must be made available to the state child-support enforcement agency (Children's Defense Fund, 1988, pp. 32–36).

Still, it is doubtful whether tough child-support legislation will have much effect on welfare families, because of the low earnings of the fathers. Child-support payments have dropped in real terms. According to the latest Census Bureau report, after adjusting for inflation, the average annual child-support payment fell from $2,528 in 1983 to $2,215 in 1985, a drop of 12.4%, while men's real average income rose from $19,630 to $20,650 (there are no data on income for absent fathers alone) ("Average Child Support," 1987; Kosterlitz, 1987). The amounts awarded by judges had declined by about the same amount as the drop in actual payments. The situation is even worse for the poor. Of all mothers in poverty, less than one-third were awarded child support and, of these, more than one-third received nothing. And, of this group, minorities, the less well educated, and the young were even worse off ("Average Child Support," 1987).

It has been charged that one of the reasons for the decline in collections is that the states have been slow in implementing the 1984 law. On the other hand, there is a coincidence in the decline in child-support payments, the one-third decline in the income of low-income families, and the declining level of child support awarded by judges. "It seems entirely likely that less is being awarded and less is being paid because fathers have less" (Schorr, 1987). In a recent study of three states (Colorado, Hawaii, and Illinois) that have implemented guidelines, while it was found that the number of zero awards fell somewhat, the overall increase was quite modest (about 15%). More significantly, the awards did little to improve the financial position of the custodial parent, especially with lower- and middle-income families. Child-support guidelines simply cannot alter the basic lack of resources (Pearson, Thoenes, & Tjaden, 1989).

Even if all child-support payments awarded were collected, the impact on welfare still might not be significant. According to HHS projections, higher child-support payments would lift less than 10% of families off the rolls. Others would be prevented from going on welfare. Estimates of savings to the federal government range from $178 million (Congressional Budget Office) to $367 million (the Ways and Means Committee) (see Kosterlitz, 1987).

How much can absent fathers of AFDC children contribute? A recent study showed that between 1973 and 1984, the average annual income for men between the ages of 20 and 24 fell almost 30%, from $11,572 to $8,072 in 1984 dollars; the decline for young African-American men was nearly 50%. On the other hand, another study showed that young men do contribute. Almost 60% reported paying child support, with average annual payments of $2,500— more than half the average annual AFDC payment. Even poor young men reported some contributions—a fourth reported an annual average of $925 (Kosterlitz, 1987).

It should be pointed out that there is strong support for tough child support even if the antipoverty results may be problematic, even if there may be resulting economic hardship to low-income fathers, and even though more fundamental problems have to do with the deplorable economic prospects of young African-American males. Many believe that the benefits of tough child-support measures lie as much in the message they send as in the money collected (Kosterlitz, 1987).

Education Reforms

Although education has been emphasized in several of the OBRA state experiments and the Family Support Act, education reform is more broadly based and extends throughout society. In this sense, it is similar to child support. However, unlike child support, which will probably have only a small impact on the poor female-headed household, education reforms could well have a large and adverse impact on poor children.

We discuss two aspects of education reform—the specific FSA provisions and the broader education reforms. FSA requires that states provide educational activities (subject to available resources) for teenage welfare parents who lack high school diplomas or the equivalent. For those parents over 20 who lack high school diplomas or the equivalent, a state can require JOBS participation, but then must provide educational activities unless the parent has basic literacy skills or a long-term employment goal that does not require a high school diploma or equivalent. Even though a state cannot require a parent of a child under 6 to participate in JOBS more than part-time, a state can require a teen parent to participate in school full-time as soon as her child is born. On the other hand, a state may require work instead of education for a custodial parent age 18 or 19 who is not progressing satisfactorily in school or if, in view of the individual's employability plan, education would be "inappropriate." If a participant is expelled from school, she might be subject to sanction for "failure to participate" (Greenberg, 1990, pp. 60–62).[24]

Consistent with the overall philosophy of FSA, with some exceptions,[25] the states have substantial leeway in deciding the key elements of the requirements—what constitutes participation and what activities are to be provided, ranging from counseling and supportive services for pregnant teenagers, to assessments of educational opportunities, to on-site or near-site child-care arrangements, to postsecondary education. With regard to welfare recipients, most state attention is focused on "learnfare," a mandatory school attendance program for teenage recipients pioneered by Wisconsin.[26]

The impetus behind Wisconsin's learnfare reflected national concerns: (a) the specter of the young welfare mother with a poor work history and no high school diploma becoming a long-term dependent, (b) the impending national labor shortage coexisting with a chronically unemployed group, and (c) fear of a growing underclass (Corbett, Deloya, Manning, & Uhr, 1989). With widespread support, Wisconsin quickly enacted a program that provides that if a welfare recipient (a parent or a child) aged 13 through 19 fails to meet strict attendance requirements, he or she is sanctioned for each month that a violation occurs.[27] The governor vetoed all provisions for services, including referral to the State Department of Instruction's Children-at-Risk program, before sanctions are imposed.[28] The amount of the sanction is determined by ignoring the noncompliant family member in calculating the family grant. For example, in a two-person family, the grant is reduced from $440 to $248. There are exceptions—if the student is expelled and an alternative school is not available, the teen has a child under 3 months of age, licensed day care is not available, transportation problems are prohibitive, or the teen is over 16 and not expected to graduate from school by age 20. On the other hand, once the unexcused absences are verified, no investigation is undertaken before the sanctions are imposed. The families can appeal, however (Corbett et al., 1989).

When the Wisconsin program was instituted there was no evaluation component, and there is no control group. Consequently, it is impossible to determine what effects the program has had on either school attendance or performance. What can be said, however, is that during the program's first year a lot of teen welfare recipients received sanctions. Over the course of the year, more than 18% were sanctioned in at least one month; this sanction rate exceeds considerably the rates typically associated with workfare programs. Moreover, teen *parents* were disproportionately sanctioned, mostly in Milwaukee, the state's one large urban area (Greenberg & Sherman, 1989).

Learnfare is a popular idea. A large number of states are developing programs, but, in contrast to Wisconsin, which is only a sanction program, the other states are attempting to take seriously the idea of reciprocal obligations. Typically, plans call for case managers to work with at-risk teens for supportive services and, in at least one state, both positive and negative sanctions (Corbett et al., 1989).

Thus learnfare, at least as planned in states other than Wisconsin, has two aspects. One is the familiar theme of getting tough on welfare recipients; this is the Wisconsin approach. But the other theme, which stresses services, taps into the broader concern about education reform in general. The impetus behind the education reforms is the widespread feeling that our public schools have failed; that vast numbers of young people are growing up without basic, minimal math or reading competence, and thus lack the skills to be mail carriers, clerks, cashiers, or even to do delivery work, let alone hold higher-paying jobs (Glazer, 1985). There are distressingly large numbers of high school dropouts, but even those who complete high school lack a basic, minimum education. Many believe that the poor and their children will never escape poverty without improving their educational competence.

Nationwide, the focus of education reform is the public high school. The effort includes implementing competency standards for graduation; requiring more courses in sciences, mathematics, English, and foreign languages; increasing the length of the school day and school year; and upgrading textbooks, instructional materials, and teaching (Levin, 1986).

According to Levin (1986), a major shortcoming of the proposed reforms is that they have little to offer those he calls "educationally disadvantaged" students. Students who are minorities or who are from immigrant or non-English-speaking families, or who are poor, tend to have low academic achievement and high dropout rates. Because of poverty, cultural obstacles, and language differences, schools are least successful in teaching this population compared with children whose parents have graduated from high school or have had some post-high school education, where there is adequate income, shelter, and privacy, and standard English is spoken.

Levin (1986, p. 15) estimates that a least a third of elementary and secondary students are educationally disadvantaged, that their proportion will rise rapidly, and that one important consequence will be a serious deterioration in the quality of the labor force. High dropout rates, low test scores, and poor academic performance will mean that a larger and larger proportion of the school population will be undereducated for even lower-level service and assembly work. Thus increasing numbers of our population will face unemployment, or employment at menial jobs with low earnings.

While our country seems to have recognized the failure of its public schools, in Levin's view the educational reforms being undertaken now will not help the educationally disadvantaged, and may actually make matters worse. Setting competency standards for high school graduation and increasing the time spent in school may actually increase dropout rates. The problem is that disadvantaged students enter secondary school with a two- or three-year handicap, and it is unlikely that any but a few will be able to make up the difference in order to graduate. In the past, schools have met the competency problem by setting very low levels for graduation. But without strong compensatory programs, higher competency requirements will just increase the pressure on the disadvantaged to drop out. Increasing the course requirements in high school, when the disadvantaged are already behind, only exacerbates the problem. The problem has to be attacked at the earliest grades, with major funding and programs. Otherwise, too many of the disadvantaged will be required to repeat grades, at a great cost to the schools.

To the extent that Levin's analysis is correct—and incoming data tend to support his view ("Average Child Support," 1987)—the current educational reforms could very well make matters worse for AFDC families. Depending on state funding, some mothers will receive education and training, and might even obtain permanent unsubsidized employment, which ought to help them serve as positive role models for their children. But the current educational reforms (to the extent that they are implemented) will tend to work at cross-purposes with such changes. AFDC children are the educationally disadvantaged, and there will be increased pressure on them to fail.

State Discretion

The fifth area of consensus is a shift of responsibility for welfare policy from the federal government to the states. The Reagan administration was long in favor of this reallocation (Kamerman & Kahn, 1989). It initially tried, but failed, to turn AFDC and food stamps completely over to the states. When its effort to require states to institute workfare also stalled, it encouraged the states to seek waivers, and most have by now exercised that option. Now, as we have seen, a considerable share of the funding for work requirements comes from the states. The Family Support Act completes the Reagan victory. Under the guise of federal reform, state authority to fashion work and welfare has been codified and increased.

The shift in responsibility has had a number of important political consequences. Conflict is now at the state and local levels, and it will be more difficult to sustain effective political action on behalf of the poor. It will be more difficult to enforce the legal rights of the poor, and shifting costs will make it more difficult to sustain generous programs (Butler, 1985; Hasenfeld, 1987). Local communities will have a greater incentive to reduce costs by requiring work. The simultaneous reduction of federal funding and granting of more autonomy to the states mobilized local interest groups and, as anticipated, a significant number of states adopted workfare. States varied in their responses, depending on their economic and political conditions. States with higher economic growth and lower unemployment tended to emphasize job placement, training, and supportive services, and to deemphasize work-relief. Economically depressed and more rural states tended to emphasize straight work-relief.

The shift in responsibility through the option and waiver policies, and now under FSA, brings us back full circle to the initial discussion of the allocation of jurisdictional authority over social welfare programs. We have argued that the allocation of authority coincided with social and political attitudes toward the category of recipients that the particular program served: Those considered deserving were served by a federal program; those undeserving, at the local level. Although AFDC has federal elements, the weight of the program has always been centered at the state and local levels, reflecting the undeserving status of poor mother-only families. Now, most of AFDC is increasingly more state and locally controlled. Categorical eligibility (i.e., the definition of a dependent child) is still subject to federal regulation, but the FSA only partially modifies the state's option to include the unemployed father. And while there are federal rules governing many aspects of the budget (e.g., work expenses, rules defining the composition of a family for purposes of welfare), *financial* eligibility and the all-important level of benefits remain state matters, and this is a major form of exclusion. The amount of benefits has always been at the heart of welfare. And now, a major condition of benefits—the whole complex of work requirements—has also been allocated to the states. As a result of the welfare rights and legal rights activities of the 1960s and 1970s, the states have lost most of their discretion over categorical eligibility—for example, they can no longer exclude women on the basis of race or moral behavior—but over the years, they have been given the authority to regulate, sanction, and, if necessary, terminate these people from welfare for a variety of other reasons. In short, the "undeserving" can be excluded for financial reasons and now for violating work requirements as well.

The fundamental distinction between the deserving poor and the undeserving poor is whether a category is morally excused from work. When the class is not excluded, and distinctions have to be made within the category, then this test has historically been administered at the local level. Historically, the control of deviant behavior, including the enforcement of industrial discipline, has been primarily a local matter; this is still true today. The moral issues, the dilemmas, the fears, the hatreds, the passions and compassion that arise out of close contact with deviant behavior are most keenly felt at the local level. Communities care about enforcing their values. Welfare has always involved great moral issues— work, moral redemption, pauperism, vice, crime, delinquency, sex, family relations, child rearing, race, and ethnicity. The anger and hostility between social classes and categories is more keenly felt the closer the proximity; the more deviant the category is considered, the more local the program. Increasing the work requirements for AFDC recipients and delegating administration to states makes stunningly clear our social and political attitudes toward poor mothers and their children.

Local control of deviant behavior also suits the institutional needs of state and federal legislatures. Legislatures are busy institutions; they have to deal with the overall budget, and all other matters compete for scarce time. Deviant behavior, including welfare, is controversial, and most legislators try to stay away from controversial issues. From time to time, problems boil up at the local level and various interest groups demand state and/or federal intervention. The favored legislative response is to purport to deal with the problem primarily through the production of symbols while, in reality, redelegating the problem back to the local level, sometimes altering local political struggles. At the top level of government (federal or state), dominant values will be affirmed, but it will be at the local level that the contradictions and conflicts will be fought out. Moreover, at the local level, the controversies are more likely to be of low visibility, operating in the silent interstices of the bureaucracy. There may be more federal or state requirements, and more financial incentives, but a close look at actual administration will usually show a great deal of local-level flexibility. In welfare, it is the local offices that pick and choose who is worthy or who will be turned away. This is exactly what is happening as the current workfare consensus unfolds, and the reason behind the "renewed" interest in state discretion. The Family Support Act confirms the historic jurisdictional allocation of welfare policy.

WHICH DIRECTION?

There are three likely paths for AFDC. The least likely is that the current consensus on welfare reform will be enacted and will work.

By *work*, we mean that there will be sufficient energy, political will, patience, and resources to implement the programs at a reasonable and sustained level. There will be education and training slots, the services will be relevant to the skills required by the economy, there will be adequate levels of day care, and there will be a sufficient number of unsubsidized suitable jobs. In addition, two important innovations of FSA must be continued, if not expanded: More broadly based child-care and health care programs for low-income families in general and subsidized day care and health care for welfare families must be continued for a significant period *after* mothers leave welfare; otherwise, the costs of leaving welfare through employment become too high. If these reforms were to happen, then welfare dependency could be reduced, if not eliminated, for a reasonable number of recipients.

If two other important changes were to be made, then we would really have turned a corner in our welfare policy. First, there is no justification for the mandatory features of the work programs. They are expensive, and they divert scarce resources. There have always been many more volunteers, even among the so-called hard to employ, than there are available training slots and jobs, and volunteers are invariably more successful in these programs (Mitchell et al., 1979). There is no credible evidence that the vast majority of welfare mothers need a "message." What they need is hope and opportunity, not the threat of sanctions (Goodwin, 1983). There are, no doubt, some people who are reluctant to prepare themselves for an independent life—teenagers form one frequently noted group—but special, targeted efforts should be made rather than distorting an entire program. Mandatory workfare is neither fair to the recipients nor cost-effective. It is also unnecessary.

The second change would be a decent income-support system. Garfinkel and McLanahan (1986) and Ellwood (1988) have described such a program at length. It is premised on the fact that even with a good work program and good jobs, most mothers of young children will not be able to support themselves even at poverty-line levels with full-time jobs. Indeed, as noted, only a third of nonwelfare mothers have full-time jobs; the rest either work part-time or are not in the paid labor force.

If these two changes were made, along with a good work program, then AFDC would be altered in a fundamental way. It would be a program of *inclusion*—poor mothers and their children would be treated the same as the nonpoor. They would be given the same choices that other mothers have—full- or part-time paid labor or homemaking and child rearing. Like the nonpoor, they could choose independent life or marriage. They would not be stigmatized or considered deviant because they would have the same options as the nonpoor; as with the nonpoor, none of the options would be privileged. It would be choice, not coercion, that brings the two groups together.

But the adoption of a decently funded work program, let alone a good income-support system, is not likely. Reischauer (1989), whose description of the consensus on welfare reform opens this chapter, is doubtful that much will change. First, he points out that while there is broad agreement on the major elements of the consensus, there is sharp disagreement on the details—and it is on details that policies and programs founder. Second, Reischauer recognizes the fundamental problem of cost. As has been emphasized in our discussion of the work requirements, in the short run at least, any kind of serious work and training program, including work-relief, will be very expensive, especially when day care and transportation are included. Given the present pressure on public budgets, costs will be a serious obstacle.[29] Third, it is difficult to administer these kinds of people-changing programs. The technology is uncertain. A great deal of interorganizational coordination is needed. The participants, moreover, often have significant employability deficits. As stated earlier, the results of even the best of the work programs, programs that probably could not be replicated nationwide, show only modest success (Sawhill, 1988). The final reason, notes Reischauer, is the state of the economy. In recessionary periods, there is little that work requirements can do to increase the employment and earnings of welfare recipients.

The second possible path for AFDC is that the current consensus will come to resemble the history of the WIN program—the laws and regulations will remain on the books for symbolic reassurance; the overwhelming majority of recipients will somehow be shunted out of the system, be declared "inappropriate for referral" or put on hold; and the bureaucrats will go on as before. As previously noted, the FSA attempts to prevent a broad-scale administrative use of deferral or hold. The statute provides that mere registration does not count toward the state's required participation rate, and there are detailed regulations as to what constitutes "participation" in various activities. However, there are loopholes and considerable room for states to exclude substantial numbers of people without reducing their participation rate. And, as usual, there are provisions for HHS to waive the participation rate penalties if the state is showing "good faith." In any event, a conflict between the states and the regulations seems inevitable since the participation rate requirements increase far more rapidly than JOBS funding, and JOBS funding is capped (Greenberg, 1990, pp. 105–113).

Faced with fewer options because of reduced funding, welfare agency staff will have to either try to force recipients into unpleasant choices or impose sanctions. But imposing sanctions also involves costs. GAIN, for example, has a very complex sanction and hearing process, requiring a lot of paperwork and energy on the part of the staff. The easier course of action for the staff would be to take the WIN route—somehow defer action. Deferral has no unpleasant consequences for recipients (except, of course, if they are looking for work, services, or child care), and, what is more important, the task of the staff is far more pleasant. There is no need to go through a complicated assessment, a search for a scarce slot, finding day care, trying to persuade or threaten the recipient, and invoking the complicated sanction procedure if there is a refusal.

Sanctions, on the other hand, imply failure. In order for the staff to be willing to invoke the sanction process, there has to be a sufficiently strong incentive system. A motivated field-level staff will be insufficient to invoke the sanction process. The top officers in the welfare bureaucracy must believe that the higher costs the work requirements impose on their agency are justified. Furthermore, a sanctioned person does not help the state meet the federal participation rate requirements (Greenberg, 1990, p. 115). Unless the drive behind the current welfare reform consensus is deep and sustained, a likely scenario is that the immediate past—the WIN experience—will reassert itself and not much will change. The difficulties that Los Angeles County is already experiencing under the GAIN program point strongly toward this outcome (see Chapter 5). There are numerous strategies that states can use to satisfy the FSA's "registration plus" requirement and still avoid spending scarce resources.[30]

A recent report by the Illinois Conference of Churches on that state's Project Chance—also touted as one of the models for the Family Support Act—seems to confirm the prediction that the FSA will be no more successful than WIN (Reardon & Silverman, 1988). After three years and spending about $43.3 million per year, the results were modest at best. Over 50,000 participants found jobs, but these were the easiest to employ—downstate whites with good job skills. It is estimated that more than 80% would have obtained jobs without the program. Only a third of those employed were African-Americans, despite the fact that more than 70% of the program's caseload is African-American; only 40% of the jobholders were from Cook County, which claims 80% of participants. A third of the jobs required additional welfare support, about half of the families were still in poverty, and about a third of those who found jobs were back on welfare within a year and a half. The program is seriously understaffed and underbudgeted. By the second year, sanctions were reduced by more than two-thirds.[31] With statistics resembling the WIN experience, only about a third of the participants are actively involved (17% in job search, the cheapest component because clients shoulder most of the responsibility), with two-thirds in various stages of administrative "holding patterns." [32] Instead of concentrating on voluntary, hard-to-employ clients (the most cost-effective), the state still insists on handling a monthly caseload of 150,000 mandatory participants in order to send a proper message.[33]

The Illinois program as well as the unfolding of GAIN are an uncanny echo from the past. The disjuncture between the rhetoric and the reality of the mothers' pension movement has been explained in terms of symbolic status politics. As part of the movement to glorify motherhood in the home, both the reformers and the opponents drew a status distinction between the fit and proper (i.e., patriarchal) mother and the poor, unworthy mother who was excluded from ADC and forced into the paid labor market. Those mothers who conformed—the worthy white widows—received the benefits from the program. Today, the status symbols have been reversed. Now, female paid labor and the working mother are privileged and the welfare mother is told to work, to become independent, to become worthy. But, as the Illinois and California programs and the past WIN experience demonstrate, most of these poor mothers cannot become independent through paid work. As with the select white widows of the mothers' pension days, a few privileged welfare recipients will succeed through the creaming efforts of the bureaucracy. State service programs seek to justify this approach as demonstrating that underfunded service programs can train only the few. But since the chosen few will be those who conform to the expectations of the nonpoor—mostly white, better educated, and skilled—their success will reinforce negative attitudes toward the unworthy.

Thus the current consensus on welfare reform draws the same status line again: The worthy support themselves; dependent people remain the deviant. The majority of nonpoor women are struggling for independence, choice, and autonomy, whereas the second alternative—a poor, stigmatized income-support system and a poor work and training program—increases dependency and patriarchy for welfare mothers by making reliance on a male breadwinner more attractive (Block, Cloward, Ehrenreich, & Piven, 1987). Even under the best of circumstances, the planned work and training programs will help only a small number of families. In no sense is the FSA a comprehensive response to the needs of poor families; instead, it offers a continuation of low benefits, restrictive eligibility and other conditions, lack of adequate child and health care, and very poor employment prospects (Greenberg, 1990).

AFDC may take a third path. If the economy continues to falter and poverty and welfare increase, then, given our present budgetary crisis, pressure will increase to cut welfare costs. However, while reducing welfare costs is a major impetus behind the current consensus, we do not think that position will hold; it is simply too costly to fund the current approach in the short run, and the long-run benefits are uncertain. Perhaps the latest developments in California are predictive. As noted, the governor has already significantly reduced the initial state budgetary estimates for GAIN. He is now pressing for more reductions in education and services. As a result, private service contractors are reluctant to bid. As stated earlier, one of the provisions of GAIN is that a portion of contract money is to be withheld depending on the outcome of the employment training and placement. The service providers are now claiming that with the small amounts of money available, the risk is too great. The counties petitioned the state for permission to use volunteers, to allow the counties to cream. Thus far, they have been unsuccessful.

In a declining economy, the services and support parts of the consensus will be reduced over time, and may even disappear altogether, but the work requirements will remain. The regulatory work test will be stripped of costly and meaningful services and simplified to a few alternatives. There are a number of ways this approach will manifest itself. For example, job search will be mandated, but without support; recipients will be required to produce evidence of job seeking on pain of sanction, much as we find in general relief today.[34] Work-relief will spread as public agencies will be more amenable to free labor. The sanction rules will be strengthened and imposed more readily for infractions—for example, missed or late appointments, failure to perform the required number of job searches, or reporting late for work. This is where the real cost savings come in—the number of recipients who are off the rolls during the sanction period.

In this sense, AFDC will come to resemble general relief, where the work requirements and the sanctions are used to deter applicants from applying and to reduce the rolls through computer-driven, automatic sanctioning (Handler, 1987–1988). There is no pretense at skill enhancement or preparation for the general economy. The regulatory work test is used to force applicants back into the labor market.

When this happens to AFDC—a tightening of the work requirements—then AFDC will only partially resemble general relief. General relief not only applies its tough work test to those on the rolls, it also denies entry to those who are considered able-bodied. AFDC may also be moving in this direction. Perhaps one of the early warning signals was Carter's stillborn Program for Better Jobs and Income for welfare recipients. It will be recalled that one of the interesting features of that proposal was the division of AFDC recipients into those who were considered employable and those who were not. The former were to be given only one-half of the AFDC benefit; this would provide a sufficient incentive for them to choose work and training over welfare. If benefits are sufficiently low, then the wage for the job does not have to be that high before the recipient is better off working. To make that plan work, under a more liberal political climate, there had to be a guarantee of a job; otherwise, the family would be far below a subsistence level. It was the expense of funding those jobs that sank the proposal.

The ideological significance of Carter's program, for our purposes, was in the proposed legislative division of AFDC mothers into the two categories, and in the presumption that one category was able-bodied and therefore subject to a lower benefit. Was this approach a straw in the wind? Will we eventually see large segments of poor mothers legislatively declared to be employable and then treated differently from those who are not employable? This is precisely what Garfinkel and McLanahan (1986) advocate.

In contrast to conventional wisdom, Garfinkel and McLanahan argue that work and welfare do not go together. Under the current approach, all AFDC recipients—the able-bodied and those not expected to work—receive the same subsistence benefit, which has to be high enough to allow those not expected to work to maintain a minimally decent standard of living (nevertheless, well below the poverty line). When the able-bodied begin to work, the following dilemma is created: If the able-bodied are allowed to keep enough of their earnings without reducing their welfare benefits to maximize incentives, then financial eligibility will soar and many of the working poor will become eligible for welfare—the rolls will increase.[35] On the other hand, if there are sharp reductions in the welfare grant as earnings rise, this amounts to heavy taxation on earnings and strong disincentives to work. Garfinkel and McLanahan would create separate programs for the two groups—those who are able-bodied and expected to work, and those who are excused from work. In addition, Garfinkel and McLanahan (1986) think that the present combined program sends an ambiguous message:

> For a society that values work, a clear distinction reinforces the values of work and independence. . . . With two separate programs . . . those poor single mothers who are physically and mentally capable of work should work enough to be independent of welfare. By creating two separate programs, the social message to those who temporarily cannot find work and therefore must have recourse to welfare is clear: Society expects their dependence on welfare to be short term. (p. 178)

How would AFDC look if it were primarily work-relief rather than cash relief? For those who are expected to work, Garfinkel and McLanahan would provide a universal benefit. The programs should provide lower benefits than AFDC cash relief and would not be reduced so drastically as under AFDC when earnings increase, thus giving the greatest incentive for the poor to work. However, no matter how successful the universal programs in drawing mothers into the labor market and off welfare, there will always be a need for a program to provide cash assistance. Some mothers will be unemployed for a time; some will be incapable of working. For those not disabled, Garfinkel and McLanahan would provide more work-relief and less cash relief to the unemployed. The amount of time for receiving cash benefits without either working or proceeding satisfactorily in education or training would be limited by how long it takes to place beneficiaries efficiently. Garfinkel and McLanahan think that two or three months would be a reasonable time, after which time the welfare would be terminated. But, in order to make work-relief a "reality," there have to be guaranteed jobs for all who are capable of working. Garfinkel and McLanahan would apply the minimum wage to work-relief and services "to facilitate independence" (pp. 185–186).

Thus Garfinkel and McLanahan, along with other prominent liberals, such as David Ellwood, have joined with conservatives such as Mead and Murray in seeking to redirect AFDC from cash relief into basically a work program for the able-bodied welfare recipient.[36] This is the underlying social policy of the state WIN demonstration projects, the major state programs such as GAIN, Project Chance, and ET, and now the Family Support Act. To be sure, there are significant differences in these approaches: Liberals such as Garfinkel, McLanahan, and Ellwood insist that a required work program can be justified *only* if there are also meaningful support services and, most significant, *both* a guaranteed income and suitable jobs. Mead, who strongly argues in favor of replacing the ideology of entitlement with responsibility and work and training programs, is equally adamant in support of services and adequate child care.

The important point is the emerging consensus, from all directions, that mothers with very young children should now be legislatively classified as a matter of public policy as the "able-bodied poor." Several justifications have been offered. These recipients (i.e., young, never-married women who become AFDC recipients while they have children younger than 3 years old) are at the greatest risk of falling into long-term dependency. However, as previously discussed, targeting will be neither easy nor necessarily successful; the main route out of welfare is not employment, but marriage, and targeting will be expensive in the short run (Ellwood, 1988). Childcare costs become increasingly expensive the younger the children. An equity argument is also used for the lower age requirement.

Large numbers of women with very young children are in the paid labor force; therefore, why should welfare mothers be excused from working? Aside from the fact that the difference between voluntary employment and mandatory work requirements in the welfare context is conveniently ignored, it is this kind of thinking that leads liberals such as Garfinkel, McLanahan, and Ellwood to propose that AFDC be converted from cash relief into a work-relief program. Now, in fairness to Garfinkel, McLanahan, and Ellwood, they make their proposal *only* on the condition that other income support is available (their child-support allowance and/or universal benefit) and that jobs are *guaranteed*. But, of course, that's the rub. Looking at the economic future, where are the resources for the income support and appropriate, guaranteed jobs?

It is Garfinkel and McLanahan's and Ellwood's reconceptualization that is most interesting. They have arrived at their position from the standard liberal analysis—the mother in poverty was the deserving poor, but now that our attitudes toward mothers of young children working have changed, poor mothers of young children should work. Under this conceptual framework, poor mothers are still considered to be one with nonpoor mothers—at first excused from work, but now considered employable due to changing norms. The Reagan administration came to the same position from an entirely different route. As we have argued, the dominant (nonliberal) view is that the vast bulk of poor mothers were *always* considered undeserving, that is, subject to the labor market. Through liberal excesses, they were let into the AFDC program, but now that program must be changed to reflect its clientele and become more clearly an undeserving poor program. AFDC mothers must be subjected to a clear, simple, effectively administered work test or, better still, a labor market work requirement. This is what it means to be considered the able-bodied poor, the FSA classification for poor mothers with very young children. Under the conservative view, poor mothers were never, and are not now, the deserving poor.

The Garfinkel-McLanahan-Ellwood approach does have antecedents, in addition to the Carter proposal. A sharply reduced welfare grant means subjecting the recipients to the labor market. Low-benefit states take this approach, distinguishing AFDC recipients from the "deserving" categories. In many states, the per capita AFDC grant is less than the other programs; the differences have been justified, and legitimated by the U.S. Supreme Court, on the grounds that AFDC recipients are more likely than the aged and disabled to supplement their grants (*Dandridge v. Williams*, 1970; *Jefferson v. Hackney*, 1972). In the low-benefit states, it is assumed that there will be supplementation—people could not survive on the grants alone. AFDC thus is used as a low-level income stopgap, like the mothers' pensions and early ADC programs, rather than as a substitute for employment (Bell, 1965). General relief performs the same function; it is a temporary, low-benefit program; rather than being a substitute for work, it is designed to enforce labor discipline. AFDC, as a work-relief program, with lower, short-term benefits, would do the same.

The third path will add teeth to the symbolic, status politics of welfare policy. A tough, stripped-down regulatory work requirement, especially if there are reduced benefits for the able-bodied, will ensure that large numbers of the most desperate AFDC families will be forced off the program. Who are these people, and why are these hard approaches appealing? For almost a decade and until recently, welfare rolls and costs had stabilized. Why is welfare still a "problem"? It is because we have constructed a new enemy. It is the specter of the ghetto African-American mother and her out-of-wedlock children as part of the crime-ridden, drug-infested underclass that is the dark side of the current consensus on welfare reform. We return to familiar themes: Our attitudes and responses to the visible presence of the poor are danger, containment, stigmatization, and deterrence. The third path will seek to treat the unworthy African-American mother and her children as it does the single male—containment and exclusion, stigma, and the sanctions of the market and a harsh welfare program.

The third path will not be taken tomorrow. Social welfare policy is a complex process. There are many different voices seeking changes and directions. Much depends on the state of the economy. In good times, we seem to be more generous with the poor. In hard times, the calls for reducing welfare costs and enforcing the work ethic become more strident. What we are impressed with is the durability of basic values toward the moral issues of work and welfare, gender and family, and race and ethnicity, and the lack of purchase that the lower social classes, the unfortunates, and deviants have on the larger society. The deinstitutionalization experience is a grim reminder. There, the liberals and conservatives united to remove the mentally ill from the institutions; this would save money and we would provide humane treatment in the community. The coalition fell apart when the mentally ill came home, and community care never materialized. There is some evidence that this is happening with education reforms as well; the Pennsylvania legislature has refused to appropriate sufficient money for remedial education, even though 60% of Philadelphia students failed to pass the school norm (Levin, 1986). We are seeing another consensus now between liberals and conservatives. The conservatives will firmly place poor mothers in the employable category, and the liberals have only the promise of services and support. In time, the AFDC program will work itself pure again: A few of the clearly unemployable (the disabled) will be supported, and the rest will be back with the undeserving poor, primarily subject to the labor market.

NOTES

1. There is some controversy over the term *workfare*. Prior to the current reform initiatives, *workfare* meant only work-relief, that is, a system under which recipients have to work a certain number of hours for their welfare grants. The present package of employment preparation and work requirements is now also called *workfare* in the current political debates and the popular press. Throughout this book, we have been using the new definition of *workfare*; workfare in the old sense has been called *work-relief*. For an explanation of the new terminology, see Wiseman (1988, p. 17).

2. While the majority of married mothers are in the paid labor force, only 27% work full-time, about 40% work part-time, and about a third do not work at all (Ellwood, 1988).

3. This perception is exaggerated. The ghetto poor are a tiny fraction of the poverty population—Ellwood (1988, p. 193) estimates less than 7%; the African-American ghetto poor are only 5% of the poor. Patricia Ruggles (1989), in a recent paper, says that if the "underclass" means those who are urban and in a lifetime of poverty (20–30 years), then we are talking about less than 1% of the population.

4. Compare with Mead (1986) the following from Heidi Hartmann (1987): "In general, I believe that most [welfare] benefits should be tied to employment or participation in training programs. As working for wages increasingly becomes the norm for all women, the fact that poor, young minority women are 'stockpiled' on welfare programs increasingly disadvantages them. They, like all women, need to learn labor market skills and progress toward self-sufficiency. Of course, not everyone is able to work, and social programs that provide a decent standard of living for those unable to work are needed as well" (p. 58).

5. The AFDC-UP obligation does not go into effect until fiscal year 1994, when states are required to have a 40% participation rate. The required participation rate rises to 75% by fiscal year 1998.

6. A state can be excused from the target requirements if it can demonstrate that, because of the characteristics of its caseload, the requirements are not feasible and the state is targeting other long-term or potential long-term recipients (Greenberg, 1990, p. 21).

7. There are some circumstances in which basic education is mandated.

8. The maximum hours are calculated by taking the AFDC grant, less the portion of aid for which the state is reimbursed by a child-support collection, and divided by the greater of the federal or applicable state minimum wage. After six months, the rate of pay for individuals employed in the same or similar occupations by the employer at the same site enters into the calculation (Greenberg, 1990, p. 26).

9. There are some restrictions; for instance, recipients must continue working (unless they terminate with good cause), cooperate with child-support enforcement, and contribute to the cost of child care under a sliding-scale arrangement (Greenberg, 1990, p. 35).

10. There are some exceptions to transitional Medicaid; for example, with OJT, the family must have been on AFDC at least three of the six months prior to losing AFDC due to employment (Greenberg, 1990, pp. 79–80).

11. Refusal without good cause requires a bona fide offer of suitable employment.

12. Net loss of cash income is defined as gross income less necessary work-related expenses amounting to less than cash assistance. In-kind benefits, such as housing subsidies, are not included (Greenberg, 1990, p. 51).

13. In 1988, 21% of recipient children were in age category 3–5, 33.3% were in age category 6–11, and 22.4% were in age category 12 and older (U.S. Congress, 1990, p. 580).

14. Recall the experience of California's GAIN allocations (see Chapter 5).

15. The recipient would refuse what is offered, and sanctions would be imposed; at that point, she would decide whether to leave welfare, acquiesce, or invoke the appeal process.

16. This is always the situation when benefits are rationed. Legal rights can only assure fairness in the process; they cannot deliver the benefits. Legal rights can deliver benefits only if they are *both* nondiscretionary and divisible (e.g., cash or close substitutes) (Handler, 1986).

17. In the words of the report: "Care can be as basic as a responsible child taking care of himself or herself or care by a babysitter" (Strassburger, 1987, p. 13).

18. The 1982 legislation increased the credit to 30% of those with incomes of $10,000 or less (including those who do not itemize); the credit then declines on a sliding scale to 20% for families with incomes above $28,000 (Liebman, 1989).

19. It is not clear whether the increase in supply is attributable to the increase in credit-induced demand or the increased participation of mothers in the paid labor force (Kamerman & Kahn, 1989).

20. For each child under 4, families would receive a credit equal to 14% of wages, with a maximum of $1,000 per child. The benefit would decrease as income rises, up to $20,000. However, only families with incomes below $15,000 would get the maximum benefit (Liebman, 1989).

21. For a more sobering view, see Duncan, Hill, and Hoffman (1988).

22. For example, working 2,000 hours at the minimum wage of $3.35 per hour would earn only $6,700, which is below the 1985 poverty level for a family of two ($7,050). To earn more than the poverty level for a family of three ($8,850), the family would have to work 2,000 hours per year at more than $4.40 per hour. Large percentages of mothers of small children work part-time. While increased efforts to enforce payment of child support will help prevent some women from going on welfare, most fathers of AFDC children earn too little to make much of a difference for welfare recipients (Garfinkel & McLanahan, 1986, p. 23).

23. Roughly, the percentage is the ratio obtained by dividing the total number of children born out of wedlock who are receiving AFDC or child-support services and have had paternity established by the total number of children born out of wedlock who are receiving AFDC or child-support services. There are other provisions designed to make establishment of paternity easier, including genetic testing, simplified civil procedures, and extending the statute of limitations (Children's Defense Fund, 1988, p. 32).

24. However, if no appropriate alternative activities are available, the participant would not be required to participate or be sanctioned.

25. A state JOBS program must provide education in English proficiency, although the states decide the standards (Greenberg, 1990, p. 65).

26. There are some inconsistencies between the Wisconsin learnfare and the FSA requirements. For example, in Wisconsin, teens between 13 and 19 are subject to the program; FSA applies only to ages 16 and over. FSA does not apply to children who are not parents; Wisconsin applies to all welfare recipients (see Greenberg, 1990, pp. 63–65).

27. If a student has 10 or more days of unexcused absences in a semester, she becomes subject to a "monthly attendance requirement." She will be sanctioned for each month in which she has two or more days of unexcused absences without good cause (Greenberg & Sherman, 1989).

28. The state now only notifies the family that the at-risk program is available. The governor also vetoed additional resources to support outreach and family-based interventions designed to deal with truancy and other educational difficulties (Corbett et al., 1989).

29. At present, the law requires maintenance of efforts in state JOBS programs (Greenberg, 1990, p. 118), but, of course, that also assumes both the maintenance of federal funding and willingness to enforce state obligations.

30. For example, states have wide discretion in defining *job search*. Presumably, they could make the most perfunctory task sufficient to satisfy this requirement (Greenberg, 1990, pp. 28–30).

31. Initially, there were high levels of sanctions. The agency calculated its budget, in part, on the basis of cost savings due to a certain level of sanctions; lower-level staff were given "quotas," and sanctions were imposed summarily, contrary to federal due-process requirements. These practices were discovered, and abandoned, as part of a consent settlement in a lawsuit brought by the local legal services office. More than 18 pages of procedural conditions were agreed to by the state (*Elkins v. Coler*, 1986).

32. Of these, 12% are in education and 4% in work experience.

33. In the words of the director: "Most welfare recipients do not want to be on welfare, but do not know how to get off or, worse, have given up" (quoted in Reardon & Silverman, 1988).

34. This is an onerous requirement. Employers have to be persuaded to acknowledge in writing or remember, if the welfare agency calls, that the particular recipient sought work. There are no incentives for employers to perform these tasks; in fact, there are disincentives if they do not want welfare recipients coming to their places of business.

35. Recall that it was the projected huge expansion of the number of working people who would also receive welfare benefits that turned conservatives against Nixon's proposed Family Assistance Plan (see Chapter 4).

36. Ellwood (1988) generally supports Garfinkel and McLanahan's plan, but would be more generous for the transitional period.

References

Aaron, H. J. (1973). *Why is welfare so hard to reform?* Washington, DC: Brookings Institution.

Abbott, G. (1938). *The child and the state: Vol. 2. The dependent and the delinquent child: The child of unmarried parents.* Chicago: University of Chicago Press.

Abramovitz, M. (1988). *Regulating the lives of women: Social welfare policy from colonial times to the present.* Boston: South End.

Albert, V., & Wiseman, M. (1986). *What's to be GAINed: Welfare in California since 1971* (Research Paper in Economics No. 86–10: 1–40). Berkeley: University of California Press.

Amenta, E., & Carruthers, B. G. (1986). The political origins of unemployment insurance in five American states. In K. Orren & S. Skowronek (Eds.), *Studies in American political development* (Vol. 2, pp. 137–182). New Haven, CT: Yale University Press.

Amenta, E., & Carruthers, B. G. (1988). The formative years of U.S. social spending policies. *American Sociological Review, 53,* 661–678.

Anderson, M. (1978). *Welfare: The political economy of welfare reform in the United States.* Stanford, CA: Hoover Institution.

Asher, R. (1983). Failure and fulfillment: Agitation for employers' liability legislation and the origins of workmen's compensation in New York State, 1876–1910. *Labor History, 24,* 198–222.

Average child support payment drops by 12%. (1987, August 23). *New York Times,* p. 26.

Axinn, J., & Levin, H. (1975). *Social welfare: A history of the American response to need.* New York: Harper & Row.

Ball, R. (1988). The original understanding on social security: Implications for later developments. In T. Marmor & J. Mashaw (Eds.), *Social security: Beyond the rhetoric of crisis* (pp. 17–39). Princeton, NJ: Princeton University Press.

Bane, M. J. (1986). Household composition and poverty. In S. Danziger & D. Weinberg (Eds.), *Fighting poverty: What works and what doesn't* (pp. 209–231). Cambridge, MA: Harvard University Press.

Becker, J. (1960). Twenty-five years of unemployment insurance: An experiment in competitive collectivism. *Political Science Quarterly, 75,* 481–499.

Bell, W. (1965). *Aid to dependent children.* New York: Columbia University Press.

Block, F., Cloward, R. A., Ehrenreich, B., & Piven, F. F. (1987). *The mean season: The attack on the welfare state.* New York: Pantheon.

Bowler, M. K. (1974). *The Nixon guaranteed income proposal: Substance and process in policy change.* Cambridge, MA: Ballinger.

Boyer, P. (1978). *Urban masses and moral order in America, 1820–1920.* Cambridge, MA: Harvard University Press.

Bremer, W. (1975). Along the "American way": The New Deal's work relief programs for the unemployed. *Journal of American History, 62,* 636–652.

Brenner, J., & Ramas, M. (1984). Rethinking women's oppression. *New Left Review, 144,* 33–71.

Brodkin, E., & Lipsky, M. (1983). Quality control in AFDC as an administrative strategy. *Social Service Review, 57,* 1–34.

Brown, J. C. (1940). *Public relief 1929–1939.* New York: Henry Holt.

Burbridge, L. C., & Nightingale, D. S. (1989). *Local coordination of employment and training services to welfare recipients.* Washington, DC: Urban Institute.

Burke, V. J., & Burke, V. (1974). *Nixon's good deed: Welfare reform.* New York: Columbia University Press.

Burtless, G. (1989). The effects of reform on employment, earnings, and income. In P. H. Cottingham & D. T. Ellwood (Eds.), *Welfare policy for the 1990s* (pp. 103–145). Cambridge, MA: Harvard University Press.

Butler, S. (1985). *Privatizing federal spending: A strategy to eliminate the deficit.* New York: Universe.

Cain, G. G., & Wissoker, D. A. (1990). A reanalysis of marital stability in the Seattle-Denver Income Maintenance Experiment. *American Journal of Sociology, 95(5),* 1235–1269.

Campbell, C., & Pierce, W. (1980). *The earned income credit.* Washington, DC: American Enterprise Institute.

Cates, J. (1983). *Insuring inequality: Administrative leadership in social security, 1935–54.* Ann Arbor: University of Michigan Press.

Chassman, D. (1987). *The future of quality control in the management of public welfare.* Unpublished manuscript.

Children's Defense Fund. (1988). *A children's defense budget.* Washington, DC: Author.

Coll, B. (1988). Public assistance: Reviving the original comprehensive concept of social security. In G. Nash, N. Pugach, & R. Tomasson (Eds.), *Social security: The first half century* (pp. 221–241). Albuquerque: University of New Mexico Press.

Corbett, T., Deloya, J., Manning, W., & Uhr, L. (1989). Learnfare: The Wisconsin experience. *Focus, 12,* 1–10.

Dandridge v. Williams. (1970). 397 U.S. 491.

Danziger, S., & Gottschalk, P. (1990). Unemployment insurance and the safety net for the unemployed. In W. L. Hansen & J. Byers (Eds.), *Unemployment insurance: The second half-century*. Madison: University of Wisconsin Press.

Danziger, S. H., & Gottschalk, P. (1985). The impact of budget cuts and economic conditions on poverty. *Journal of Policy Analysis and Management, 5,* 587–593.

Danziger, S. H., Haveman, R. H., & Plotnick, R. D. (1986). Antipoverty policy: Effects on the poor and the non-poor. In S. H. Danziger & D. H. Weinberg (Eds.), *Fighting poverty: What works and what doesn't* (pp. 50–77). Cambridge, MA: Harvard University Press.

Dehavenon, A. (1987–1988). Administrative closings of public assistance cases: The rise of hunger and homelessness in New York City. *NYU Review of Law and Social Change, 16,* 741–746. (Abstract)

Derthick, M. (1979). *Policymaking for social security.* Washington, DC: Brookings Institution.

Deukmejian, G. (1990, July 27). Clear away obstacles to workfare. *Los Angeles Times,* part B, p. 7.

Downs, G. W., Jr. (1976). *Bureaucracy, innovation, and public policy.* Lexington, MA: Lexington.

Duncan G. J., Hill, M. S., & Hoffman, S. D. (1988). Welfare dependence within and across generations. *Science, 239,* 467–471.

Durman, E. (1973). Have the poor been regulated? Toward a multivariate understanding of welfare growth. *Social Service Review, 47,* 339–359.

Edelman, M. (1988). *Constructing the political spectacle.* Chicago: University of Chicago Press.

Elkins v. Coler. (1986). U.S. Dist. Ct., Central Dist. IL, 83–4019.

Ellwood, D. (1988). *Poor support: Poverty in the American family.* New York: Basic Books.

Ferber, R., & Hirsch, W. Z. (1978). Social experimentation and economic policy: A survey. *Journal of Economic Literature, 16,* 379–414.

Finegold, K. (1988). Agriculture and the politics of U.S. social provision: Social insurance and food stamps. In M. Weir, A. S. Orloff, & T. Skocpol (Eds.), *The politics of social policy in the United States.* Princeton, NJ: Princeton University Press.

First, R., & Toomey, B. (1989). Homeless men and the work ethic. *Social Service Review, 63,* 113–126.

Fraker, T., Moffitt, R., & Wolf, D. (1985). Effective tax rates and guarantees in the AFDC program 1967–82. *Journal of Human Resources, 20,* 264–277.

Fraser, N. (1989). *Unruly practices: Power, discourse and gender in contemporary social theory.* Minneapolis: University of Minnesota Press.

Friedlander, D., Erickson, M., Hamilton, G., & Knox, V. (1986). *West Virginia: Final report on the community work experience.* New York: Manpower Demonstration Research Corporation.

Friedlander, D., Hoerz, G., Quint, J., & Riccio, J. (1985). *Arkansas: Final report on the WORK program in two counties.* New York: Manpower Demonstration Research Corporation.

Friedman, B., & Hausman, L. (1977). *Work, welfare, and the Program for Better Jobs and Income* (study prepared for U.S. Congress, Joint Economic Committee). Washington, DC: Government Printing Office.

Friedman, L., & Ladinsky, J. (1988). Social change and the law of industrial accidents. In L. Friedman & H. Scheiber, *American law and the constitutional order: Historical perspectives* (pp. 269–282). Cambridge, MA: Harvard University Press.

Friedman, M. (1962). *Capitalism and freedom.* Chicago: University of Chicago Press.

Gabe, T. (1989). *Distributional effects of selected proposals to modify the earned income tax credit.* Washington, DC: Congressional Research Service.

Galm, S. (1972). *Welfare: An administrative nightmare* (staff study prepared for U.S. Congress, Subcommittee on Fiscal Policy of the Joint Economic Committee, Studies in Public Welfare, 5[1]). Washington, DC: Government Printing Office.

Garfinkel, I., & McLanahan, S. (1986). *Single mothers and their children: A new American dilemma.* Washington, DC: Urban Institute Press.

Glazer, N. (1985). The problem with competence. In J. Brunzel (Ed.), *Challenge to American schools: The case for standards and values* (pp. 216–231). New York: Oxford University Press.

Goldman, B., Friedlander, D., Gueron, J., & Long, D. (1985). *California—the demonstration of state work/welfare initiatives: Findings from the San Diego Job Search and Work Experience Demonstration.* New York: Manpower Demonstration Research Corporation.

Goodwin, L. (1972). *Do the poor want to work? A social-psychological study of work orientations.* Washington, DC: Brookings Institution.

Goodwin, L. (1983). *Causes and cures of welfare: New evidence on the social psychology of the poor.* Lexington, MA: Lexington.

Gordon, J. E. (1978). WIN research: A review of the findings. In C. Garvin, A. Smith, & W. Reid (Eds.), *The work incentive experience* (pp. 24–87). Montclair, NJ: Allanheld, Osmun.

Gordon, L. (1988). *Heroes of their own lives: The politics and history of family violence—Boston, 1880–1960.* New York: Viking.

Greenberg, M. (1990). *The JOBS program: Answers and questions.* Washington, DC: Center for Law and Social Policy.

Greenberg, M., & Sherman, A. (1989). *Wisconsin learnfare: What the data does (and doesn't) tell us.* Washington, DC: Center for Law and Social Policy.

Groeneveld, L. P., Tuma, N. B., & Hannan, M. T. (1980). Marital dissolution and remarriage. In P. K. Robins, R. G. Spiegelman, S. Weiner, & J. G. Bell (Eds.), *A guaranteed annual income: Evidence from a social experiment* (pp. 163–182). New York: Academic Press.

Grossman, J. B., Maynard, R., & Roberts, J. (1985). *Reanalysis of the effects of selected employment and training programs for welfare recipients.* Princeton, NJ: Mathematica Policy Research.

Grossman, J. B., & Mirsky, A. (1985). *A survey of recent programs designed to reduce long-term welfare dependency.* Princeton, NJ: Mathematica Policy Research.

Gueron, J. (1990). Work and welfare: Lessons on employment programs. *Journal of Economic Perspectives, 4,* 79–98.

Hall, A. R. (1980). Education and training. In P. K. Robins, R. G. Spiegelman, S. Weiner, & J. G. Bell (Eds.), *A guaranteed annual income: Evidence from a social experiment* (pp. 263–280). New York: Academic Press.

Hamilton, G., & Friedlander, D. (1989). *Saturated work initiative model in San Diego.* New York: Manpower Demonstration Research Corporation.

Handler, J. (1986). *The conditions of discretion: Autonomy, community, bureaucracy.* New York: Russell Sage Foundation.

Handler, J. (1987–1988). The transformation of Aid to Families with Dependent Children: The Family Support Act in historical context. *NYU Review of Law and Social Change, 16,* 457–533.

Handler, J., & Hollingsworth, E. (1971). The "deserving poor": A study of welfare administration. New York: Markham.

Handler, J., Hollingsworth, E., & Erlanger, H. (1978). *Lawyers and the pursuit of legal rights.* New York: Academic Press.

Hartmann, H. (1987). Changes in women's economic and family roles. In L. Beneria & C. R. Stimpson (Eds.), *Women, households, and the economy* (pp. 33–64). New Brunswick, NJ: Rutgers University Press.

Hasenfeld, Y. (1987). *Welfare and work: The institutionalization of moral ambiguity* (Working Paper, Series 147). Los Angeles: University of California, Institute of Industrial Relations.

Himmelfarb, G. (1984). *The idea of poverty: England in the early industrial age.* New York: Knopf.

Hoagland, W., & Korbel, J. (1978). *The administration's welfare reform proposal: An analysis of the Program for Better Jobs and Income.* Washington, DC: U.S. Congress, Congressional Budget Office.

Houseman, A. (1990). Poverty law developments and options for the 1990's. *Clearinghouse Review, 23,* 2–16.

Illinois statutes. (1911). Ch. 23, Sec. 175: Laws 126.

Irwin, R., & McKay, E. (1936). The Social Security Act and the blind. *Law & Contemporary Problems, 3,* 271–278.

Isaac, L., & Kelly, W. R. (1981). Racial insurgency, the state and welfare expansion: Local and national level evidence from the postwar United States. *American Journal of Sociology, 86,* 1348–1386.

Jefferson v. Hackney. (1972). 406 U.S. 535.

Jones, J. (1985). *Labor of love, labor of sorrow: Black women, work, and the family from slavery to the present.* New York: Vintage.

Kamerman, S., & Kahn, A. (1989). *Privatization and the welfare state.* Princeton, NJ: Princeton University Press.

Kasarda, J. (1989). Urban industrial transition and the underclass. *Annals of the American Academy of Political and Social Science, 501,* 25–47.

Katz, M. (1986). *In the shadow of the poorhouse: A social history of welfare in America.* New York: Basic Books.

Katz, M. (1989). *The undeserving poor: From the War on Poverty to the war on welfare.* New York: Pantheon.

Kemper, P., Long, D., & Thornton, C. (1981). *The supported work evaluation: Final benefit-cost analysis.* New York: Manpower Demonstration Research Corporation.

Kessler-Harris, A. (1982). *Out to work: A history of wage-earning women in the United States.* New York: Oxford University Press.

Kirp, D. (1986). The California work/welfare scheme. *Public Interest, 83,* 34–48.

Kosterlitz, J. (1987). Fading fathers. *National Journal, 38,* 2337–2339.

Kramer, F. (Ed.). (1988). *From quality control to quality improvement in AFDC and Medicaid.* Washington, DC: National Academy Press.

Law, S. (1983). Women, work, welfare, and the preservation of patriarchy. *University of Pennsylvania Law Review, 131*, 1249–1339.

Leff, M. (1983). Consensus for reform: The mothers'-pension movement in the progressive era. *Social Service Review, 47*, 397–417.

Leman, C. (1980). *The collapse of welfare reform: Political institutions, policy, and the poor in Canada and the United States.* Cambridge: MIT Press.

Levin, H. (1986). *Educational reform for disadvantaged students: An emerging crisis.* West Haven, CT: NEA Professional Library.

Levine, R. A. (1975). How and why the experiment came about. In J. Pechman & M. P. Timpane (Eds.), *Work incentives and income guarantees: The New Jersey Negative Tax Experiment* (pp. 15–25). Washington, DC: Brookings Institution.

Levitan, S. A., & Mangum, G. L. (1969). *Federal training and work programs in the sixties.* Ann Arbor, MI: Institute of Labor and Industrial Relations.

Liebman, L. (1989). Evaluating child care legislation: Program structures and political consequences. *Harvard Journal on Legislation, 26*, 357–390.

Lipsky, M. (1980). *Street-level bureaucracy: Dilemmas of the individual in public services.* New York: Russell Sage Foundation.

Lipsky, M. (1984). Bureaucratic disentitlement in social welfare programs. *Social Service Review, 58*, 3–27.

Lipsky, M., & Thibodeau, M. (1990). Domestic food policy in the United States. *Journal of Health Politics, Policy, and Law, 15*, 319–339.

Long, R. (1971, August 6). *Welfare reform—or is it?* Address to the U.S. Senate Committee on Finance.

Lubove, R. (1967). Workmen's compensation and the prerogatives of voluntarism. *Labor History, 8*, 254–279.

Lynn, L. E., & Whitman, D. D. (1981). *The president as policymaker: Jimmy Carter and welfare reform.* Philadelphia: Temple University Press.

Malone, M. S. (1986). *Work and welfare* (prepared for U.S. Senate, Subcommittee on Employment and Productivity of the Committee on Labor and Human Resources and the Subcommittee on Social Security and Income Maintenance of the Committee on Finance). Washington, DC: Government Printing Office.

Marmor, T. R., & Rein, M. (1973). Reforming "the welfare mess": The fate of the Family Assistance Plan, 1969–72. In A. Sindler (Ed.), *Policy and politics in America* (pp. 2–28). Boston: Little, Brown.

Massachusetts Taxpayers Foundation. (1987). *Training people to live without welfare.* Boston: Author.

Massey, D. (1990). American apartheid: Segregation and the making of the underclass. *American Journal of Sociology, 96*, 329–357.

Massey, D., & Eggers, M. (1990). The ecology of inequality: Minorities and the concentration of poverty, 1970–1980. *American Journal of Sociology, 95*, 1153–1188.

May, M. (1986). *The "problem of duty": The regulation of male breadwinning and desertion in the progressive era* (Working Paper, Series 1). Madison, WI: Institute for Legal Studies.

McDonald, M. (1977). *Food, stamps, and income maintenance.* New York: Academic Press.

Mead, L. (1986). *Beyond entitlement: The social obligations of citizenship.* New York: Free Press.

Mead, L. (1989). The logic of workfare: The underclass and work policy. *Annals of the American Academy of Political and Social Science, 501,* 156–169.

Meyer, J. W., & Rowan, B. (1977). Institutionalized organizations: Formal structure as myth and ceremony. *American Journal of Sociology, 83,* 340–363.

Michel, S. (1988). *The nineteenth-century origins of American child care policy.* Unpublished manuscript, University of Illinois, Champaign, Department of History.

Mitchell, J., Chadwin, M., & Nightingale, D. (1979). *Implementing welfare-employment programs: An institutional analysis of the Work Incentive (WIN) program.* Washington, DC: Government Printing Office.

Moffitt, R. A. (1982). The effects of a negative income tax on work effort. In P. Sommers (Ed.), *Welfare reform in America: Perspectives and prospects* (pp. 209–229). Boston: Kluwer-Nijhoff.

Moffitt, R. A. (1985). Evaluating the effects of changes in AFDC: Methodological issues and challenges. *Journal of Policy Analysis and Management, 4,* 537–553.

Moffitt, R. A. (1986). The lagged effect of the 1981 federal AFDC legislation on work effort. *Journal of Policy Analysis and Management, 5,* 596–597.

Moffitt, R. A., & Wolf, D. A. (1987). The effects of the 1981 Omnibus Budget Reconciliation Act on welfare recipients and work incentives. *Social Service Review, 61,* 247–260.

Moynihan, D. P. (1965). *The Negro family: The case for national action.* Washington, DC: U.S. Department of Labor, Office of Planning and Research.

Moynihan, D. P. (1973). *The politics of a guaranteed income: The Nixon administration and the Family Assistance Plan.* New York: Random House.

Murray, C. (1984). *Losing ground: American social policy, 1950–80.* New York: Basic Books.

Myles, J. (1988). Postwar capitalism and the extension of social security into a retirement wage. In M. Weir, A. S. Orloff, & T. Skocpol (Eds.), *The politics of social policy in the United States* (pp. 265–292). Princeton, NJ: Princeton University Press.

Nash, G. (1976). Poverty and poor relief in pre-revolutionary Philadelphia. *William & Mary Quarterly, 33,* 3–30.

Nash, G. (1979). The failure of female factory labor in colonial Boston. *Labor History, 20,* 165–188.

Nelkin, D. (1987). The use of "contract" as a social work technique. In R. Rideout & J. Jowell (Eds.), *Current legal problems 1987.* London: Sweet & Maxwell.

Nelson, B. (1988). The gender, race, and class origins of early welfare policy and the welfare state: A comparison of workmen's compensation and mothers' aid. In L. Tilly & P. Gurin (Eds.), *Women, change, and politics.* New York: Russell Sage Foundation.

Neubeck, K. J., & Roach, J. L. (1981). Income maintenance experiments, politics, and the perpetuation of poverty. *Social Problems, 28,* 308–320.

Nightingale, D. S., & Burbridge, L. C. (1987). *The status of state work-welfare programs in 1986: Implications for welfare reform.* Washington, DC: Urban Institute.

Nightingale, D. S., Burbridge, L. C., Wissoker, D., Bawden, L., Sonenstein, F. L., & Jeffries, N. (1989, November 2–4). *Experiences of Massachusetts ET job finders: Preliminary findings.* Paper prepared for the annual meeting of the Association for Public Policy Analysis and Management, Washington, DC.

O'Neill, J. (1990). *Work and welfare in Massachusetts: An evaluation of the ET program*. Boston: Pioneer Institute for Public Policy Research.

Orfield, G. (1988). Race and the liberal agenda: The loss of the integrationist dream, 1965–74. In M. Weir, A. S. Orloff, & T. Skocpol (Eds.), *The politics of social policy in the United States* (pp. 313–356). Princeton, NJ: Princeton University Press.

Orloff, A. (1988a). The political origins of America's belated welfare state. In M. Weir, A. S. Orloff, & T. Skocpol (Eds.), *The politics of social policy in the United States* (pp. 37–80). Princeton, NJ: Princeton University Press.

Orloff, A. (1988b, November 6). Women in the American welfare state: The implications of the social insurance approach. Paper presented at the annual meeting of the Social Science History Association, Chicago.

Orloff, A., & Skocpol, T. (1984). Why not equal protection? Explaining the politics of public social spending in Britain, 1900–1911, and the United States, 1880s-1920. *American Sociological Review, 49,* 726–750.

Patterson, J. (1981). *America's struggle against poverty, 1900–1980.* Cambridge, MA: Harvard University Press.

Pearson, J., Thoenes, N., & Tjaden, P. (1989). Legislating adequacy: The impact of child support guidelines. *Law and Society Review, 23,* 569–590.

Peterson, G. E. (1984). Federalism and the states: An experiment in decentralization. In J. L. Palmer & I. V. Sawhill (Eds.), *The Reagan record* (pp. 217–256). Washington, DC: Urban Institute.

Peterson, P., & Rom, M. (1989). American federalism, welfare policy, and residential choices. *American Political Science Review, 83,* 711–728.

Piven, F., & Cloward, R. (1971). *Regulating the poor: The functions of public welfare.* New York: Pantheon.

Piven, F., & Cloward, R. (1977). *Poor people's movements: Why they succeed, how they fail.* New York: Pantheon.

Piven, F., & Cloward, R. (1988a). Popular power and the welfare state. In M. Brown (Ed.), *Remaking the welfare state: Retrenchment and social policy in America and Europe.* Philadelphia: Temple University Press.

Piven, F., & Cloward, R. (1988b). Welfare doesn't shore up traditional family roles: A reply to Linda Gordon. *Social Research, 55,* 631–647.

Piven, F., & Cloward, R. (1990). *Normalizing collective protest.* Paper prepared for the conference of the Fund for Dispute Resolution, Washington, DC.

Quadagno, J. (1988). *The transformation of old age security: Class and politics in the American welfare state.* Chicago: University of Chicago Press.

Reardon, P., & Silverman, D. (1988, October 23). Welfare-to-work plan fails neediest. *Chicago Tribune,* pp. 1, 18.

Rein, M. (1982). *Dilemmas of welfare policy: Why work strategies haven't worked.* New York: Praeger.

Reischauer, R. (1989). The welfare reform legislation: Directions for the future. In P. Cottingham & D. Ellwood (Eds.), *Welfare policy for the 1990s* (pp. 10–40). Cambridge, MA: Harvard University Press.

Riccio, J., Goldman, B., Hamilton, G., Martinson, K., & Orenstein, A. (1989). *GAIN: Early implementation experiences and lessons.* New York: Manpower Demonstration Research Corporation.

Robins, P. K. (1980). Labor supply response of family heads and implications for a national program. In P. K. Robins, R. G. Spiegelman, S. Weiner, & J. G. Bell

(Eds.), *A guaranteed annual income: Evidence from a social experiment* (pp. 59–72). New York: Academic Press.

Robins, P. K., & West, R. W. (1980). Labor supply response of family heads. In P. K. Robins, R. G. Spiegelman, S. Weiner, & J. G. Bell (Eds.), *A guaranteed annual income: Evidence from a social experiment* (pp. 86–99). New York: Academic Press.

Rose, N. (1989). Work relief in the 1930s and the origins of the Social Security Act. *Social Service Review, 63,* 63–91.

Rosenheim, M. (1966). Vagrancy concepts in welfare law. In J. tenBroek (Ed.), *Law of the poor* (pp. 187–242). San Francisco: Chandler.

Ruggles, P. (1989). *Short and long term poverty in the United States: Measuring the American "underclass."* Unpublished manuscript, Urban Institute.

Savner, S., Williams, L., & Halas, M. (1986). The Massachusetts Employment and Training Program. *Clearinghouse Review, 20,* 123–131.

Sawhill, I. (1988). Poverty in the U.S.: Why is it so persistent? *Journal of Economic Literature, 26,* 1073–1119.

Schiller, B. (1978). Lessons from WIN: A manpower evaluation. *Journal of Human Resources, 13,* 503–523.

Schneider, S. K. (1982). The sequential development of social programs in eighteen welfare states. *Comparative Social Research, 5,* 195–200.

Schorr, A. (1987). Welfare reform, once (or twice) again. *Tikkun, 2*(5), 15–88.

Shapiro, I., & Nichols, M. (1989). *Unprotected: Unemployment insurance and jobless workers in 1988.* Washington, DC: Center on Budget and Policy Priorities.

Sharkansky, I., & Hofferbert, R. (1969). Dimensions of state politics, economics, and public policy. *American Political Science Review, 63,* 867–878.

Sheehan, S. (1976). *A welfare mother.* Boston: Houghton Mifflin.

Simon, W. (1985). The invention and reinvention of welfare rights. *Maryland Law Review, 44,* 1–37.

Skocpol, T. (1986). States and social policies. *Annual Review of Sociology, 12,* 131–157.

Skocpol, T., & Ikenberry, J. (1983). The political formation of the American welfare state. *Comparative Social Research, 6,* 87–148.

Sosin, M., Colson, P., & Grossman, S. (1988). *Homelessness in Chicago: Poverty and pathology, social institutions and social change.* Unpublished manuscript, University of Chicago, School of Social Services Administration.

Stansell, C. (1987). *City of women: Sex and class in New York, 1789–1860.* Urbana: University of Illinois Press.

State Board of Control. (1939). *A history of the State Board of Wisconsin and the state institutions 1849–1939.* Madison: Author.

State of California Employment Development Department. (1976). *Third year and final report on the Community Work Experience Program.* Sacramento: Author.

Steiner, G. (1966). *Social insecurity: The politics of welfare.* Chicago: Rand McNally.

Steiner, G. Y. (1981). *The futility of family policy.* Washington, DC: Brookings Institution.

Stewart, B. (1938). *Planning and administration of unemployment compensation in the United States.* New York: Industrial Relations Counselors.

Stone, D. (1984). *The disabled state.* Philadelphia: Temple University Press.

Storey, J. R., Harris, R., Levy, F., Fechter, A., & Michel, R. C. (1978). *The better jobs and income plan.* Washington, DC: Urban Institute.

Strassburger, H. (1987). California's GAIN program falls short in meeting child care needs. *Youth Law News, 12,* 12–19.

Sutton, J. (1985). The juvenile court and social welfare: Dynamics of progressive reform. *Law and Society Review, 19,* 112–146.

Testa, M., Atone, N., Krogh, M., & Neckerman, K. (1989). Employment and marriage among inner-city fathers. *Annals of the American Academy of Political and Social Science, 501,* 79–91.

Tienda, M., Smith, S., & Ortiz, V. (1987). Industrial restructuring, gender segregation, and sex differences in earnings. *American Sociological Review, 52,* 195–210.

Tishler, H. (1971). *Self-reliance and social security: 1870–1917.* Port Washington, NY: Kennikat.

U.S. Bureau of the Census. (1989). *Statistical abstract of the United States, 1988.* Washington, DC: Government Printing Office.

U.S. Committee on Economic Security. (1937). *Social security in America: The factual background of the Social Security Act as summarized from staff reports to the Committee on Economic Security by the Social Security Board* (Social Security Board Publication No. 20). Washington, DC: Government Printing Office.

U.S. Congress, House of Representatives. (1967). 90th Congress, 1st session. *Congressional Record, 117*(17). Washington, DC: Government Printing Office.

U.S. Congress, House of Representatives, Committee on Ways and Means. (1981). *Background material and data on programs within the jurisdiction of the Committee on Ways and Means.* Washington, DC: Government Printing Office.

U.S. Congress, House of Representatives, Committee on Ways and Means. (1989). *Background material and data on programs within the jurisdiction of the Committee on Ways and Means.* Washington, DC: Government Printing Office.

U.S. Congress, House of Representatives, Committee on Ways and Means. (1990). *Background material and data on programs within the jurisdiction of the Committee on Ways and Means.* Washington, DC: Government Printing Office.

U.S. Congress, Senate, Committee on Finance. (1972). *Report on H.R. 1, Social Security Amendments of 1972* (92nd Congress, 2nd session). Washington, DC: Government Printing Office.

U.S. Congress, Senate, Committee on Finance, Subcommittee on Public Assistance. (1978). *Hearings, welfare reform proposals* (95th Congress, 2nd session). Washington, DC: Government Printing Office.

U.S. Department of Labor. (1934). *A tabular summary of state laws relating to public aid to children in their own homes, in effect January 1, 1934.* Washington, DC: Government Printing Office.

U.S. Department of Labor. (1970). *Reports on the work incentive program.* Washington, DC: Government Printing Office.

U.S. Department of Labor. (1980). *Implementing welfare-employment programs: An institutional analysis of the work incentive (WIN) program.* Washington, DC: Government Printing Office.

U.S. Department of Labor. (1988). *An examination of declining UI claims during the 1980's* (Unemployment Insurance Occasional Paper 88–3). Princeton, NJ: Mathematica Policy Research for the Employment and Training Administration.

U.S. Department of Labor, Bureau of Labor Statistics. (1989). *Handbook of labor statistics.* Washington, DC: Government Printing Office.

U.S. General Accounting Office. (1982). *An overview of the WIN program: Its objectives, accomplishments, and problems.* Washington, DC: Government Printing Office.

U.S. General Accounting Office. (1985). *An evaluation of the 1981 AFDC changes: Final report.* Washington, DC: Government Printing Office.

U.S. General Accounting Office. (1987). *Work and welfare.* Washington, DC: Government Printing Office.

Walker, J. L. (1969). The diffusion of innovation among the American states. *American Political Science Review, 63,* 880–899.

Wallace, J., & Long, D. (1987). *GAIN: Planning and early implementation.* New York: Manpower Demonstration Research Corporation.

Webb, S., & Webb, B. (1927). *English poor law history.* London: Longmans, Green.

Weinstein, J. (1968). *The corporate ideal in the liberal state: 1900–1918.* Boston: Beacon.

Weir, M. (1988). The federal government and unemployment: The frustration of policy innovation from the New Deal to the Great Society. In M. Weir, A. S. Orloff, & T. Skocpol (Eds.), *The politics of social policy in the United States* (pp. 149–198). Princeton, NJ: Princeton University Press.

Weir, M., Orloff, A. S., & Skocpol, T. (1988). The political origins of America's belated welfare state. In M. Weir, A. S. Orloff, & T. Skocpol (Eds.), *The politics of social policy in the United States* (pp. 3–36). Princeton, NJ: Princeton University Press.

White, L. (1990). Subordination, rhetorical survival skills, and Sunday shoes: Notes on the hearing of Mrs. G. *Buffalo Law Review, 38,* 1–58.

White, L. (in press). On "homelessness": Moving beyond the rhetoric of retrenchment. *Miami Law Review.*

Wilson, W. (1987). *The truly disadvantaged: The inner city, the underclass, and public policy.* Chicago: University of Chicago Press.

Wisconsin revised statutes. (1849). Ch. 28, Sec. 1.

Wiseman, M. (1988). Workfare and welfare reform. In H. Rodgers (Ed.), *Beyond welfare: New approaches to the problem of poverty in America* (pp. 14–36). Armonk, NY: M. E. Sharpe.

Zedlewski, S., & Meyer, J. (1989). *Toward ending poverty among the elderly and disabled through SSI reform* (Report 89-1). Washington, DC: Urban Institute Press.

Author Index

Subject Index

ADC. *See* Aid to Dependent Children
Adequate Income Act of 1970, 151
AFDC. *See* Aid to Families with Dependent Children
AFDC-UP. *See* Aid to Families with Dependent Children with an Unemployed Parent
African-Americans, 7, 23, 83, 117, 206, 234; ADC and, 34, 70; AFDC and, 25, 27, 35, 85, 113, 123; as low-wage labor, 89; as NWRO members, 28, 118–119; as percentage of the poor, 241; as underclass, 204, 240, 241; domestic code and, 52, 57; economic and political subjugation of, 6; electoral politics of, 129; exclusion of from welfare programs, 7, 26–27, 34, 82, 85, 87, 91, 94, 99, 129; FAP and, 152; feminists among, 7; general relief and, 21; income decline of, 224; in Seattle-Denver study, 144, 145; Johnson administration and, 116; Kennedy administration and, 116; lower benefits for, 102; male unemployment among, 6, 38, 115; migration of from farm to city, 108, 114, 127; NIT and, 168; single mothers among, 27, 114; subordination of in South, 34–35, 84–

85, 97; underrepresentation in social security system, 38, 43, 85; underrepresentation on relief rolls, 101; unemployment compensation coverage for, 112; wage-earning women among, 56; work relief discrimination of, 85
Aid to Dependent Children (ADC), 24, 50, 51, 63–74, 75, 79, 81, 84, 96, 134, 203, 234; as exclusive program, 21–22, 34, 70, 71, 80, 8; as grant-in-aid program, 85, 103–105; as low-level income stopgap, 240; as state and local program, 204; changes in clientele in post-New Deal period, 106; maximum payment of, 130. *See also* Mothers' pensions
Aid to Families with Dependent Children (AFDC), 1, 5, 6, 13, 14, 34, 35, 42, 44, 106, 113–123, 126, 134, 140, 141, 148, 151, 159, 160, 175, 178, 185, 192, 199, 210, 212, 237; administration of, 131, 172; African-American mothers and, 25, 27, 85, 113, 123; as exclusive program, 21, 113; as inclusive program, 21, 231–232; benefit levels frozen, 35; calculating benefits of, 169; collecting of child support by

About the Authors

Joel F. Handler is Professor of Law at the University of California, Los Angeles. He received an A.B. degree from Princeton University and a J.D. degree from Harvard Law School. Previously, he was the Vilas Research Professor and the George A. Wiley Professor at the University of Wisconsin Law School and served on the senior research staff at the university's Institute for Research on Poverty. He has served on several committees of the National Research Council and as Chair of the Panel on Public Policies Contributing to the Deinstitutionalization of Children and Youth, the Panel of the Political Participation and the Administration of Justice, Committee on the Status of Black America, and the Panel on High-Risk Youth. He has been a Guggenheim Fellow and a member of the board of trustees, executive committee, and President-Elect of the Law and Society Association. His primary research interests are in the areas of poverty law and administration, social welfare programs, race, social movements, public interest law, legal services, and law reform activities. He has published more than a dozen books and numerous articles on these subjects.

Yeheskel Hasenfeld is Professor of Social Welfare at the School of Social Welfare, University of California, Los Angeles. He has an M.S.W. degree from Rutgers University, and a Ph.D. in social work and sociology from the University of Michigan. He has a long-standing interest in studying the impact of the institutional and organizational arrangements of human services on their clients. He has published extensively on the organizational determinants of service delivery patterns, client-organization relations, and the management of social services. Currently, he is engaged in a study of the implementation of welfare-work programs.